The Problem-Solving Approach to Adjustment

A Guide to Research and Intervention

George Spivack
Jerome J. Platt
Myrna B. Shure

The Problem-Solving Approach to Adjustment

Jossey-Bass Publishers
San Francisco · Washington · London · 1976

Cop 1

The Problem-Solving Approach to Adjustment
A Guide to Research and Intervention
  by George Spivack, Jerome J. Platt, and Myrna B. Shure

JACKET DESIGN BY WILLI BAUM

FIRST EDITION

Code 7616

The Jossey-Bass
Behavioral Science Series

Preface

To assert that human beings are problem-solvers would seem to be asserting the obvious. It also would not be startling to further assert that the social adjustment of humans may be related to how adept they are in solving problems of an interpersonal nature. We all know that the rational handling of social problems—our capacity to think "straight" with others —would be a central feature of any definition of healthy psychological functioning. Given these truths, however, one might wonder why the thinking processes that underlie interpersonal problem solving have been relatively neglected as a field of study. Certainly the fact that it is obvious rarely protects a natural or social phenomenon from the careful scrutiny of the scientist.

But the fact is that *how* we think when confronted with personal and interpersonal problems has been a neglected area. We know little about those parameters of thought that might determine our sensitivity to problems, whether we think of solutions, how we plan what to do, whether we appreciate consequences, how well we understand the other person's point of view, and whether in fact these or other cognitive processes are the significant mediators of successful resolution.

The kernel of the idea that there may be certain properties of thought or thinking skills that specifically mediate social adjustment occurred to one of the authors and a colleague a little more than a decade ago. One of them was engaged in therapy with a delinquent teenaged boy, who left the campus of the residential treatment center without permission. When discovered on his way to a nearby city, the boy was not upset or concerned. He said he had wanted to purchase something and so decided to get it. His explanation seemed weak, in light of the circumstances—that the route into town the youngster selected was in fact dangerous, that going AWOL was a serious offense (the consequences of which would interfere with other things he wished to do), and that by the time of his arrival in town the stores would have been closed anyway. Therefore, an attempt was made to explore the entire event "therapeutically." During the week following this episode, the therapist explored with the youngster his awareness of the consequences of what he did, his possible "unconscious" motives, and whether he might have thought of legitimate and more practical ways to get what he wanted. The therapist hypothesized that the act might signify a hostile desire to worry others, or a symbolic way of challenging authority and social limits, or perhaps even a masochistic need to be caught and punished.

During therapy sessions, questions and answers revealed nothing in support of such conjecture. Repeatedly, the youngster indicated that he had wanted something, knew "they" had it in town, and so decided to "take off." There was no evidence of anger or resentment associated with his action, nor even a compelling need for what he had wanted at that moment. When asked, he said he had not thought of what might happen when he returned and was confronted by staff. He smiled in a self-deprecating manner when it was pointed out how his method would not have worked, and seemed genuinely apologetic at the inconvenience he had caused others. His most frequent response to questions about what he had done was, "I didn't think of that at the time" or "No, that didn't occur to me." Only slowly did the therapist come to accept the possibility that what the youngster was offering by way of explanation might in fact explain what happened. The simplest explanation for his behavior was that he just did not think and that it was lack of a certain kind of thought that had gotten him into difficulty. Further, his failure to think beforehand of the implications and consequences of his actions could not be ascribed to a limitation in measured intellectual ability. He was a boy of above-average intelligence. While described by staff as impulsive and seemingly impatient at times, he was not characteristically defiant or difficult to manage. When he wanted something, apparently his thinking quickly focused on his desire for it and the act of consummation, with little concern with the pros and cons of different methods, the need for a plan, or consideration of consequences for him or others beyond the relatively obvious and immediate. His problem was not one of conflict or aberrant motivation. He suffered from a form of cognitive deficit that repeatedly led him into social difficulties.

This clinical incident soon led to an extensive study of a group of such teenagers, in the course of which a variety of specially designed measures of social cognition (Spivack and Levine, 1963) were identified. The relevant results of this study will be reported in Chapter Four. At this point, suffice it to say that the hypothesis of a social cognitive deficit was confirmed.

The initial research study stimulated subsequent theorizing and research, especially in the Division of Research and Evaluation of the Hahnemann Community Mental Health/Mental Retardation Center, Department of Mental Health Sciences at Hahnemann Medical College and Hospital, Philadelphia. What has now emerged is a beginning statement about the nature of healthy human functioning and a set of working postulates relevant to social adjustment and the ways in which certain cognitive skills function in social adjustment:

(1) A key and common element in any theory of adjustment is the quality of social relationships (capacity to relate to and deal with other people).

(2) A significant and heretofore largely neglected determinant of the quality of social relationships is a group of mediating cognitive processes that define abilities to solve interpersonal problems.

(3) These processes, while perhaps delimited in their broad outline by general intellectual ability, are not the same as abstract, impersonal intellectual ability.

(4) These essential mediating processes are learned from experience in our culture (for example, family and childrearing).

(5) Given the above, any educational/therapeutic interventions that enhance or "free up" these processes will enhance the quality of social adjustment.

Our effort since 1968 has been to identify and measure, over a broad age span, what have come to be called interpersonal cognitive problem-solving skills, to appreciate their meaning within the broader question of what defines healthy human functioning, and to explore how intervention programs may enhance their operation. An earlier book, *Social Adjustment of Young Children* (Spivack and Shure, 1974), has presented knowledge in the area up to that date, focusing on work with young children and presenting a complete mental health curriculum for preschool children. The present book is broader in scope, encompassing the work of others at Hahnemann as well as those elsewhere who have begun to work in this area. The attempt is to present the current state of the art, bringing together the newest information about these interpersonal thinking processes and about programs specifically designed to affect them. The authors are aware that such an attempt will very likely highlight what is not known more than what is known. They judge that the effort is still worthwhile, if for no other reason than to arouse interest in a heretofore neglected area that shows exciting promise for researchers and practitioners alike. If one can demonstrate specific interpersonal cognitive problem-solving processes that mediate social adjustment, one may then devise educational means of supporting healthy adjustment. In doing so, one will have provided another needed link between education and therapy.

This book should be of value to those interested in cognitive functioning and social adjustment, and to those in the psychiatric and mental health fields responsible for creating and maintaining treatment and preventive mental health programs. It should also be of interest to teachers and school curriculum directors. Some of the programs described have been developed in and for schools. Schools often wish to incorporate a mental health component into their overall curriculum, particularly if it is "educational" in the strictest sense and avoids the problems of privacy and confidentiality that mental health programs in schools often raise. Programs deriving from the present work avoid these issues.

In presenting both research findings on interpersonal cognitive problem-solving skills and outlines of training/therapy programs based upon these findings, the attempt has been to keep a proper balance in emphasis. Since one proof of any research pudding in this area is the effectiveness of the intervention programs it inspires, an attempt is made in Chapter Eight to provide sufficient detail so that the reader can evaluate the intervention approach and decide whether to seek more detail from the program developer. On the other hand, the authors have judged it necessary to summarize what is known from research about the processes being taught and to suggest what more must be known in order to increase our confidence in any intervention programs devised.

Much of what follows derives from work that involved teachers, parents, and children in schools in the greater Philadelphia area, staff and clients of the Hahnemann Community Mental Health/Mental Retardation Center, research assistants in the Division of Research and Evaluation of the Department of Mental Health Sciences, and secretarial staff who through the years tolerated with patience and good humor our scribbles, last-minute changes, and altered deadlines. Whatever has been accomplished could not have been without the assistance and support of these people. While too numerous to mention by name, they all will know we mean them when they read these lines.

Considering the depth of their involvement in this work, however, specific mention must be made of Denise Altman, Marsha Bloom, Joan Bryson, Steve Kaplan, Christina Labate, and Stanley Silver, who as research assistants shared their knowledge and collected and analyzed data. Many Philadelphia Get Set day care staff supported our efforts, especially Rosemary Mazzatenta, Vivian Ray, and Bertram Snead and Get Set supervisors Sarah Bowers, Robert Dorso, Sarah Reid, Esther Waters, and Phyllis Williams. Appreciation also goes to the administrative staff of Friends Hospital, especially Dr. William Camp, Director. And, finally but by no means least, the authors express their warmest appreciation to Zakia Amin, Patricia Erdenberger, and Grace Verna, all of whom worked creatively with our manuscript and produced clean copy.

Research work was supported in part by Hahnemann NIH Institutional Grants 720-20-0150, 751-22-9966, 751-20-9951, and 751-20-9897 through its Daughter Grant mechanism. Research was also supported in part by Grant R01-MH20372, awarded by the Applied Research Branch of the National Institute of Mental Health.

Philadelphia, Pennsylvania
September 1976

George Spivack
Jerome J. Platt
Myrna B. Shure

Contents

The Problem-Solving Approach to Adjustment

A Guide to Research and Intervention

Part One

Interpersonal Cognitive Problem-Solving Skills

〰〰〰〰〰〰〰〰〰〰〰 1 〰〰〰〰〰〰〰〰〰〰〰

Role of Interpersonal Problem Solving and Social Cognition in Human Adjustment

〰〰〰〰〰〰〰〰〰〰〰〰〰〰〰〰〰〰〰〰〰〰〰〰

People encounter problems in their relationships with other people. In daily contacts with others, each of us is engaged with family, friends, or coworkers around a variety of personal issues, some minor and some not so minor, that have implications for how well we satisfy our desires or live up to our personal standards, values, and obligations. At one point we may want something from someone and must consider how best to approach the matter. At another we may sense a rebuff that makes us feel uncomfortable. There is a misunderstanding between husband and wife, a person new to a neighborhood

3

wants to make friends, a young girl is concerned about how well she is liked by her peers, a wife begins to feel lonely at home, a child is angry with what another child has said about him. How well the individual handles these very human, everyday problems is a major determinant of his or her emotional well-being.

Interpersonal Problem Solving

The quality of resolution of interpersonal problems is probably due to a complex of interacting factors, including the material and social resources available to the person at the time to aid and support him during the problem-solving process. However, to fully appreciate the efficiency with which the person navigates through the problem to a satisfactory solution, it is necessary to understand how well he thinks about and works through the interpersonal situation. It is this process, manifest in a set of cognitive skills, that defines his social problem-solving capacity. It is the manner in which he proceeds that largely determines the quality of the outcome. It is *how* he thinks it through, rather than what he might think at any given instant, that becomes the important issue in understanding the likelihood of long-range social success or failure. These are the assumptions about people that form the basis of what follows.

In essence, a theory of cognitive problem-solving is being proposed that suggests that there is a grouping of interpersonal cognitive problem-solving (ICPS) skills that mediate the quality of our social adjustment. The purpose of research in the area is to identify and measure these skills, to demonstrate their relationship to social adjustment, to discover how they are learned and how they evolve and change through the life span, to understand their relationship to motivational and affective elements in the person, and to develop educational and treatment programs to enhance their operation. While such a broad research and program development effort is still in its early stages, available evidence offers some support for the theory and provides details that create some structure for its operation.

Interpersonal Cognitive Problem-Solving Skills

There would appear to be a series of ICPS skills rather than a single unitary ability, and the significance of each in determining degree of social adjustment may differ as a function of age. Among these skills is an awareness of the variety of possible problems that beset human interactions and a sensitivity to the existence of an interpersonal problem or at least to the potential for such problems whenever people get together. Such qualities imply not a seeking for trouble where none exists but rather a readiness to view human interaction in terms of real people who desire things, who attempt to manipulate others to achieve their ends, and who may therefore at times rub one another the wrong way. It may also be a willingness to see at any given moment that a human interaction has gone sour and that something has been done or said by one or another person that may have altered the situation—an ability to look at how one relates to others and an ability to examine self in relationship to others right now.

Another ICPS skill is the capacity to generate alternative solutions to problems. This would seem to closely parallel group brainstorming, wherein participants offer a variety of possible solutions, no matter how far-fetched, suspending judgment and withholding censorship of ideas. The key feature, as an individual ICPS skill, is that of *generating* different solution possibilities and not the ability to recognize what might be a "best" solution among those offered. The individual manifests this skill when he draws from a repertoire of ideas that are not merely variations on a single theme but rather different categories of solution to a given problem. The issue is whether the person thinks in terms of options: "I could do this, or that, or I could even do that . . ." or, in contrast, characteristically forecloses without considering alternative routes.

A third ICPS skill is that of articulating the step-by-step means that may be necessary in order to carry out the solution to any interpersonal problem. This spelling out of the so-called means-ends, which often incorporates recognition of obstacles that must be overcome, implies at least foresight, if not necessarily an awareness of others or of how they may react and have to be reacted to during the process of solving a problem. It contrasts markedly with thinking which, having specified a goal, jumps immediately to thoughts of consummation and satisfaction or, at the opposite extreme, so dwells upon the impelling motives or feelings as to forestall necessary action or planning for the attainment of real satisfaction. Means-ends thinking may be viewed as a defining of an interpersonal road map that lays out, in some detail, how one may proceed and what one might do if a block occurs along the way. Implied is a sensitivity to the idea that a solution may take time to carry out and that interpersonal problem solving may at times be a complicated process of interaction.

A fourth ICPS skill is that of considering the consequences of one's social acts, in terms of their impact both on other people and on oneself. The process is one of pursuing an act to the point of asking: "What might happen as a result of my doing this?" There may be more than one feature to such consequential thinking as it pertains to social adjustment. Initially, there is the question of whether or not the idea of consequences spontaneously occurs at all in the mind of someone who is pursuing a course of action. Very often the individual who says, "I'm sorry for what I did—I just didn't think," is essentially saying that he knew what he wanted, and thought of how to get it, but did not consider the consequences of his means-ends in terms of impact upon others and their reactions to his methods. But beyond whether or not the mind moves to consequential thinking at all is the matter of the mind's ability to generate alternative consequences to any act of social significance before the individual decides what to do. As with alternative-solution thinking described earlier, the skill here is manifest in the tendency to generate alternative possible consequences to any one problem solution: "If I yell at him for what he did, he might better appreciate the seriousness of the matter . . . *or* he might only feel hurt and not really listen to me . . . *or* he might not be my friend when I need him . . ." and so forth.

A fifth ICPS skill studied to date reflects the degree to which the individual understands and is ready to appreciate that how one feels and acts may have been influenced by (and, in turn, may have influenced) how others feel and act. In a general sense, this skill reflects an awareness of social and personal motivation in oneself and others and an awareness that current interpersonal events have a continuity with past events that helps us appreciate the meaning of the present. At a more specific level, it reflects the tendency to think: "I am unhappy because he is irritated with me. But maybe he is irritated with me because I ignored him today." Such thoughts reflect a readiness to understand events that propel us toward action. Unwillingness or inability to consider such events narrows the range of rationales available to justify why we act as we do and makes our reactions unduly subservient to our immediate needs and moods, regardless of the context in which they arose.

These ICPS skills are not personality traits as such traits are usually measured by personality tests, nor are they merely one facet of general intelligence as measured by standard IQ tests. There is good reason to believe that they emerge as skills at different ages, depending on the capacity of the developing child and the cognitive demands of the skill, and that one skill may play a more significant role than another in the social adjustment of the individual, depending on age. These skills comprise a grouping of skills that are learned through experiences with other people, particularly childrearers. How well the growing child evolves these skills will reflect how much these forms of ICPS thought are manifest in adults around him at home, especially during the resolution of real interpersonal problems in the family. How childrearers talk to the growing child and handle actual problems involving him probably plays a major role in determining whether or not the child evolves a problem-solving style of thought of his own. Since ICPS skills reflect in part a tendency to *generate* thought in a problem situation, it would be reasonable to expect that they would best be nourished in interpersonal circumstances that encourage the child to express his ideas when problems arise, without undue anxiety and threat to security.

It is proposed that in any instance ICPS skills may not be manifest for two broad classes of reason. On the one hand, the child may not have learned such cognitive skills adequately or may not have been exposed to them at all. In this instance one might speak of a general social cognitive deficit of function in an individual. The deficit could occur as part of a general deficiency in all areas of intellectual stimulation in the home or as a consequence of family emotional dynamics that specifically restrict any opportunity to acquire the ICPS skills needed to face and grapple with interpersonal issues. On the other hand, a person may fail to manifest good interpersonal problem-solving thinking on a particular occasion because the particular situation arouses emotions that destroy his usual social sensitivities or inhibit him from freely exploring options available. He may be so pressured for premature action that appropriate planning, or appreciation of causes and consequences, does not take place. In either case, it is the failure of these mediating thought processes to function that leads to interpersonal misjudgment and social frustration. As a helping agent, one's intervention strategy may be to augment the skills, resolve the interfering emotional components, or both, depending upon one's diagnosis.

Impersonal and Interpersonal Problem Solving

While it may appear self-evident that the kinds of thought processes described above would relate to social adjustment, the fact remains that such processes have rarely been theorized about or studied experimentally. Very few attempts have been made to affect them and, through such intervention, the quality of adjustment. Rapaport (1951) quotes from a theoretical paper written by Heinz Hartmann in 1939 that discusses ego mechanisms and the problem of adaptation and that, at one point, alludes to these kinds of processes. After noting that Freud held that the ego achieves a delay of motor discharge by interpolating thought processes and adding that such thought processes become preparatory trial activity increasingly displaced from overt motor actions into the interior of the organism, Hartmann adds (Rapaport, 1951, p. 388):

The intellect implies an enormous extension

> and differentiation of reaction-possibilities; it sub-
> jects the reactions to its selective control; it creates and
> utilizes means-ends relationships. By means of causal
> thinking connected with space- and time-perception,
> and particularly by turning his thinking back upon the
> self, the individual liberates himself from his slavery to
> the . . . immediate here and now. The intellect under-
> stands and invents; according to some views its function
> is more to pose than to solve problems. . . . The intel-
> lect creates derivative needs; it turns means into ends
> and ends into means. . . ."

The earliest statement relating problem-solving thinking to adjustment was made by Jahoda (1953). According to
Jahoda, one major tendency toward psychological health may
be noted in the sequential tendency to admit to a problem, consider it, make a decision, and take action. An important affective element in this process is the tendency not to avoid the
strain involved and to feel dissatisfied until some resolution
emerges. Another facet is the directness with which the person
approaches the root of the problem. Subsequently, Jahoda
(1958) offered the problem-solving process as one element in
positive mental health: "Going through the process, rather
than finding a successful resolution is taken as the indication
for mental health" (p. 4). No research followed directly upon
such a reasonable conjecture. D'Zurilla and Goldfried (1971)
described what they view as likely stages of interpersonal problem solving, having extensively reviewed research in problem
solving dealing almost exclusively with impersonal tasks.
They suggested ways in which training and psychotherapy
might be viewed as teaching the person *how* to solve problems.
In addition, Weinstein (1969) has offered a speculative paper on
interpersonal competence, viewed as the ability of people to
achieve their purposes when dealing with others. Such competence is said to depend upon one's empathy, defined by
Weinstein as the ability to see the other's perspective, acquiring
a repertoire of tactics to use with and on others, and a variety of
personality parameters that may inhibit or augment such competence (for example, rigidity, internal locus of control, self-

esteem). On January 23–25, 1973, a panel of experts met under the auspices of the Office of Child Development to attempt a definition of social competence in young children (Anderson and Messick, 1974). They agreed that social competence was something more than general intelligence. Among the varied facets noted were intrapersonal and interpersonal sensitivity, appreciation of varied perspectives, and problem-solving skills.

Despite such scattered and rather infrequent references relating problem solving to adjustment, little evidence has been forthcoming. This is interesting in view of the fact that human problem solving has a long and respected history in psychology that has justified periodic review (Duncan, 1959; Davis, 1966; Simon and Newell, 1971). These studies have focused solely on the measurement of cognitive styles and abilities when the individual is confronted with purely intellectual tasks such as puzzles, anagram problems, an array of physical stimuli that offer a conceptual problem to solve, or tasks requiring intellectual creativity. The purpose of such studies is often to determine the cognitive strategies used by the subject in the experiment or how solution efficiency relates to other variables. Other studies have attempted to determine developmental differences or differences between advantaged and disadvantaged groups (see Gray and Miller, 1967).

To date no one except the present authors (see Spivack and Shure, 1974) has stressed the necessity to distinguish between the problem-solving processes called forth by such impersonal intellectual tasks and the thinking demanded when one is confronted with interpersonal problems. While data regarding this issue will be presented subsequently, it is interesting to note at this point that, after reviewing research on the development of social cognition in children, Shantz (1975) concludes: "To date, there seem to be no data to support the view that children's social cognitive skills are 'nothing more' than a reflection of their brightness as measured by conventional intelligence tests" (p. 302). Shantz notes that such correlations are in the low-to-moderate range at best and vary with sex of child, social-economic status, and type of IQ test used. In contrast,

Dudek and others (1969) found consistent significant correlations in the .50s between Piagetian impersonal tasks and WISC IQ scores in primary grade children.

Muuss (1960a) has reported that social causal thinking does not relate to measured intelligence, whereas scores on a test measuring causal thinking about impersonal events do. Feffer and Gourevitch (1960) found a significant relationship between Piagetian impersonal decentering tasks and a social role-taking task, after controlling for IQ. However, Turnure (1975) found no relationship between Feffer's role-taking task and scores and measures of concrete and formal operational thought in children seven to nine years of age. Similarly, Rardin and Moan (1971) found that while measures of popularity and social awareness relate in young children, neither bears a significant relationship to the development of physical concepts. Kurdek and Rodgon (1975) found little or no relationship between affective, perceptual, and cognitive role-taking skills among preschoolers. Awareness of how another child might feel if he saw his brother take away his favorite toy (affective perspective taking) showed no consistent relationship to whether a child could turn his tray so that he could see cut-out characters from the same perspective as the experimenter (perceptual perspective taking) or the ability to predict a story his friend would tell based on differential information (cognitive perspective taking). The findings of Jennings (1975) essentially confirm these findings, adding evidence indicating that IQ test measures and tests of impersonal object classification represent a distinct and separate system from that of social knowledge.

A different order of evidence suggests caution in assuming the unitary operation of impersonal and interpersonal task behaviors. As part of a broader study, Epstein and Radin (1975) factor-analyzed ratings made by testers following administration of the Stanford-Binet to preschoolers. Two factors emerged, one describing the adequacy with which the child responded to the test tasks and the other dealing with the manner in which the child related to the adult and appeared to feel about himself. Epstein and Radin report similar findings having emerged in the work of Hess and others (1968).

Evidence from the study of social intelligence also bears upon the issue of the relationship between impersonal and interpersonal problem-solving abilities. Thorndike (1920) was among the first to propose a social intelligence distinct from the conventional definition of intelligence, but attempts through the years to measure social intelligence, especially independent of verbal ability, have met with many problems. Guilford (1967) has used factor analysis to construct measures to fit his structure-of-intellect model. Social intelligence is viewed as the ability to understand the thoughts, feelings, and intentions of others, and is measured using tasks that have a low loading on a verbal comprehension factor (O'Sullivan and Guilford, 1966). The fact of such low loadings itself suggests that it is necessary to maintain separate consideration of traditional and social intelligence. Two other types of evidence are also relevant, however. Hoepfner and O'Sullivan (1968) found correlations between a traditional IQ measure and Guilford's measures of social intelligence to fall mainly in the .30s and .40s, and findings of Shanley, Walker and Foley (1971) largely confirm this. Thus, while correlations are statistically significant, they actually account for little of the variance. Data of Hoepfner and O'Sullivan also indicate that the two measures exhibit a bivariate triangular distribution indicating that while high-IQ people usually have high social intelligence scores, low-IQ people range from low to high on social intelligence scores. The overall evidence would indicate that while skill in understanding certain aspects of social affairs is not totally independent of traditionally conceived intelligence, there remains good reason not to conceive of them as merely two facets of the same thing or manifestations of the same underlying processes.

Social Cognition as an Area of Study

The social cognition of adults has been studied for many years, especially by social psychologists focusing on the accuracy of social judgments and the processes used in making

social judgments. The latter area has been given more attention in recent years. Until a decade or so ago, however, the
focus in child research has been on understanding his non-
social world. His social behavior was studied independently of
his conceptions of other people or any social cognitive processes that might pertain to his behavior.

Shantz (1975) has recently critically reviewed and discussed the status of theory and research on social cognition,
especially as it pertains to role-taking ability. The evidence presented deals with perceptual perspective taking, empathy, ability to infer what another person is thinking or knows (and
intends), and how growing children evolve in their perceptions of others' traits. While the data pertain mostly to children
and youth, this excellent review summarizes work in this area
most relevant to our present purposes. The evidence suggests
that:

(1) The ability to understand what another person sees,
    feels, thinks, and intends and how he perceives others
    is a developmental phenomenon.
(2) The preschooler has a beginning understanding that
    others have a different perceptual experience, though
    no perspective on how things appear to another per-
    son; he can take into account certain characteristics
    of a listener, and in these respects demonstrates a sim-
    ple form of role-taking ability; he can identify simple
    emotions from facial cues and in situations familiar
    to him; he does not anticipate another's thoughts,
    and probably characterizes others in terms of physi-
    cal appearance.
(3) Between five and seven years of age, there is clear rec-
    ognition of different spatial perspective and an
    understanding that others may have different
    thoughts than he himself, and many at this age are
    able to distinguish accidental from intended action;
    some can blame on the basis of intention, as long as
    consequences of an act are not too negative (if they
    are, consequences and not intention determine

blame); people are described by their appearance and possessions, and by simple evaluative traits.

(4) Middle childhood marks the period of dramatic changes in social understanding. The child comes to understand that his own feelings, thoughts and intentions can be the object of another person's thinking. He can appreciate simple social situations from another's perspective. Blame is ascribed on the basis of intention more than the damage done, spatial perspective is well developed, and the feelings of others may be inferred even in situations unfamiliar to the child. He becomes alert to the inner experiences of others more than merely attending to obvious aspects of social interactions.

(5) In early and middle adolescence, the perspective extends further to the point the youngster can assume the role of a third-party observer of himself and others in interaction, encompassing the feelings, thoughts, and intentions of all involved. There is a spontaneous tendency to try to explain thoughts and feelings, increased refinement in the ways others are described, and recognition of contradictory tendencies in people.

Findings from this research area would suggest that if preschool children should demonstrate the cognitive capacity to problem-solve their social relationships, such problem solving would be quite rudimentary and egocentric. One might even doubt whether differences emerging in ICPS skills between children would bear any relationship to actual behavioral adjustment, but merely reflect differences in general intellectual capacity. It would seem irrelevant to consider sensitivity to interpersonal problems or social causality at this age, considering the child's egocentricity, and certainly means-ends planning would be far beyond his scope. To the extent that appreciation of consequences plays a part in such problem solving, this appreciation should not emerge until somewhere between five and seven years of age.

In middle years, and especially adolescence, dramatic changes should occur in degree and subtlety of interpersonal problem solving. Means-ends planning should emerge as a significant skill, and there should be a gradual increase in sensitivity to social motivation and consequences. Evidence to be presented subsequently bears out some of these suggestions but not others.

Social Cognition and Social Adjustment

Much of the work in social cognition has concerned itself with developmental issues and focused upon role-taking capacity. This probably derives from Piaget's influence on the work of many in the field and from the assumption of an isomorphic correspondence between how we deal with impersonal and social tasks.

Relatively little effort has gone into relating social cognition to social behavior, although results have been promising. Rubin and Schneider (1973) found moderate correlations between communicative role-taking and measures of altruism and helpfulness. Ceresnie (1974) found no relationship between egocentrism and cooperative behavior while studying children working together, but Feffer and Suchotliff (1966) found that dyads with higher scores on a role-taking task did better communicating with one another through one-word association clues than dyads with lower scores.

While no relationship has been found between role-taking ability and popularity in most studies (Rothenberg, 1970; Finley, French, and Cowan, 1973; Rubin, 1973), a significant relationship has emerged between role-taking skill and positive social interaction (Deutsch, in press; Rothenberg, 1970). Jennings (1975) found that four- and five-year-old children exhibiting good interpersonal awareness and social role-taking ability were not only more popular than others but also tended to display more leadership ability, initiative, and ability to get along with others. Iannotti (1975) found that training in role-taking increased willingness of six-year-olds to share candy but that training did not affect scores on a test of empathy or alter frequency with which aggressive outcomes were selected in hypothetical situations.

Studies of a more clinical nature have suggested the fruitfulness of exploring social cognition as a mediator of social adjustment. Noting previous studies relating empathic ability to psychological adjustment (Dymond, 1950; Cline, 1955; Wittick, 1955), Milgram (1960) studied the ability of schizophrenic and brain-damaged patients to assume different roles and respond accordingly to a free-association task. Data suggested that the schizophrenic group had a specific deficiency in this ability, while the brain-damaged were deficient in the capacity to shift from one mental set to another, a trait that underlies this ability. Feshbach and Feshbach (1969) and Feshbach (1973) have found an inverse relationship between measured empathy and antisocial behavior in boys after five years of age, and Chandler (1973) has shown that a training program to enhance ability to take different social perspectives decreases frequency of subsequent delinquent behavior. A similar program has enhanced the behavioral adjustment of institutionalized emotionally disturbed children (Chandler and others, 1974).

Rothenberg (1970) found that appreciation of the feelings of others was directly related to positiveness of self-evaluation and lack of defensiveness (as shown by willingness to face uncomfortable feelings and concern about self and relationship to others). One very interesting finding was that the relationship between appreciation of others' feelings and positive social adjustment emerged most clearly when appreciation of others' feelings was tested in social situations involving negative feelings. These more stressful contexts closely approximate the social situations that require resolution through the kinds of problem-solving cognitive skills that are the focus of the present book.

The work of Muuss (1960a) and Ojemann (1967) on social causal thinking has suggested that an appropriate orientation to causality in human affairs significantly influences the quality of adjustment and that such an orientation may be learned. They present evidence that social causal thinking relates positively to frustration tolerance and tolerance of ambiguity and relates negatively to anxiety level and tendency to lie. Training in social causality has been shown to decrease personal conflicts and to lower scores on tests of anxiety level and insecurity. Unfortunately, none of these studies measured behavioral adjustment as observed in the overt behavior of the children and youth studied. According to Muuss (1960a), "A child might operate causally in his thinking processes and then be able to give the kind of answer that is indicative of mental health while still unable to emotionally apply causal thinking to actual situations such as conflict. . . . Thus, there is a great need for an investigation of the same variables according to more direct behavior indices of mental health" (p. 155).

Giebink, Stover, and Fahl (1968) taught ten- to twelve-year-old impulsive boys alternative adaptive ways to handle frustrating situations. Boys who received instructions in what to do improved in their ability to handle frustrating situations more than did boys who did not receive instructions. Holzworth (1964) taught socially acceptable verbal solutions to and consequences of problem situations to four-year-olds showing deviant classroom behavior. He found significant improvement in isolated play activity. Unfortunately, in both the Giebink and others and Holzworth studies, few children were trained, and so it is difficult to assess the significance of their results.

The body of evidence relating specific ICPS skills to social adjustment is covered in detail in the chapters that follow. An attempt is made to define the issues, describe methods of measurement, demonstrate the relationship of ICPS scores to social adjustment, discuss the relationship of ICPS to IQ and other measures of ability and personality, show how ICPS skills may be learned in the family and childrearing context, and present the outlines of programs that have been developed to enhance these skills in children and in adults.

ᗷᗷᗷᗷᗷᗷᗷᗷᗷᗷᗷ 2 ᗡᗡᗡᗡᗡᗡᗡᗡᗡᗡᗡ

Early Childhood

ᗷᗷᗷᗷᗷᗷᗷᗷᗷᗷᗷᗷᗷᗷᗡᗡᗡᗡᗡᗡᗡᗡᗡᗡᗡᗡᗡᗡ

This chapter will describe the nature of ICPS skills and associated behaviors in preschool and kindergarten children four and five years of age.

Four interpersonal thinking skills have been identified that differentiate children in this age group: (1) ability to conceptualize alternative solutions to typical age-relevant interpersonal problems (for example, wanting a toy another child has); (2) ability to conceptualize potential consequences of an interpersonal act (for example, grabbing that toy); (3) ability to conceptualize causality to explain the occurrence of particular

18

acts (for example, hitting the other child); and (4) a tendency to perceive a problem situation as an interpersonal one.

These interpersonal thinking skills will be examined in light of their unique role as ICPS skills, the extent to which they relate to social adjustment, and their function as mediators significant in determining the quality of social relationships and interpersonal adjustment.

Alternative-Solution Thinking

An individual's ability to generate in his own mind different options (solutions) that could potentially be put into action to solve a problem defines his capacity for *alternative-solution thinking* (also referred to as *alternative thinking*). Interest in alternative thinking in children specifically centers around ability to generate options in solving interpersonal problems with peers and figures of authority. Among four- and five-year-olds, for instance, a girl may want her sister to let her play with her doll. She may ask her, and her sister may say no. Of interest is whether the child who wants the toy would conceive of an alternative way to get her sister to let her play with the doll. Any further attempt that the girl might make to solve her problem is, in the present view, largely dependent upon her ability to generate in her own mind other ways to go about it.

If an individual has only one or two options available to him, his chances of success are less than they might be for someone who can turn to alternative solutions in case his first attempt fails. If the girl's sister consistently says no every time she is asked for something, and no other options are available to the girl, she would soon become frustrated with her sister. She might react aggressively and exhibit impulsive behavior (for example, she might grab the toy) or she might avoid the problem entirely by withdrawing. Either impulsive or withdrawn behavior could come to predominate if problem after problem remains unresolved.

Ability to generate alternative solutions is judged important for successful resolution of problems other than those involving covetousness. For example, children often find themselves in situations in which another person might become angry with them because of something they did. A mother may become angry when her four-year-old spills water on the floor. A child deficient in problem-solving thinking may simply say, "I didn't do it," and when his mother responds by becoming still angrier, the child may retreat and begin to cry. A more efficient problem-solving child may think of ways to avert the mother's anger, such as offering to wipe the water up or explaining how it happened. If no damage has been done, he may even think to wipe it up before his mother discovers it, thus avoiding interpersonal confrontation completely.

One research goal was to determine whether alternative thinking could be identified as an ICPS skill vis-à-vis a testable measure that could distinguish those who could conceptualize alternative solutions to interpersonal problems from those who could not.

Measuring alternative thinking. Children four and five years of age were the first target groups investigated for specific identification of alternative thinking (also referred to as alternative-solution thinking) as an ICPS skill. This skill was measured by the Preschool Interpersonal Problem Solving (PIPS) Test (Shure and Spivack, 1974b). The PIPS Test is a technique designed to elicit from the child as many alternative solutions as he can think of to two age-relevant interpersonal problems. Supplemented with pictures, the first problem (peer-type) depicts one child as wanting a toy another child has. The child is told, "Johnny has been playing with this truck for a long time, all morning, and now Jimmy wants a chance to play with it." After the child identifies the characters, he is asked, "What can Jimmy do or say so he can have a chance to play with this truck?" Because young children lose interest or are unable to respond with more than one idea to the same question, new characters and a new toy (for example, a shovel) are presented after one relevant solution is given; then the question is repeated. In this way the child, in responding to what he thinks is a "new" story, is in fact naming a new solution to the same general peer-type problem. The same procedure is followed in the second type of problem (authority), depicting a child as having damaged property important to his mother. For example, the child is told that Peter broke his mommy's favorite flowerpot and his mommy might be mad at him. He is then asked what Peter could say or do so that his mommy will not be mad. After the child offers one relevant idea, such as "buy her a new one," new characters and a new act of damage to property (for example, scratching her table) are introduced. The idea is to examine the number of different relevant solutions that the child gives to these two interpersonal problems.

With the number of solutions for the peer-type problem correlating between .51 and .59 with the number given to the authority-type problem, a child's score consists of the combined total of different, relevant solutions.

Just as the girl described earlier may become frustrated and aggressive or perhaps withdrawn if problems in interaction with her sister remain consistently unresolved, varying degrees and types of maladaptive behaviors may frequently accompany deficiencies in problem-solving thinking. Having used the PIPS test to identify alternative-solution thinking as a measurable process in children, we next investigated the relationship of this thinking skill to overt behavioral adjustment in children four and five years of age.

Alternative thinking and behavioral adjustment. Seven studies relating alternative thinking to behavioral adjustment have been conducted, each as part of a larger series of investigations and each adding new information about the role alternative thinking plays in the child's ability to adjust and to relate to the world of other people. All youngsters studied in this series were normal preschoolers, displaying varying degrees of behavioral difficulty as observed in the classroom.

The major hypothesis tested was that, regardless of content, better adjusted youngsters could conceptualize a greater number and a wider range of problem-solving strategies for interpersonal problems than could those displaying social behaviors judged to be less adaptive. The child's adjustment was always assessed by rating scales completed by teachers who had known the child for at least one full month and who had had ample opportunity to observe the child's daily behavior patterns in school. In all studies conducted, at least 80% rater reliability was provided by teacher-aides who, like the teacher, had known each child for at least one month.

In the first study Shure and Spivack (1970b) administered the PIPS Test and obtained behavior ratings for 60 four-year-olds—35 lower-class attending inner-city Get Set day-care (mean age, 4.4) and 25 middle-class attending a private down-town nursery school (mean age, 4.3). The behavior scale consisted of twenty separate items, such as: amount of disturbance displayed in the classroom; disrespect and defiance; inability to delay, wait, take turns; comprehension of general classroom discussion; and need to be close to the teacher. Each scale had a statistically defined normal range as established by 200 previously rated children of the same age. Children rated outside of the normal range in either direction were considered aberrant —below the normal range if tending in the inhibited direction; above it, if acting out. The results indicated that while middle-class youngsters as a group could conceptualize a greater number and a broader range of categories of solution, the more poorly adjusted scored significantly below the better adjusted within *each* social class group. Among lower-class youngsters, the deficiencies were particularly marked among those displaying inability to wait a turn, nagging and demanding behavior, and a general impatience with respect to needs and wants requested from peers and adults. In the middle class, the deficiencies were greater among youngsters classified as shy, inhibited, or generally withdrawn—youngsters whose ratings fell predominantly below the normal range.

The purpose of the second study was to gain a more comprehensive picture of problem-solving thinking in four-year-olds by adding new measures of interpersonal cognition to be described later in this chapter. Shure and others (1971) focused attention upon low SES youngsters who had previously shown clear deficiencies relative to their middle-class age-mates. Sixty-two inner-city day-care youngsters (mean age, 4.5) were included. Indices of behavioral adjustment were modified and expanded. Seven items, analyzed into three factors describing behavior "control" problems, were adapted from the Devereux

Child Behavior (DCB) Rating Scale (Spivack and Spotts, 1966b). On a scale from one ("rarely" or "never") to nine ("very, very much") teachers rated each child on items describing: (1) inability to delay, (2) emotionality, and (3) aggression. With intercorrelations of the three factors each significant at the .01 level, the seven items were combined into a single score. The aberrant group consisted of those youngsters considered to be "acting out"—those whose adjustment ratings exceeded those of the "average child" as defined in the rating instructions—and those whose adjustment ratings were so far below the average that they would be considered inhibited or withdrawn.

Youngsters whose behavior ratings indicated a predominance of acting-out behaviors and those classifiable as inhibited were found to conceptualize significantly fewer solutions than did those whose ratings suggested healthy, adaptive adjustment. Among the thirty-two boys and thirty girls, there were no overall sex differences, nor were there any sex differences within any one behavior group classification. These findings were replicated by Shure, Spivack, and Powell (1972).

Given that alternative-thinking skills varied consistently with behavior, being lowest in children with behavioral difficulties, the next goal was to examine more closely the types of behavioral difficulties associated with such thinking deficiency (Shure, Newman, and Silver, 1973). The final version of the scale, called the Hahnemann Pre-School Behavior (HPSB) Rating Scale, included the seven items from the previous study plus new ones obtained from ratings in a sample of 257 inner-city day-care four-year-olds. Instructions to the teacher were clarified and specific scoring criteria were developed so that the seven items (again highly intercorrelated) could clearly define each of the three behavior group classifications. Youngsters classified as impulsive were less able than the average child to wait, share, or take turns. They were more likely to grab toys, nag, and demand when they could not have what they wanted—a general tendency toward impatience. Such youngsters may also have displayed a greater tendency to become easily upset by their peers (when teased or pushed) or by adults, if things did not go their way. They may have reacted with immediate anger if another child interfered with their play or possessions. These youngsters were also more likely to aggress against other children, physically and/or verbally. Youngsters classified as inhibited were likely to retreat or shy away from others at the least sign of frustration, displaying excessive control of behavior or feelings. Such a child may be too timid to exhibit even normal amounts of aggression. Those classified within the adjusted category were rated within the normal range as defined by the scoring system.

Regardless of sex, youngsters rated within the adjusted behavior group range conceptualized the most number of solutions, impulsive youngsters significantly less, and those judged as displaying inhibited behaviors significantly fewer still. From an array of additional specific overt classroom behaviors, alternative problem-solving thinking showed the strongest relationship to four. Well-adjusted youngsters were most liked by their peers, most likely to display concern and/or to offer help to another child in distress, most likely to display autonomy in the classroom (as evidenced by a child's ability to overcome obstacles and complete activities by himself), and most likely to show initiative when appropriate.

The relationship between alternative thinking and behavioral adjustment has appeared consistently. In a study designed to investigate the relationship between a child's alternative-thinking skills and various measures of mother's problem-solving cognition (see Chapter Six) the only consistent finding for both boys and girls was the marked deficiencies in alternative-thinking skill among poorly adjusted children. Another study investigating 113 five-year-olds attending inner-city kindergarten classes revealed the same strength of relationship between interpersonal alternative-thinking skills and overt classroom behavioral adjustment (Shure and Spivack, 1975a).

Solution relevancy.   To learn more about the cognitive process operating among youngsters able to conceptualize alternative solutions to interpersonal problems, five of the seven described studies also investigated the child's ability to focus upon a given task. In the PIPS Test procedure, each child was allowed four attempts to give a relevant solution for each instance of a damaged toy or object. If he responded with a statement such as "his mommy will beat him [for having broken the flowerpot]" the response was considered irrelevant to the problem as stated. Instead of telling what Tommy could do or say so that his mother would not be mad, the child was telling what the *mother* would do as a result of his having broken the pot. Since probing stopped as soon as a new, relevant solution was given, it was possible that children with the same alternative-solution score could give differential numbers of irrelevant responses, indicating differences in another aspect of the cognitive process of alternative thinking. In both four- and five-year-olds, the proportion of relevant solutions to nonrelevant responses has consistently been higher among high problem-solvers and better-adjusted youngsters than among low problem-solvers and the less well adjusted. Inhibited children, usually the poorest problem-solvers, also have exhibited the greatest proportion of nonrelevancies, indicating the least understanding of how a child could solve a problem in interaction with other children or adults.

Solution content. Given that the better-adjusted and high problem-solvers could conceptualize a greater number and variety of new, relevant solutions to interpersonal problems, a further question was whether differences would also occur in solution content. In the six studies that examined this issue, a major interest was the number of solutions describing some form of force as a way to obtain a toy from another child. In every study it was consistently found that while most children conceptualized force, most typically in the form of replies such as "hit him" and "snatch [the toy]," high problem-solvers also conceptualized a greater proportion of nonforceful solutions, typically expressed by "ask," "say please," "I'll let you play with my [toy]," and "take turns."

Differences in priority of thought have also been considered. Low problem-solvers (scoring below the group mean) who had at least one forceful and one nonforceful solution expressed the forceful one first significantly more often than did high problem-solvers with similar content. Apparently young-sters who can think of only a few ways to obtain what they want from others think the fastest and surest way is through some kind of attack.

While low problem-solvers have exhibited a higher ratio and priority of force relative to nonforce, a direct relationship between the force-ratio score and behavior adjustment group classification has not emerged. In general, the thinking of inhibited youngsters contains as much force as that of young-sters in the other adjustment groups, and this has been found for both girls and boys. These findings suggest that while high problem-solvers conceptualize a lower proportion of force, *it is the ability to think of a wide range of solutions, rather than specific content, that most directly accompanies adjusted, adaptable behavior as measured.*

Alternative thinking and language ability, IQ, and test verbosity. Analyses have also been undertaken to discover whether the ability to generate alternative solutions is a unique ICPS skill or whether high problem-solving scores are merely a function of language ability, general intelligence, or ability or motivation to try.

Among both four- and five-year-olds, the number of relevant solutions has never related to items on a teacher rating scale describing the degree to which the child was able to talk in complete sentences or to make himself understood with words. This finding makes sense because it was cognitive thought that was scored and not the way in which that thought was expressed. A child therefore received the same credit on the PIPS Test for "ask" as he would have had he said, "He can ask him for the toy."

In one study, Shure and Spivack (1975a) investigated the possibility that understanding certain key words may have been an operating factor on a child's PIPS score. A significant number of low problem-solvers and poorly adjusted children suggested that the mother will "beat him," "send him to bed," or "make him stay inside" in response to the child's having damaged property. Offering statements about what the mother would do, instead of what the child could do so that the mother would *not* be mad (or beat him), might have been due to lack of understanding or ability to think the negation, that is, the word *not*. Also, inherent in conceptualizing multiple alternatives may have been an understanding of the word *and*. By administering a separate test for the child's understanding of the words *not* and *and*, it was discovered that knowledge of these words was not sufficient to explain high problem-solving scores. (A fuller description of this issue can be found in Spivack and Shure, 1974). This is not to say that some minimal language ability is not necessary. Most inner-city three-year-olds could not even respond to the PIPS testing procedure, because they did not have enough language skill. Important at this point, however, is that varying degrees of comprehension and usage of the English language among four- and five-year-olds did not account for the number of relevant solutions conceptualized to interpersonal problems.

Considering the possible contribution of IQ to both interpersonal alternative thinking and social adjustment, three different IQ tests have been administered in four of the seven studies (Shure and others, 1971; Shure and others, 1972; Shure and others, 1973; Shure and Spivack, 1975a). Little or no relationship emerged between alternative thinking and the Slosson test, the Peabody Picture Vocabulary Test (PPVT), or the Stanford-Binet (long form L-M) test of intelligence. Where low but significant relationships did occur, analyses revealed the cognitive deficiency of impulsive and inhibited children to be still significantly greater than that of adjusted youngsters, regardless of the effect of IQ. Such was true of both the number and proportion of relevant solutions given. A series of discriminative analyses also indicated that while the Stanford-Binet IQ test could predict behavior adjustment group classification, a child's alternative thinking score could add significantly to the distinction of the three behavior groups over and above that provided by IQ. Testing the reverse order, it was discovered that when IQ was added to the alternative-thinking score, it failed to effect increased classifiability of children into behavior groups. With respect to four additional social adjustment behaviors studied, the significant predictability of alternative thinking was completely unaffected by IQ in two of them: a child's concern for others and the degree to which the child was liked by his peers. Such was not the case for behaviors describing autonomy and initiative. For the latter two behaviors, the best predictive power was provided by the combination of alternative thinking and IQ.

It is noteworthy that just as alternative thinking accounted for the predictive power of IQ on the three behavior group classifications (adjusted, impulsive, inhibited), it also accounted for the role played by IQ in predicting a child's concern for others and how well liked he was by his peers. This finding is important in that the latter two behaviors, just as those defining the three classification groups, are interpersonal in nature, whereas those defining the degree of autonomy and initiative are not. Consonant with the interpersonal problem-solving structure of this research, the data suggest that ability to think through and solve problems concerning interaction with others relates more intimately to overt behaviors that are interpersonal in nature than to behaviors defining other abilities to adapt to demands created by the child's environment.

Given that alternative thinking and its relationship to interpersonal behavioral adjustment reflect processes other than those defining general intellectual functioning and that better problem-solvers and better-adjusted youngsters also had a greater tendency to state relevant solutions without also stating nonrelevancies, it was important to determine whether high PIPS scores might be a function of mere tendency to talk or willingness to try. Within the four opportunities given for each example of a broken toy or object, it was possible for a child to *enumerate* or *repeat* earlier relevant solutions or, as described earlier, state an irrelevancy. For example, "I'll let you play with my new ball" to obtain a drum is considered an *enumeration* if "I'll let you play with my new puzzle" was given to obtain an earlier toy. Variations of the same idea, such as "snatch [the kite]" and "take it," are considered *repetitions* if a child had already offered "grab it" as a way to get another toy. It was possible that a child would offer some verbalization to each probe or simply stop and say "I don't know" after one attempt. In six of the seven studies that examined this issue, both four- and five-year-olds responded in some way when probed, and no relationship occurred between the number of relevant solutions and the number of total verbalizations offered. In addition, inhibited youngsters in every study offered as many verbalizations as the adjusted. These findings indicate that interpersonal alternative-thinking skills as measured do not reflect merely a child's motivation to respond or the extent of verbalization during the testing session.

Alternative thinking as a mediator of adjustment. Up to this point, evidence reviewed has consistently indicated that the process of alternative-solution thinking significantly relates to interpersonal overt behaviors, and is an ICPS skill independent of general intellectual functioning, language ability, and a mere tendency to verbalize. An implicit assumption has been that ability to conceptualize alternative solutions to interpersonal problems is an antecedent condition for adjustment and that such thinking ability serves as a *mediator* of healthy human functioning. The tenability of this assumption has been put to empirical test through a series of training programs designed to improve the behavior of impulsive and inhibited children, *not* by direct modification of the behavior itself, but by altering a child's problem-solving thinking style. (See Chapters Eight and Ten for description of program content.) Results of intervention have demonstrated consistently that, irrespective of sex and any change in IQ, four- and five-year-olds displaying behaviors characteristic of impulsivity or inhibition prior to training, and behaviors within the adjusted range following it, improved in interpersonal alternative thinking to a greater extent than did those who remained aberrant. That youngsters who improved in the trained thinking skills were the *same* as those who improved in behavior adjustment suggests a direct link between the two, and alternative thinking as a direct mediator of overt behavioral adjustment. Considering all behaviors measured, impulsive youngsters who improved most in the trained alternative skills became more able to wait for what they wanted and became less nagging and demanding. They were better able to share and take turns and less easily upset in the face of frustration. Inhibited youngsters who learned how to think of alternative solutions to interpersonal problems became more socially outgoing, more able to express feelings and desires to both peers and adults, and less timid in the face of frustration. The degree to which youngsters were liked by their peers and showed concern or offered help to another child in distress also increased as a direct function of improvement in the trained alternative-thinking skills.

Findings from the series of programs to train mothers to enhance problem-solving thinking skills of young children further substantiate interpersonal alternative thinking as a significant mediator of overt behavioral adjustment:

(1) Prior to training, girls learn a significant portion of their problem-solving skills from their mothers, whereas boys appear to learn them through other channels (see Chapter Six). Nevertheless, boys as well as girls displaying healthy, adaptive adjustment were significantly more efficient in alternative thinking than those showing signs of impulsivity or inhibition.

(2) From whomever the child initially learns how to think about solutions to interpersonal problems, boys as well as girls could enhance these skills from highly specialized training. Whether trained by the teacher or the child's own mother, improvement in these thinking skills was related to improvement in behavioral adjustment [the direct link].

(3) Though improvement in the child's alternative-thinking skills did relate to improvement in the mother's problem-solving style of communication with her child as a consequence of training (in boys as well as girls), the direct link between the child's alternative thinking and overt behavior was independent of that relationship.

This last finding (Shure and Spivack, 1975a) clearly suggests that the mother's problem-solving interaction with her child does not affect behavior directly, but has a direct influence on the child's problem-solving thinking skills, which in turn affect his behavior.

The results of these investigations have clearly identified interpersonal alternative thinking as one ICPS skill functioning as a significant determinant of the quality of social relationships and interpersonal behavioral adjustment.

Consequential Thinking

Consequential thinking is defined as the ability to generate in one's own mind what might happen as a direct result of carrying out an interpersonal act.

The girl who was refused her sister's doll may, for example, impulsively hit her sister as a reaction to the frustration of having been denied her wish, or she may think through different options and decide that, at that particular moment, hitting is one alternative way to get her sister to give in and let her have that doll. If she thought about it and decided to hit her, the new question of relevance is whether the girl also thought through the potential interpersonal consequences of her hitting and whether having done so might have influenced her decision to hit.

Whether consequential thinking guides behavior is an important question. If the girl had thought to herself, "If I hit her she might hit me back," it is possible that she would not have cared about that and would have proceeded to hit her sister. However, it is also possible that, if she thought of other potential consequences that might have occurred, she might have chosen a different option. Would a child who spilled water on the floor tell his mother, "I didn't do it," if he thought that might make his mother still angrier?

In four- and five-year-olds, initial research attempted to discover whether children so young could think in terms of consequences of an act and whether it would be possible to develop a test that could distinguish youngsters efficient and deficient in such skills.

Measuring consequential thinking. The first pilot test

developed by Shure and Spivack quickly indicated that a large majority of four-year-olds were unable to respond to a procedure wherein the child had to make a choice between two given solutions and then state why the choice was made. For example, in one part of the test the child was shown pictures and told: "Here is Johnny and he wants to play with this truck, but Jimmy is playing with it. Here are two things Johnny did to get Jimmy to let him play with this truck. One time he said, 'If you let me play with the truck, I'll give you a ball to play with.' One time he punched him." After the child repeated the given solutions he was asked: "Which idea do you like better, giving him a ball or punching him?" After the child made a choice, he was asked: "Why do you like [giving the ball] better than [punching him]?" or "What might happen next if he [gives him the ball]?" The child was then asked: "Why don't you like [punching him]?" or "Why isn't [punching] as good as [giving the ball]?" or "What might happen next if he [punches him]?" Although most children did make a choice, their reasoning was often irrelevant. Some children, when asked a question such as, "Why don't you like [punching him]?" responded, " 'Cause then he'll get the truck." Either the language of the test was beyond the comprehension of children this age, or the process of relevantly explaining one choice over another was too difficult for children this age.

It was not yet possible to clearly ascertain whether consequential thinking was beyond the developmental ability of four-year-olds, whether the measuring device was not sensitive enough to tap these skills, or whether consequential thinking was not an ICPS skill that would bear relevance to mental health functioning of young children.

The procedure was changed to measure a different process, that of a child's ability to conceptualize *alternative* consequences to a given interpersonal act. It was assumed that if consequential thinking does have relevance to the behavioral adjustment of young children, the identification of it would require designing a test with maximum sensitivity to the cognitive skills developed in children four years of age. Based on responses to the PIPS Test, it was evident that ability to conceptualize *alternatives* was within the cognitive capacity of these children, and a test was developed paralleling that procedure to measure consequential thinking.

After two attempts to create a procedure that would be similar to yet distinguishable from the PIPS Test and story content that would hold maximum interest (Shure and others, 1971; Shure and others, 1972), the third design focused upon eliminating the difficulties of the first two. First, small wooden stick figures were made to represent child and adult characters, replacing the PIPS Test pictures previously used in consequences testing. This change was necessary to eliminate any "set" established from having given problem solutions to the same pictures. The questioning procedure was similar to that of the PIPS Test, except the child was given one solution to a problem—that of grabbing a wanted toy from another child— and asked to tell what might happen next or what [Johnny] might do or say if [Jimmy] grabs the toy. As in the PIPS procedure, new sets of characters and toys were shown after one relevant consequence was given, and the question about grabbing was repeated. Of the fifteen categories of consequences that emerged, the most typical for the act of grabbing included "snatch it back," "hit him," "he'll tell his mother," and "he won't be his friend." The second series of stories depicted a child having taken an object from an adult without asking first. Then the four-year-old was asked, "What might happen next?" or "What might [Mrs. Smith] do or say when she sees her [flashlight] was taken?" Each new story represented a new adult character and different object taken, such as a wooden statue or a tablecloth. Of the thirteen categories that emerged, typical were "she'll tell her mother," "she'll beat him," "give it back!" As in the PIPS procedure, new stories continued until the child could no longer offer new, relevant consequences, with each child given a minimum of five toys and five objects taken. Interest level was high, a wide range of relevant consequences was obtained, and the final version of the consequences test, called the "What Happens Next Game" (WHNG), was incorporated into the research program.

Consequential thinking and behavioral adjustment. Using

the final revised version of the testing procedure, it was found that regardless of sex, inner-city day-care four-year-olds rated as behaviorally adjusted on the previously described HPSB scale conceptualized a greater number of different, relevant consequences to acts of grabbing toys and taking objects without permission than did those judged to be displaying behaviors of impulsivity and inhibition (Shure, Newman, and Silver, 1973; Spivack and Shure, 1975; Shure and Spivack, 1975b). In one of these studies (Shure, Newman, and Silver) analyses were conducted to further examine the role of consequential thinking in the child's overt behavioral adjustment. It had already been established that ability to conceptualize solutions and the separate ability to conceptualize consequences could each predict with significant accuracy the behavior adjustment group of inner-city four-year-old children. Stepwise discriminant analyses revealed that knowledge of a child's alternative-solution thinking was sufficient to predict healthy, adaptive behavioral adjustment. If one could measure skills in both alternative *and* consequential thinking, it was significantly more possible to predict which of the two aberrant behavior groups would describe a particular child. If a child was a high problem-solver (high in alternative thinking) he was likely to have displayed healthy, adjusted behavior regardless of his consequential-thinking ability. A child low in alternative thinking was likely to have displayed either impulsive or inhibited behaviors. A child deficient in both alternative *and* consequential thinking was most likely to have exhibited behaviors classified as inhibited.

Youngsters most liked by their peers who showed concern for others and tended to display initiative in the classroom conceptualized more consequences than did youngsters not displaying these behaviors. However, knowledge of a child's consequential-thinking skills did not add to ability to predict these behaviors beyond that which could be predicted by alternative thinking alone.

While consequential thinking provided added predictability of a child's impulsivity or inhibition at age four, the relationship to adjustment group classification was less clear among the five-year-old kindergarten youngsters (Shure and Spivack, 1975*b*). Nevertheless, adjusted youngsters did conceptualize the most consequences to an interpersonal act, the impulsive group an intermediate amount, and the inhibited the least. Among kindergarten youngsters, however, consequential thinking did not add to the power to predict specific aberrant behavior classification above and beyond that provided by alternative thinking alone. Among the five-year-olds, consequential thinking did relate to the degree to which the child was liked by his peers, but further analyses also revealed that solution thinking alone was sufficient to predict this measure of social competence.

Consequences relevancy. Just as in the PIPS Test procedure, the child was given four opportunities for each toy grabbed and each object taken, and a ratio of relevant to nonrelevant statements examined. The child was probed for any irrelevancy ("he'll get another toy," "he'll be happy"); a statement of nonconsequence ("nothing will happen"); any apparent solution to obtain the toy ("he'll give him his bike"); or, in the case of the object taken, a shift to the mother's viewpoint ("she'll look for it"). Repetitions or enumerations of earlier relevant consequences were also probed. Among both four- and five-year-olds, youngsters who conceptualized the most consequences also had a higher proportion of relevant responses than did those with low scores, though this finding was less consistent across studies in the preschool groups. In stating fewer irrelevancies among the total number of responses allowed, high scorers did indicate a greater understanding of the concept than did low scorers.

Consequential thinking and language ability, IQ, and test verbosity. As in the case of alternative-solution thinking, consequential thinking did not relate to verbal skills as displayed in the classroom in any of the studies in the described series. Again, this is no doubt due to crediting any words that indicate cognition ("can't have candy") with the same value as "He'll show him all his candy and say you can't have any 'cause you snatched my boat." Similarly, neither IQ nor ability or tendency to verbalize had any effect on a child's consequences score or on any significant relationship between consequential thinking and behavioral adjustment as measured. It might be of interest to note that youngsters relatively incapable of conceptualizing relevant consequences were also more likely to state that "nothing" would happen if a child grabbed a toy or took an object from an adult without asking permission. Whether these youngsters really believed that no consequence would result from these acts or were unable to conceptualize consequences that might ensue has not been ascertained. Given that the same child would generally state one relevant consequence for grabbing a truck, followed by "nothing would happen" for grabbing a shovel, low scores were more likely a function of cognitive deficiency than of a real belief of no consequence.

Consequential thinking as a mediator of adjustment. One goal of the previously described intervention training program was to enhance the child's alternative thinking skills. Another was to increase the child's ability to think about how an act might affect other people and his relationships with them—his ability to think about the consequences of what he does.

If teachers train a group of aberrant (impulsive or inhibited) four-year-olds in consequential thinking, some will respond and some will not (Shure and Spivack, 1973). The direct link between the teacher's training effort and the children's response is not as dramatic for consequential as for alternative-solution thinking at this age, apparently. But the link is markedly stronger between training and improved consequential thinking among children only a year older. Shure and Spivack (1975a) found the increase in number of consequences given by aberrant youngsters who became behaviorally adjusted following training, when compared to those who remained aberrant (the direct link), was more impressive among five-year-olds than among four-year-olds. In addition, five-year-olds verbalized fewer irrelevant statements prior to offering a relevant consequence after training, while the proportions of irrelevancies given by four-year-olds did not change. While both age groups did increase the total amount of consequences given, the more frequent irrelevant statements given by the younger children suggest that the older children could "catch on" to the cognitive processes involved in consequential thinking more quickly than the younger ones and that conceptualizing "what might happen next" is a relatively demanding task for prekindergarten youngsters. This assumption was further strengthened by four-year-olds trained by their mothers (Shure and Spivack, 1975a). The relatively weaker mediating function served by consequential thinking as compared to alternative thinking showed patterns similar to those of four-year-olds trained by their teachers.

Regarding the other measured behaviors in the classroom, no consistent correlation with improvements in consequential thinking was evident for the degree to which the child was liked, showed concern, or displayed initiative or autonomy, for either four- or five-year-olds.

The results of all these studies suggest that consequential thinking does play a mediating role for youngsters who can wait for what they want and who display normal amounts of emotionality and aggressiveness. *Lack* of skill (especially in combination with lack of alternative-solution thinking) also affects the behavior of inhibited youngsters. The significance of consequential thinking in determining the behavior of impulsive youngsters is less consistent and its mediating function more questionable.

Although impulsive youngsters conceptualize potential consequences more than inhibited youngsters, such thinking may not always play a role in guiding their behavior. There are at least two possible reasons. The thinking of the impulsive youngster seems to be typified by a relatively narrow repertoire of solutions. Perhaps his awareness of potential consequences of an act is of limited use to him because in carrying out an act he chooses from such a relatively limited range of options to begin with that feedback about consequences does not result in significantly expanded choices for action. Or perhaps a child displaying impatience or more than normal amounts of emotionality and aggression may be aware of the potential consequences of, say, his grabbing or hitting, but is more concerned about what "will work [now]" than about what "might happen [later]." As one child told another, "If you don't play [Lotto] with me I'll rip your pants." When asked by the teacher what might happen if he did that, the child responded, "He won't be my friend but I don't care." Thus, impulsive children may be less prone than adjusted youngsters to seek out or consider a different, more effective solution in case of actual failure, because for impulsive children thoughts of consequences are less likely to play a self-corrective function.

For youngsters not able to exhibit even normal amounts of impatience, emotion, and/or aggression, consequences do not seem even to enter into their thinking. With evidence indicating that inhibited youngsters have even fewer problem solutions available to them than are available to impulsive youngsters, it is possible that they have simply withdrawn from potential problem situations, attempting to consider neither possible solutions nor "what might happen next." If the withdrawn, inhibited child is involved in thought, such thought is not about what he might do about his problems or what might happen if he does do something.

In sum, consequential thinking does play a significant mediating role in the behavioral adjustment of young children, with lack of such skills particularly affecting youngsters who display shy, withdrawn, inhibited behaviors. In adjusted and especially among impulsive youngsters, the presence or absence of consequential thinking has a secondary impact on guiding behavior relative to the presence or absence of alternative-thinking skills.

Causal Thinking

To gain a more comprehensive picture of problem-solving thinking of young children and to further assess such skills in relationship to behavioral adjustment, a third cognitive process was introduced early in the research series, that of cause-and-effect thinking associated with interpersonal problem situations.

Causal thinking is the ability to relate one event to

another over time with regard to the "why" that might have precipitated an act.

It seems reasonable to assume that if the girl described earlier thinks through her decision to hit her sister, she might also be aware that she hit her "because she wouldn't let me play with her doll," or "because I am angry at her for not letting me play with her doll." If her sister should hit her back as a consequence of having been hit, it is reasonable to assume that the girl is aware that her sister hit her "because I hit her first."

The reasons for investigating causal thinking in four- and five-year-olds were, first, to determine whether interpersonal cause-and-effect could be found among children of that age and, second, to determine its role as an ICPS skill both by itself and in combination with alternative and consequential thinking. For example, one question raised is whether a child who can conceptualize solutions to a problem as well as their potential consequences is also a child more prone to think of cause-and-effect when confronted with situations pertaining to typical human interactions.

Causal thinking in four-year-olds.   In two studies, the question of interest was the child's tendency to think of cause-and-effect when presented with a hypothetical interpersonal event. For example, in one test the child was told: "Billy's knee is bleeding. He is talking to his mother." He was then asked: "What do you think he is saying to her?" The child was given no indication that a causal explanation was of interest. Measured was the child's spontaneous inclination to state a causal explanation. Credit was given only if the child's response indicated a possible cause *of* the event, not what might be caused by the event. Therefore, responses such as "I cut myself on glass" or "I fell" were scored, but "I need a Band-Aid because my knee is bleeding" was not.

In both studies using this procedure, causal thinking either did not relate to behavioral adjustment (Shure, Spivack, and Jaeger, 1971) or any relationship that did occur was relatively weaker than that of alternative-solution and consequential thinking (Shure and Spivack, 1975*b*). Knowledge of the child's score in causal thinking did not add to the power of scores in alternative-solution and consequential thinking to classify children as adjusted, impulsive, or inhibited.

An important point must be made here. After training, the training group increased in causal thinking to a significantly greater extent than did the nontrained controls. The training group also improved in behavioral adjustment to a significantly greater extent than did the controls. From these data one might conclude that improvement in causal thinking improves behavioral adjustment. Further analyses revealed, however, that the children who improved in causal thinking were not the same children who improved in behavioral adjustment, and this result was unlike the result for alternative-solution and consequential thinking. That is, the direct link established between improvement in social adjustment and training for alternative and consequential thinking was not established for causal thinking. Thus, causal thinking as a mediator of adjustment in four-year-olds has not been empirically demonstrated. It has not been clearly ascertained, however, whether lack of a direct link is due to the impact of causal thinking on children this age, to relative lack of emphasis in the training program itself, or to lack of sufficient sensitivity to causal thinking in the measuring instrument itself.

Causal thinking in five-year-olds. When ICPS ability of five-year-old inner-city kindergarteners was studied, Shure and Spivack (1975a) made a further attempt to discover whether any causal-thinking processes have been developed by this age. It was judged reasonable to measure causal thinking via the general procedure that successfully discriminated skills in alternative-solution and consequential thinking.

In the revised measure, the child was specifically asked why an event might have happened, and the research questions were to determine (1) whether children who could conceptualize alternative causes would differ in behavioral adjustment from those who could not; and (2) whether causal thinking serves as a mediator of adjustment.

Using small wooden dowel sticks to represent child characters, the child was told: "This is Peter and this is Tommy.

Peter and Tommy are at school. Peter is hitting Tommy." The child was then asked: "Why is Peter hitting Tommy?" As in the procedures measuring alternative-solution and consequential thinking, new characters were presented as soon as the child gave one relevant causal statement. Several variations of the test questions were used, such as, "He might be hitting Tommy because _____"; "How come this boy hit Tommy?" or "What made Peter hit Tommy?" After a minimum of five situations depicting one child hitting another, the children were shown a series of pictures of children laughing. Each child was given four opportunities per story to state a causal explanation, and was probed if he gave an irrelevancy (for example, "Tommy should tell his mother Peter hit him" or " 'Cause he just did") or if he enumerated or repeated earlier relevant causal statements.

Initial analyses revealed that, regardless of IQ, the number of relevant causal statements was significantly related to behavior adjustment group, with adjusted youngsters stating the most and inhibited the least. Scores were not attributable to lack of willingness to talk on the part of inhibited youngsters. The total number of verbal statements was as high for inhibited youngsters as for those in the other adjustment groups. Further, a significant negative correlation between causal and noncausal statements indicated that youngsters with fewer causal responses did at least respond with some kind of verbalization.

Optimism about causal thinking as a potential mediator of behavioral adjustment has diminished with further analyses. Unlike findings for consequential thinking, test results have indicated that the relationship between causality and behavior is attributable to the child's alternative-solution thinking skills. As in the case of four-year-olds, causal thinking added no predictive power to behavioral classification above and beyond that provided by alternative-thinking skills. Initial relationships of causal thinking to the other behaviors measured—that is, concern for others, liked-by-peers, initiative, and autonomy—were also lost when the child's ability to conceptualize solutions to interpersonal problems was accounted for. Finally, there was no significant increase in causal thinking as children improved in behavioral adjustment as a function of training.

At least as currently measured, causal thinking does not appear to function as a direct mediator of behavioral adjustment in four- and five-year-olds.

Sensitivity to Interpersonal Problems

Interpersonal sensitivity involves the cognitive ability to perceive a problem when it exists and the tendency to focus on those aspects of interpersonal confrontation that create a problem for one or more individuals involved.

To carry our example of the girl who wanted her sister's doll one step further, it seems reasonable to assume that if she were aware that a problem or potential problem could develop once she decides to ask for the doll, her behavior and/or problem-solving strategies may differ from what might ensue in the absence of such sensitivity. Further, if she were also sensitive to the fact that a new problem might emerge once she "hits her" in retaliation to having been told no, her behavior and/or problem-solving strategies might differ from the course pursued in the absence of such sensitivity.

Whether such cognitive sensitivity to interpersonal problems is part of the repertoire of thinking processes in four- and five-year-olds and whether such sensitivity could be identified as an ICPS skill provided the rationale for designing a test to measure such a skill.

Measuring sensitivity to interpersonal problems. The goal was to measure the child's readiness to perceive a problem situation as interpersonal. Each child was shown nine commercial pictures (from Kerr, Good Manners Posters [Primary], Hayes Publishing Company) illustrating children in interaction with peers or adults in potential interpersonal problem situations. For example, one picture shows a girl walking a dog, with a boy in ripped pants, hands on hips, angrily looking on. The child was then told: "Oh, oh, something's wrong. What's wrong in this picture?" Interpersonal responses included, "She won't let him walk the dog," "He's mad at her," and "It's his dog and she took it." Statements such as "His pants are ripped" were considered a personal problem for the boy, but not interpersonal because the girl was not included in the problem. "The dog is sick" was regarded as an impersonal problem, and "She'll let him walk the dog," a statement of a *solution* but not of a problem (even though interpersonal). Statements such as "He wants the dog" were considered a state of need, and "His hands are on his hips," irrelevant. Each child was shown two warm-up pictures illustrating an obvious interpersonal problem, one showing a boy pushing a girl off a bike. The child was not told, however, that a statement of an interpersonal problem was of interest.

The final version of the test included those pictures that interrelated with each other (five of them), each of which provided a range of responses including statements about interpersonal problems. This measure was used for both four- and five-year-olds, as both age groups provided a wide range of responses.

Interpersonal sensitivity and behavioral adjustment. Results of two studies of four-year-olds (Spivack and Shure, 1975; Shure and Spivack, 1975a) revealed that differences in cognitive sensitivity did not significantly relate to behavior adjustment, although inhibited youngsters, especially boys, did show less readiness to perceive interpersonal problems than did the impulsive or adjusted.

In the kindergarten year, the initial relationship of interpersonal sensitivity to the three behavioral adjustment groups suggested borderline significance, with adjusted youngsters most sensitive, inhibited the least. Analyses combining sensitivity and alternative-solution thinking showed that both contributed to significant mean differences between each behavior pair, with inhibited youngsters most deficient, impulsive youngsters intermediate, and adjusted youngsters most efficient. These analyses also showed, however, that alternative thinking was still the single most significant predictor of behavior adjustment. While sensitivity also related to three of the four additional behaviors measured—concern for others, initiative, and autonomy—further analyses indicated that sensitivity did not add to the power of alternative-solution thinking in predicting these behaviors.

Interpersonal sensitivity as a mediator of adjustment. Though a child's tendency to perceive a potential interpersonal problem did show a trend in differentiating youngsters with varying degrees of behavioral difficulties, no direct link as a consequence of training was evident for either four- or five-year-olds. In other words, any improvement in behavioral adjustment was not a function of increased cognitive sensitivity to interpersonal problems.

Whether cognitive sensitivity to interpersonal problems functions as a behavioral mediator in young children remains an open question. It has not been established whether a readiness to perceive interpersonal problems simply plays a minor role in regulating behavior in children this age or whether the measuring instrument has been unable to detect differences between behavior group classifications. That children who improved in behavioral adjustment after training did not also improve in interpersonal sensitivity could be due to relative lack of emphasis in training for this particular cognitive skill.

Interrelationships of Interpersonal Thinking Skills

Previous discussion has emphasized the varying strength of relationship between particular ICPS skills and adjustment, describing alternative thinking as the strongest, consequential thinking as intermediate, and causal thinking and interpersonal sensitivity as the weakest. Of interest now are the relationships among the four described thinking skills and whether there is any evidence suggesting that there may be a common element running through them.

Table 1 presents intercorrelations among the four thinking skills as measured, with children in adjusted, impulsive, and inhibited behavioral adjustment groups combined.

The data suggest that there is an interrelationship among the four measures. However, the percentage of overlap (variance) ranges from 29 percent (solutions and consequences,

Table 1

Interrelationships of Four Interpersonal Thinking Measures Among
Four- and Five-Year-Olds, with Behavioral Adjustment Groups Combined

	Consequences		*Causality*		*Sensitivity*	
Age	*4*	*5*	*4*	*5*	*4*	*5*
Alternative solutions	.54*	.47*	.34*	.40*	—	.40*
	(N=257)	(N=113)	(N=257)	(N=110)		(N=110)
Consequences			.38*	.31*	—	.24*
			(N=257)	(N=110)		(N=110)
Causality						.31*
						(N=110)

*p <.01

four-year-olds) to 6 percent (consequences-sensitivity, five-
year-olds), indicating that the skills measured by the four tests
cannot be considered interchangeable or assumed to be merely
measuring the same thing.

A further test of the issue of a common element in the
four thinking skills was conducted via factor analysis on data
for the five-year-olds. Using varimax rotation, Table 2 shows

Table 2

Factor Loadings of Four Interpersonal Thinking Skills
Among Five-Year-Olds Within Two Separate
Behavior Group Classifications

	Adjusted (N=41)		*Aberrant* (N=72)
Factor	*1*	*2*	*1*
Thinking Skill			
Alternative solutions	.82	.20	.78
Consequences	.62	-.26	.70
Causality	-.04	.96	.73
Interpersonal sensitivity	.67	-.08	.73

the factor loadings on analyses conducted for adjusted youngsters and separately for the aberrant groups (impulsive and
inhibited) combined.

Results of the two factor analyses are not identical but do
suggest a common element that might be termed a basic ability
in children this age. Over a broad range of children, this com-

mon element is manifest in measures of alternative problem-solution, consequential, and interpersonal problem-sensitivity thinking. Why causal thinking does not load with the other three measures of interpersonal thinking in the better adjusted behavior group is not clear. While more data are needed, it is interesting to note that the three measures that did load together in both behavior groups test skills that describe a similar time line. Alternative-solution thinking and interpersonal sensitivity describe the present, and consequential thinking as measured describes how a present act could relate to the immediate future—"If he hits him [now], he might get hit back [later]." Causal thinking, as tested, requires turning the mind back, linking present events to those that took place in the past —"He's hitting him [now] because he hit him [before]."

Impersonal Alternative Thinking

A child's ability to conceptualize alternatives to noninterpersonal referents was investigated to gain a greater understanding of ICPS functioning. The first question of concern was whether a child's ICPS ability is merely a function of his ability or motivation to conceptualize alternatives per se, and whether that general ability is really accounting for the relationships between solutions and consequences (each measured by eliciting alternatives) and overt behavioral adjustment. The second question concerns the more general relationship between impersonal alternative-thinking skills and interpersonal thinking skills other than those involving the use of alternatives in their measurement—that is, cognitive sensitivity to interpersonal problems.

In one study, each child was given a multiple usage test in which he was asked to name as many uses as he could for two items familiar to four-year-olds, a chair and water (Shure and Spivack, 1975a). Because of the importance of the questions asked of the resulting data, the complete findings relative to impersonal alternative thinking are discussed here as a separate issue.

First, the relationship between alternative problem-solution and consequential thinking, as well as the relationship of each to behavior adjustment, could not be explained by an abstract ability to conceptualize alternatives. Though there was an initial significant relationship between impersonal and interpersonal alternative-solution and consequential thinking in girls, further analyses revealed that the two interpersonal thinking skills maintained that relationship after the effect of impersonal alternative thinking was controlled. Importantly, the relationship between solution score and impersonal alternative usage score disappeared with consequences controlled. Similarly, the relationship between consequences score and impersonal usage score disappeared with alternative solutions controlled. It is of interest that inhibited girls conceptualized slightly *more* impersonal alternatives than did the adjusted, a trend never seen with respect to ICPS thinking skills.

Another difference between interpersonal and impersonal measures concerns the relationship of the number of alternatives given to the number of verbal statements made during testing. In the entire series of investigations, there was never a significant positive relationship between number of alternatives and number of verbal attempts. For both alternative solutions and consequences, lower-scoring youngsters make as many verbal attempts as do higher-scoring youngsters. These analyses have consistently indicated that when a child could not conceptualize a new, relevant solution to a problem or consequence to an act, he at least made some kind of response. Such was not the case for impersonal alternative thinking. There was a significant positive relationship for both sexes between the number of alternative usages for a chair and water and the total number of verbal attempts. Unlike interpersonal alternatives, then, impersonal alternatives may be a function of willingness to talk or to make an attempt with some kind of response. Stated another way, the child who talks the most might inadvertently hit upon more relevant alternatives in an impersonal task, but would not necessarily score higher in interpersonal ones.

In addition to lack of significant impact of impersonal alternative thinking on behavior adjustment classification

(adjusted, impulsive, inhibited), impersonal alternative thinking also bore no significant relationships for either sex to the
additional studied classroom behaviors—liked-by-peers, concern for others, initiative, and autonomy. Of the ICPS skills,
alternative-solution scores most consistently related to these
behaviors, indicating a still additional difference between the
interpersonal and impersonal cognitive skills in question.

Just as IQ does not account for the relationship between
alternative problem-solution and consequential thinking or
the relationship of these ICPS skills with adjustment in overt
behavior, the same holds true of impersonal alternative thinking. *A significant portion of a child's interpersonal alternative
thinking is independent of a general ability to conceptualize
alternatives.*

It can be concluded from all analyses that ability to conceptualize alternatives interpersonal and impersonal in nature
represents distinct and separate dimensions of cognitive
thought.

The second question is whether impersonal alternative
thinking skills relate to ICPS skills other than those measured
by eliciting alternatives. There was no significant relationship
between the child's impersonal alternative thinking and cognitive sensitivity to interpersonal problems, for boys or for girls.
The significant relationship between problem sensitivity (not
requiring thinking of alternatives) and ICPS skills wherein the
measuring procedure elicited alternatives (problem solutions
and consequences) suggests a closer relationship among the
three interpersonal cognitive skills than among any measured
personal and impersonal skills of alternative thinking. It is
also of interest to note that in the study of ICPS skills of
mothers and children (see Chapter Six), there was a low but significant relationship between the mother's reported methods of
handling real problems that arise at home and the daughter's
(but not the son's) impersonal-alternatives score. However,
this finding did not account for the significant relationship
between the mother's methods and a child's solution score. Further, the child's impersonal alternative thinking did not relate

to any measured ICPS skill in mothers, but his/her interpersonal ICPS skills did.

It is also of interest to note that youngsters with high sensitivity scores gave about an equal number of responses classified as problem-oriented and as not oriented to a problem at all. Thus, youngsters who tended to focus on interpersonal problems did not necessarily tend to also focus on all kinds of problems per se. However, when they did focus on problems, the problems were more likely to be interpersonal than noninterpersonal in nature. These findings, plus certain relationships to thinking skills of mothers (at least among girls) help define interpersonal sensitivity as an ICPS skill, suggesting that it may very well play a role as a cognitive skill important in the problem-solving thinking of the young child. *Alternative problem solutions, consequences, and sensitivity to interpersonal problems are related to each other, independent of impersonal alternative thinking.* All three are also related to mother's cognitive ability to solve problems between a hypothetical mother and child, while a child's impersonal alternative thinking is not. Furthermore, all three interpersonal thinking skills of the child have been found related to mother's problem-solving style in handling real problems that arise with her child at home, and these relationships were also genuine irrespective of impersonal alternative-thinking skills (Shure and Spivack, 1975a). Though cognitive sensitivity does not relate directly to the child's behavioral adjustment, its intimate relationship to other interpersonal thinking skills in a pattern significantly different from that of impersonal skills further suggests the identification of measured interpersonal sensitivity as a clear ICPS skill warranting continued study.

Discussion and Conclusions

It appears that some interpersonal thinking skills have a more direct bearing on a young child's behavioral adjustment than others. The most significant ICPS skill appears to be ability to conceptualize alternative solutions to interpersonal problems, reflecting how well the child generates ways of obtaining what he wants or relieving interpersonal discomfort (as measured by the PIPS Test). In both the nursery and kindergarten years, youngsters displaying such cognitive efficiency have been found to be those exhibiting healthy, adaptive behaviors with respect to: (1) ability to wait and not show excessive nagging and demanding behavior; (2) display of reasonable emotionality; and (3) reasonable degree of verbal and/or physical aggression toward peers. Youngsters judged impulsive with respect to these behaviors are significantly more deficient in their alternative-thinking skills, while those classified as inhibited were even more deficient. Alternative thinking is also the single most significant predictor of other behaviors that are interpersonal in nature—the degree to which a child shows concern and/or offers help to another child in distress and the degree to which the child is liked by his peers. Characteristic differences between high and low alternative-solution thinkers are that the former are more likely to state relevant solutions accompanied by fewer irrelevant responses and can better conceptualize solutions beyond those limited to direct force.

Alternative thinking has also been established as the most significant ICPS skill serving as a direct mediator of a child's behavioral adjustment. Youngsters who improved most in alternative thinking skills as a function of training also improved most in the interpersonal behaviors.

While consequential and alternative-solution thinking are correlated phenomena, consequential thinking as a behavioral mediator plays a significant though secondary role in a child's ability to problem-solve. Alternative-solution thinking consistently differentiates behavior adjustment groups among both four- and five-year-olds, while consequential thinking does not. The most important contribution made by the latter is that, regardless of IQ, language ability, test verbosity or ability at impersonal alternative thinking, a child's consequential skills in *combination* with alternative thinking skills provide the best indicator of the type of aberrant behavior he is displaying, that is, knowledge of both these thinking skills aids in predicting whether a child will demonstrate behavior labeled impulsive or inhibited.

Whether or not a child considers consequences to a given interpersonal act, the key indicator of aberrant behavior is *lack* of ability to think of different ways to go about solving an interpersonal problem. While an impulsive child may recognize that he may get hit if he grabs a toy, he may proceed to grab the toy anyway. The best indicators of behavioral withdrawal and inhibition, however, are the child's lack of thought about how to solve a problem as well as about any potential consequences that may ensue. Perhaps the inhibited child quickly reacts to any social failure with withdrawal from those social circumstances that would teach the kinds of ICPS skills needed to solve problems. Perhaps the very early childrearing of the inhibited child is so defective relative to the development of ICPS skills that withdrawal follows naturally from the sense of inability to face and deal effectively with interpersonal problems. In either case, it is likely that once inhibited withdrawal occurs it seriously limits the opportunity for the child to learn and exercise ICPS skills with others.

By itself, a child's cognitive sensitivity to interpersonal problems does not strongly relate to overt behavioral adjustment. Nevertheless, such thinking ability relates to both alternative-solution and consequential thinking, is part of a common element that might be termed a basic problem-solving ability in children this age, and probably plays a significant role in the child's interpersonal cognitive problem-solving thinking. Whether such sensitivity is an antecedent of or a result of ability to conceptualize solutions to a problem and consequences to an act is not known. It is possible to assume that a child's sensitivity may lead him to think about how to go about solving the problem, but is not in itself sufficient to determine behavioral adaptation. The role of causal thinking in the problem-solving life of the young child remains in question.

Following systematic ICPS training, youngsters did display more thought about the potential consequences of an act than they did prior to training. Consideration of consequences also altered behavioral adjustment when children were specifically trained in how to think about them. However, this direct link between improvement in consequential thinking and improvement in behavior as a result of training was less dramatic than that between improvement in alternative-solution thinking and improvement in behavior. That causal and problem-sensitivity thinking did not directly alter behavioral adjustment may have been due to the requirements of the thinking processes involved. It would be important to investigate how a program placing more emphasis on causal and problem-sensitivity thinking would affect social behavior and interpersonal adjustment.

The capacities for role-taking and empathy do not appear to be as directly linked to overt behavioral adjustment as do ICPS skills.

Jennings (1975) did find children of this age who were capable of social awareness and social role-taking to be more socially competent than youngsters less efficient in these social cognitive skills. The former were more likely to function as group leader, to forcefully pursue what they wanted, to be self-starting and self-propelled, and to get along well with others. These findings are consistent with those found for ICPS skills that related to similar measures of social competence in young children: concern for others, liked-by-peers, and, to a lesser extent, initiative and autonomy. While ability to recognize and/or assimilate another's feelings internally may have important implications for interpersonal competence, such as a displayed concern for others in distress, such may not be the case for behaviors describing impulse-control or inhibition. Feshbach and Feshbach (1969) found that among four- and five-year-olds, boys who displayed the most empathy also displayed the *most* physical and verbal aggression. Though ability to assimilate another's emotions (that is, empathy) was related to lower aggression in six- and seven-year-olds, this relationship was found among boys only. In girls, there was no relationship in either direction at either age level. *That ICPS skills may function as more direct mediators of behaviors characteristic of impulsivity (including aggression) and inhibition is supported not only by the relationship between ICPS and behavior in girls and in boys but by the direct change in behavior as a result of ICPS training.*

Kameya (1975) found that training improved role-taking skills in boys as young as five years of age but, unexpectedly, only among those beginning in the low-empathy group. The observed training effect, however, may have been a function of his training procedures. Children were presented with situations of conflict—such as, for example, a brother and sister wanting to watch different TV shows at the same time. The children enacted the roles with puppets and were guided to discuss solutions to the problem and how they felt about the problem and the suggested solutions. While cognitive problem solving was not measured, training did produce change in ability to tell a story about social conflict from the perspective of another person. Given that problem solutions were discussed in the training, it is possible that the training effect was due to the effects of problem-solving training. Unfortunately, behaviors such as those affected by problem-solving training (for example, impulsiveness and inhibition) were not investigated in this study.

It is possible that problem-solving ability may function as a skill prerequisite to role-taking ability. The present position, however, is that the reverse is more likely to be the case. While seeing another's perspective may enrich one's appreciation of consequences, having such perspective does not insure that it will be operative in solving social problems. A child may be aware that another person may or may not feel happy about the same thing that makes him happy. Such information would be useful in problem-solving, however, *only* if the child considers possible consequences (such as the other person's unhappiness) or thinks about solutions that take other people's feelings and potential reactions into account.

Given the above, it is possible to conjecture what goes on in the minds of young children when a problem arises. When well-adjusted children want something, such as a toy or the avoidance of their mother's anger, presumably their desire is uppermost in their minds. However, these children are likely to give some thought to how to go about what they want to accomplish. They may even think about what might happen if they choose a particular course of action. If they get hurt as a consequence of what they do (for instance, if they get hit because they grabbed a toy) they can think of some other way that will work better. Very young children may not think about problems in a very subtle way and may not always appreciate all the reasons for their getting hurt for what they do, but they can, if well adjusted, consider a concrete here-and-now problem in terms of how to satisfy their desires. This is not to say that adjusted children always get what they want. However, they are able to cope with frustration when they cannot have what they want, because they are able to think of a different course of action and its consequences and can thus more effectively deal with an unpleasant interpersonal confrontation.

Less well-adjusted youngsters probably as often as not have the same desires with the same intensity as the well-adjusted youngsters. However, they are not as likely to give as much thought to what they are doing when a problem arises. They are less likely to anticipate what will happen next and less likely to associate such possibilities with their current course of action. If their choice of action fails, they are less prone to think of another way to proceed and thus more likely to persist in the same maladaptive pattern that continually proves to be ineffective. Some of these children may give thought to the consequences of their actions but seem less able or less willing to let it affect what they are doing. Such children may feel their needs to be so intense that any delay of action based upon consideration of consequences is out of the question. On the other hand, it may be that they do the first thing that comes into their minds because that is all that comes into their minds, awareness of consequences having little corrective feedback effect. The child is stuck with the one thing he can think of doing and can only decide to do that (despite negative consequences) or do nothing. Other poorly adjusted children seem to give relatively little thought at all to what they do and end up withdrawing from social problem situations. One might assume that their minds are filled with what they want but they give little or no thought to means of obtaining it or to whether such means might succeed or fail. One might conjecture that these children have feelings of low self-esteem and little or no sense of control or command of their world.

≫≫≫≫≫≫≫≫≫≫≫ 3 ≪≪≪≪≪≪≪≪≪≪≪

Middle Childhood

≫≫≫≫≫≫≫≫≫≫≫≫≫≫≫≪≪≪≪≪≪≪≪≪≪≪≪≪≪≪

If a significant determinant of the quality of social relationships is a group of mediating processes that define abilities
to solve interpersonal problems, it is reasonable to assume that,
across the age span, differences in ICPS ability would distinguish individuals who exhibit healthy, adaptive adjustment
from those who do not. While considerably less research has
been done with older than with younger children, a group of
studies has identified processes of interpersonal cognitive
problem-solving thinking among latency-aged children, nine
to twelve years of age.

Four interpersonal thinking skills have been identified that differentiate children in this age group: (1) ability to conceptualize alternative solutions to an interpersonal problem; (2) step-by-step planning to reach an interpersonal goal (called means-ends thinking); (3) consequential thinking; and (4) ability to appreciate cause-and-effect dynamics in human relations.

These interpersonal thinking skills will be examined in light of their role as ICPS skills, how they relate to social adjustment, and the extent to which research has identified them as mediators that determine the quality of social relationships and interpersonal adjustment.

Alternative Thinking

Having found that differential alternative-thinking skills exist in children as early as age four and that deficiencies were most evident among lower-class children and the more poorly adjusted within each social-class group (Shure and Spivack, 1970*b*), the experimenters hypothesized that similar differences would be found among older children as well. Specifically, Shure and Spivack (1970*a*) hypothesized that among fifth graders attending public schools, lower-class youngsters would conceptualize fewer solutions to interpersonal problems than middle-class youngsters and that, regardless of social class, youngsters manifesting poor school adjustment would conceptualize fewer solutions than their better-adjusted classmates.

Measuring alternative thinking.   While the process of alternative thinking (also referred to as alternative-solution thinking) is conceived of as the same as that described for younger children, the technique of measurement and story content were made more sophisticated to meet the abilities and interests of older children. Instead of presenting seemingly different stories to elicit solutions to the same problem (as was needed to maintain the interest of younger children), fifth graders were given a problem situation and asked to name all the ways they could think of to solve that particular problem. For example, the experimenter said to the child, "Johnny wants his friend to go to the playground with him after school, but his friend doesn't want to go. What can Johnny do to get his friend to go with him to the playground after school?" After the child gave one response, he was told, "Tell me all the ways you can think of—everything that comes into your head." The child was persistently asked, "What else can he do?" until no new ideas could be offered. Four peer-type problems were presented, and three concerning figures of authority (for example, "David is trying to get the teacher to help him with something. What can David do to get the teacher to help him?").

Since the scores for each of the seven problems significantly intercorrelated, a child's score consisted of the total number of relevant solutions given to the seven problems.

Alternative thinking and behavioral adjustment. The child's adjustment was measured by teacher ratings on the Devereux Elementary School Behavior Rating Scale (Spivack and Swift, 1966, 1967). This scale consists of forty-seven items of observable classroom behavior, analyzed into eleven factors (for example, Classroom Disturbance, Disrespect-Defiance, Impatience). Youngsters classified as aberrant were those whose total scores on three or more factors fell outside the statistically defined normal range as previously established by ratings on over 700 children in public school settings.

In addition to finding higher scores among the middle-class youngsters, the data clearly suggested that regardless of social class, IQ (as measured by the Lorge-Thorndike), and mere test verbosity, children judged to be actively involved and personally able to adapt to the task-oriented structure of the classroom, and who, in addition, behaved in ways compatible with effective group functioning, exhibited greater cognitive capacity to generate alternative solutions to real-life problems than those demonstrating observable behavioral difficulties.

After teaching nine-year-olds how to conceptualize alternative solutions through discussion, role-playing, and role-switching techniques (Elardo and Cooper, in press), Elardo and Caldwell (in preparation *b*) found that, with IQ controlled, alternative-solution thinking improved, as did behavioral performance on four Devereux Scale factors: (1) *Disre-*

spect-defiance, the degree to which a child talks disrespectfully to the teacher, will not do what he is asked to do, belittles the subject being taught, and breaks classroom rules (for example, throws things or marks up the desk or books); (2) *External reliance*, the degree to which a child looks to see what others are doing before he does it, relies on the teacher to tell him what to do and how to do it in class, has to be prodded to finish work, and has difficulty deciding what to do when given a choice between two or more things; (3) *Inattentive-withdrawn*, the degree to which a child loses attention, becomes fidgety, makes one doubt that he is paying attention, appears oblivious to what is going on in class, is difficult to reach and preoccupied with his own thoughts, and has to be called by name to bring him out of himself; (4) *Creative initiative*, the extent to which a child brings things to class that relate to a current topic, tells stories and describes things in an interesting and colorful fashion, initiates classroom discussion, and introduces into class discussion personal experiences or things he has heard that relate to what is going on in class.

Alternative thinking, behaviors in solving "real" problems, and locus of control. In a study to teach third- and fourth-graders social problem-solving strategies, Larcen and others (1974) placed children in contrived but seemingly real problem situations and recorded the number of different relevant solutions each child offered to solve each problem. For example, the child was told that a room was occupied, that it could not be used, and the adult really wanted to play story-telling games with the child. The child was then asked to help solve the problem of how they might play these games despite the fact that the room was occupied. Trained youngsters offered more solutions than nontrained youngsters comparable in age and level of problem-solving ability prior to training. Ability to solve seemingly real problems was not a function of the child's sex or level of intellectual functioning as measured by the Peabody Picture Vocabulary Test.

McClure (1975) modified these contrived problem situations to represent problems more interpersonal in nature (for example, a "mother" (an experimental confederate) explains that "her child" is worried about the teacher after a long absence from school, or that her child has never had a chance to make many friends). In both third and fourth graders, the number of alternative solutions (which increased as a function of specific training techniques) was the most powerful predictor of solution effectiveness. Solution effectiveness was measured in terms of maximum positive and minimum negative social and personal consequences, and each solution offered by a child to solve the "real" problem was rated for effectiveness by independent judges. Measures of locus of control, IQ (Lorge-Thorndike), number of words used in trying to solve a problem, or step-by-step elaborations given to carry out a solution did not add to the predictive power of alternative solutions to solution effectiveness.

Instead of measuring cognitive sensitivity to interpersonal problems as a predictor of overt behavioral adjustment, as previously described by Shure and Spivack (1975a), McClure related capacity to conceptualize alternative solutions to a behavioral index of sensitivity to interpersonal problems in a simulated social situation. Using the term *problem sensing,* McClure was interested in how obvious a problematic situation must be before the child would recognize its existence as a problem and begin to problem-solve. Problem sensing was assessed in the dyadic interaction between the "mother" and child. If the child failed to problem-solve when the mother first introduced the problem, she initiated one or more "prods" to make him aware of the problem. The prods began with a mere statement of the problem: "Mike is really concerned about making friends here at school." Then, if necessary, a statement that she is unable to cope with the problem: "I wish I could help him make some friends." And finally, if necessary, an outright request for a solution to the problem: "How do you think Mike could make some friends?" Problem sensitivity was measured by the number and intensity of prods, with the more sensitive child requiring fewer prods. McClure found that the number of alternative solutions offered by a child to the "mother" was the most powerful predictor of a child's behavioral sensitivity, suggesting that ability to problem-solve reflected less need to be made aware of the existence of the problem by an adult.

The number of alternative solutions given in the same problem situation with the "mother" also best predicted a child's problem-solving persistence, the ability to continue problem solving in the face of obstacles presented by the experimenter. As soon as the child offered a solution to the "mother," the experimenter administered an obstacle. For example, if a child suggested that Mike could talk to someone, the obstacle presented was, "He doesn't know what to talk about." A maximum of three obstacles was administered but only if the child continued to offer solutions after the obstacle was presented. Relative to locus of control, IQ, verbosity, or step-by-step elaboration, the number of alternative solutions was the most powerful predictor of problem persistence.

While no analyses were made relating alternative solutions to overt behavioral adjustment measures, it is important that ability to generate alternative solutions in a seemingly real problem situation does play a powerful role in solution effectiveness and the child's behavioral sensitivity and persistence.

But is there a relationship between a cognitive capacity to conceptualize alternative solutions and solution effectiveness in a situation perceived by the child as purely hypothetical? Measuring the number of alternative solutions stated in a story-telling procedure (adapted from a procedure called means-ends thinking, described below), McClure found again that the number of different solutions was most related to solution effectiveness. Larcen (in Allen and others, 1976) found clear evidence that alternative-solution thinking in a hypothetical situation was related to problem-solving behavior in contrived situations, although McClure found this relationship to be less consistent.

Measures of locus of control yielded an interesting addition to alternative-solution thinking. While McClure found that locus of control played a relatively minor role in predicting solution effectiveness, both Larcen and McClure did find "internals" (who believe they themselves determine what happens to them) significantly more able than "externals" to conceptualize alternative solutions to hypothetical problems. Larcen attributes this difference to the likelihood that "internal" children are more likely to generate new strategies in the belief that a solution to a problem is contingent upon what they do (in Allen and others, 1976). Larcen and others (1974) and McClure (1975) also found that a training program emphasizing that problems could be solved and encouraging children to solve their own problems significantly increased the frequency of "internal" statements given. (For descriptions of the programs developed by Larcen and by McClure, see Chapter Eleven.)

Alternative thinking as a mediator of adjustment. While alternative thinking has been shown to relate to overall behavioral adjustment patterns as measured by the Devereux Scale (Shure and Spivack, 1970a), and Elardo and Caldwell found improvement on four Devereux behavioral factors as a result of training, a direct link analysis to determine whether the children who improved in alternatives were the *same* children who improved in these four factors was not made. However, these findings are encouraging in light of an earlier finding by Elardo (1974) that training latency-period youngsters improved neither alternative thinking nor behavioral adjustment. Elardo (1974) and Elardo and Caldwell (in preparation *a, b*) attribute improvement in thinking and behavior to increased incorporation of the program into the total school curriculum, greater teacher support, more visits to the classroom by the research team, and use of the training approach in everyday discipline situations. (The details of the program developed by Elardo and Cooper are described in Chapter Twelve.)

It is important to note, however, that Elardo and Caldwell found only a predicted trend on behaviors more similar to those showing improvement among the younger children, four and five years of age. For example, predicted but not significant change was reported for the degree to which a child had to be reprimanded or controlled because of his behavior in class and for the degree to which the child poked, tormented, or teased classmates or annoyed or interfered with their work in class, or tended to be drawn quickly into the talking or noisemaking of others. Larcen (in Allen and others, 1976) also reports that descriptive behaviors such as disruptiveness as rated on the Walker checklist did not improve significantly as a function of problem-solving training. These findings seem surprising until one recognizes that impulsive behavior in younger children also included impatience (nagging and demanding behavior, tendency to grab toys, not sharing) and overemotionality when frustrated—behaviors not measured in these studies of older children. Other factors may also have accounted for this finding. Larcen points out that possibly such behaviors are slow to change or that rater bias may have been operating as a function of a labeling process that is resistant to change even when observable changes exist. While the latter is possible, the trend found by Elardo and Caldwell suggests that obstreperous behaviors are simply slower to change in latency-period children, highlighting the importance of intervention at the preschool and kindergarten level. That more than one year of training is needed for older children is suggested by the additional finding of McClure that problem-solving training effects were lost after four months. Both cognitive and behavioral effects of nursery school training lasted for at least one full year following training (Shure and Spivack, 1975e).

The previously described results of Larcen and others (1974) and McClure (1975) provide important extensions to our knowledge about overt problem-solving behaviors affected by ICPS training, some of which strongly suggest a mediating function for alternative thinking. Unfortunately, no attempt was made to correlate, within the training group, enhanced measured alternative thinking and posttraining overt behaviors indicative of problem solving.

A direct link between alternative thinking and overt behavioral adjustment has not been demonstrated so clearly for latency-period children as it has for younger children. However, given the significant correlations between alternative-solution thinking and adjustment behavior, the enhancement of both adjustment and problem-solving behaviors as a function of training to enhance alternative thinking, and the very reasonable correlations found between alternative solutions offered and solution effectiveness, problem sensitivity, and problem-solving persistence in a simulated situation, it is not unreasonable to assume that alternative-solution thinking plays a mediating role in behavioral adjustment in this age group.

Means-Ends Thinking

Different alternative solutions to the problem of making new friends could be, "I can go visit the boy next door," "I can have a party," "I can meet them in school." The process of means-ends thinking, unlike alternative thinking, involves careful planning, step-by-step, in order to reach a stated goal: "I can do this, and then I can do that. . . . " Such planning includes insight and forethought to forestall or circumvent potential obstacles and, in addition, having at one's command alternative means if an obstacle is realistically or psychologically insurmountable. The process implies an awareness that goals are not always reached immediately and that certain times are more advantageous than others for action. A child adept at means-ends thinking may consider, "I can go visit the boy next door [means] but he won't know me and won't let me in [obstacle]. If I call first and tell him I just moved in and ask if I can come over [means], he'll say okay. But I'd better not go at dinnertime or his mother will be mad [time and obstacle] and he won't like me." Since it assumes that the child is able to put his plan into action, consider potential obstacles along the way, and evaluate the timing of his act, means-ends thinking is a more demanding task than is alternative thinking, wherein the sole requirement is to identify a particular type or category of solution.

Measuring means-ends thinking. The procedure to measure ability of latency-period youngsters to plan a route toward solving a problem is called the Children's Means-Ends Problem Solving Test, or Children's MEPS. It is similar in procedure to the MEPS Test designed for adolescents and adults described in detail in Chapters Four and Five, with story content appropriate for children in this particular age group. The test measures means-ends thinking toward socially acceptable goals (for example, making friends) and the extent to which a child is capable of achieving ends that may be considered by some as less acceptable (for example, getting even with a child who has said something nasty; stealing a diamond from a store window).

Each child is given six stories portraying hypothetical real-life problems to be solved. The child is told the beginning of the story and supplied the end of the story, and asked to "fill in the middle," "tell what happens in between," or "tell how the ending got to be that way." The child is encouraged to make up a story plot but is otherwise allowed to approach the problem in any way he wishes. For example, one story specifically depicts a child who momentarily has no friends.

> Al (Joyce) has moved into the neighborhood. He (she) didn't know anyone and felt very lonely.
> The story ends with Al (Joyce) having many good friends and feeling at home in the neighborhood. What happens in between Al's (Joyce's) moving in and feeling lonely, and when he (she) ends up with many good friends?

Other stories involved one child getting even with another for having said something nasty to him; averting mother's anger for having broken her favorite flowerpot; successfully stealing a diamond from a store window; needing money to buy mother a special birthday present; and owning a sports car just like one seen parked at a curb.

Interest is in the child's means-ends thinking to reach a stated goal, not in his determination of the goal itself. That is, if the child is asked to construct a story plot so that a sports car is obtained, he is not free to change the goal to something that might be perceived by the child as more obtainable or desirable. To secure maximum attention to the task, children are tested orally, a method that also avoids the possibility of interpreting thinking skills as a function of differential reading or writing skills.

Means-ends thinking and behavior. A study to determine differential means-ends thinking skills in latency-period children, by Shure and Spivack (1972), compared normal youngsters in regular schools with disturbed youngsters in special schools, most diagnosed as manifesting a personality disorder or psychoneurosis. Each behavior adjustment group was represented by youngsters in both the middle and lower socioeconomic groups. Middle-class children and normal youngsters within each social class group conceptualized more means (steps) to reach a goal, more obstacles that might be encountered on the way toward that goal, and more consideration of importance of time than did youngsters in the disturbed group.

A normal child typically described steps toward the goal. One eleven-year-old boy told how Al made friends in a new neighborhood.

> First Al got talking to the leader. He found out the kids liked basketball but Al didn't know how to play. When Al got to know the leader better he asked him to get the kids down to the skating rink. The kids went and saw him practicing shooting goals. So the kids asked him, "Would you teach us how to do that?" So he did and they organized two teams and the kids liked that and Al had lots of friends.

This child conceptualized a story wherein the first means, talking to the leader, uncovered an obstacle—the kids liked a game that Al didn't know how to play. The obstacle was overcome by stimulating interest in another game (hockey) that Al did know how to play. The child also recognized that it takes time to make friends, as evidenced by his statement, "When Al got to know the leader better. . . ."

A disturbed child more typically would think of the end goal rather than means to obtain it. For example, one eleven-year-old ego-disturbed girl related her story of how Joyce made new friends.

> She'll go out and meet some kids and then she'll have lots of friends. Then she won't be lonely any more

and her mother will be very happy because she went out and made lots of friends. She was happy too because she wasn't lonely any more. She and her friends had lots of fun together because they played a lot during recess and after school.

Typical of disturbed youngsters, this child revealed less ability to conceptualize means in achieving the satisfaction or goal presented. When motivated in fantasy, her thinking moved immediately to consummation with insufficient consideration given to how to get there and awareness of obstacles that might have to be overcome. Most of her story described feelings and events surrounding the resolution of the problem, all of which occurred *after* the goal (making friends) was reached.

A more stringent test of the relationship between means-ends thinking and behavioral adjustment among latency-period children was conducted by Larcen, Spivack, and Shure (1972). In a homogeneous sample of children placed in institutions largely for reasons of parental neglect, specific behaviors most intimately related to means-ends thinking were similar to those found most relevant to alternative thinking among four- and five-year-olds: inability to delay, emotionality, and social aggression. Pilot work by Shure and Spivack confirmed differential means-ends thinking skills and behavioral adjustment within a homogeneous group of latency-period youngsters. Among ten-to-twelve-year-olds attending regular public schools, youngsters judged to be better adjusted displayed means-ends thinking skills superior to those displaying behavioral difficulties in the classroom. The capacity for means-ends thinking among normal youngsters in regular schools who displayed behavioral difficulties typically fell between immediate goal attainment and a step-by-step elaboration of means toward the goal. A normal but relatively impatient eleven-year-old girl gave her account of how to make friends.

Somebody asked her her name and she said Joyce. Joyce asked the girl her name. The girl said her name was Laura and they started playing. Then somebody else came along and Laura said, 'Hi Barby, this is

Joyce.' Then more kids came along and she told them
her name and they told Joyce their names and they
made friends. People just keep coming and more people
came and they made friends.

This child conceptualized two means, one being several enumerations of asking each other their names and the other being
an introduction by one girl to others. Obstacles and recognition of time were generally less frequent in the stories of aberrant than of more adjusted youngsters in the regular school
classroom.

These studies suggest that severely impulsive or overly
inhibited youngsters suffer from a means-ends cognitive deficiency that gets them into difficulty with others and brings on
failure when confronted with important life situations. While
these deficiencies are most clearly marked among children
classed diagnostically as disturbed, relative deficiencies are also
clearly evident among normal youngsters displaying more
than average amounts of behavioral aberrance in the
classroom.

Content of means-ends stories.   Factors underlying differentiation of the capacity to conceptualize a sequence of
events leading to a goal completion were revealed, in part, by
the content of stories conceived. Relative to the disturbed, normals and better-adjusted youngsters in regular school class-
rooms saw a broader spectrum of possibilities open to satisfy
goal attainment, and this cognitive capacity was evident within both the lower and middle class groups. First of all, disturbed and normals displaying behavioral difficulties were significantly more likely to express physical retaliation ("fight" or
"kick him") as the only form of reprisal to a nasty remark. By
contrast, the best adjusted normals, more particularly in the
middle class, also elaborated nonphysical ways to counterat-
tack, such as verbal retaliation, playing a practical joke, or a
plan to make the child feel bad.

An example of extreme physical attack was given by a
twelve-year-old disturbed boy.

He hit him, talked to him, kicked him, told him, scratched him. Throw a stone. Pick up something and throw it at him. Push him in the mud. Hit him back against the wall. Hit him on the head. Push him in the water. Then he got even.

Somewhat less extreme but still predominantly physical was this story, given by a normal but overly obstreperous boy attending regular school.

George got all the kids down to the park for a picnic. He invited the boy who called him a name. When they got there they lured him to a stream full of lizards. The kids all pretended to turn over rocks and when the boy bent down to turn a rock, George pushed him in. The mud was deep and George felt happy twice because the boy's mother was mad because he was full of mud.

A well-adjusted child also thought of physical attack but included other forms of retaliation as well.

George thought he'd beat him up but when he saw him, he had lots of kids around him. So he asked his friends to beat him up but his friends said no. So George decided to have a party and not invite the boy. The next day George and his friends were standing around and, when the boy came by, George said [to one of his friends], 'Did you have fun at my party last night?' When the boy found out about the party he was feeling real bad and George got even.

Second, prolific strategies of planning and foresight were evident among many of the normals but absent among the disturbed. With the end goal in mind rather than the means to obtain it, a significant number of disturbed youngsters in both social class groups stated relatively primitive means to steal a diamond from a store window, such as, "Smash the window with a rock and take it." Normals were more likely to describe at least one strategy of careful planning, such as hiding, disguise, fooling the clerk, or removing fingerprints.

Sophistication in their "use" of people was a third differentiating factor between the normals and the disturbed, but in this case only in the middle class. As reflected in the story regarding making new friends, a significant percentage of normals thought of interpersonal helping strategies such as fixing a wound, helping someone with his or her homework, or taking a hurt child to the hospital. No disturbed children conceptualized stories including such content. Disturbed children were more likely than normals to conceptualize a story wherein the child could make friends by bribing with physical possessions such as a new toy or object of value.

In addition to mentioning fewer means, obstacles, and elements of time considered in reaching a goal, less well-adjusted youngsters also expressed stories more limited to pragmatic, impulsive means, as well as physically aggressive means. Qualitative differences were most apparent in youngsters attending special schools for the disturbed.

Means-ends thinking, language, productivity, and IQ. All studies measuring means-ends thinking to date have shown no relationship between story length and cognitive means-ends thinking capacity. As evidenced in the examples given thus far, stories of the severely disturbed, less adjusted normals, and adjusted normals were about equal in length. The latter included the most relevant steps toward the goal. The disturbed were more likely to talk about events and feelings *after* the goal was reached, such as how much fun two children had after they became friends or what the child in the story could do with the diamond (or sports car) after he had it. The less adjusted were more likely to enumerate one particular means to a greater extent than was necessary, a characteristic especially prominent among the aberrant normals. For example, to get a special present for the mother, these children frequently described how the child could do dishes for one neighbor, baby-sit for another, wash windows, and the like. Although three different jobs are stated, they are considered enumerations of only one means—

that of earning money to buy the present. While Larcen (in Allen and others, 1976) did find story length related to problem-solving score, he also found nontrained youngsters likely to use more words than those trained. Unfortunately, Larcen did not determine the relationship between problem-solving capacity and behavior with verbal productivity controlled.

Regarding the issue of IQ, one interesting finding did emerge from the Shure and Spivack (1972) study. With the effect of the Lorge-Thorndike and WISC measures of general intelligence controlled, there were still genuine differences in means-ends thinking between the adjusted groups, but the greater differences between the adjustment groups in the middle social class disappeared. This finding suggests that with the effect of IQ removed, differences in capacity for means-ends thinking are clearly a function of adjustment level and not of membership in a social-class group. Larcen and others (1972) did not find a significant correlation between the WISC and means-ends thinking among dependent and neglected children, though he did find a low but significant relationship (using Lorge-Thorndike) among normal children of the same age (in Allen and others, 1976). These findings are not inconsistent with those found for younger children (see Chapter Two) or for older adolescents and adults (see Chapters Four and Five). However, all studies analyzing the relationship between problem-solving capacity and behavior found that relationship to be genuine regardless of any effect of IQ. As was true of four- and five-year-olds, Larcen and others (1974) and McClure (1975) both found that IQ predicts neither problem-solving scores nor change in problem-solving capacity as a result of training for interpersonal cognitive problem-solving skills.

Means-ends thinking as a mediator of behavior. Means-ends thinking has been shown to relate to extreme differences in behavioral adjustment (normals vs. disturbed). Differences were found within homogeneous samples of dependent and neglected youngsters and within a sample of normal youngsters attending regular schools. However, such cognitive capacity as an antecedent requirement for adjustment has not been empirically investigated.

Consequential Thinking

In addition to an ability to solve problems of an interpersonal nature, logical components of a person's total problem-solving capacity should include an ability to consider how his actions may affect other people and himself and how they may react. The process of consequential thinking includes consideration of pros and cons to an interpersonal act that goes beyond simple naming of alternative events that might ensue. For example, if a child is trying to decide whether to go to a party on a weeknight or to study for an exam being given the next day, he can think to himself, "If I go to the party, I'll have more fun and I'll see my best friend, but my mother will be mad and I might fail my exam." In the sense that the child weighs both the pros and cons to each conflicting choice, this process of consequential thinking is more demanding than that asked of four- and five-year-olds—that of thinking about what might happen next if one particular act is carried out.

Measuring consequential thinking. Consequential thinking has been assessed by measuring what the youngster conceptualizes when faced with temptation to transgress. The child is given four stories describing a hypothetical person faced with a temptation situation. He is asked to complete each story, indicating what the hypothetical person is thinking about before he decides what to do, and what happens after that. In one story, for example,

> George is in training. The football coach has a rule that all members of the team get to bed early during the week. George gets invited to a Tuesday night social in the next town by a girl he likes a lot. If he goes, he'll end up getting to bed rather late. He would really like to go.

The child is then asked to tell everything that goes on in George's mind and then tell what happens. No suggestion is made to the child that he relate pros and cons or consequences of an act. Of interest is the child's *spontaneous* inclination to do so. A child's score consists of the total number of different statements that concern weighing the pros and cons in four "temptation" stories.

Consequential thinking and behavior. Only one study to date has investigated consequential thinking in latency-period children (Larcen and others, 1972). Among dependent and neglected youngsters, differences in such thinking skills were noted. An example of efficient consequential thinking is exemplified by this story:

> George is thinking he should go to the party. Or should he listen to what the coach says? He is thinking that if he goes to the party, he gets in more trouble. But then if he goes to bed early, he might lose the girl. She might get mad, and not speak to him again. Other people at the party who knew George would tease him. They would tease him about playing football. He could always go to bed early another night. Then the coach will be mad at him, though. But he goes anyway; when he gets back his parents remind him of the rule. George said he did not really want to go to bed early. The coach says he is suspended from football. But he was happier because he went to the party.

This child considered the pros and cons of both choices, in sharp contrast to a story given by a child showing deficiencies in consequential thinking:

> He is thinking about going to the party that night. Nothing is going to happen if he goes. Then the guy in charge of the game, the coach, catches him. Then the next time he goes out he does not get caught.

Of twenty-three children, about half demonstrated efficient and half deficient consequential thinking skills. Tendency to weigh the pros and cons of an act was independent of IQ (WISC). However, no relationship was found between consequential thinking and overt measures of behavioral impulsivity and inhibition.

Both Larcen and others (1974) and McClure (1975)

attempted to teach consequential thinking to normal third and fourth graders attending regular schools. The training included guided questions in a manner similar to that described by Spivack and Shure (1974) and Shure and Spivack (1973, 1975c; see Chapter Eight). After a solution to a problem was offered, guided questions encouraged the child to think about "What might happen next?" and "How will this make Mary feel?" and "What will happen in the short run?" and "What will happen in the long run?" That no effect of the training was observed is interesting in light of Larcen and others' (1972) finding that consequential thinking did not relate to adjustment. However, this finding is difficult to interpret because both Larcen and others (1974) and McClure (1975) assessed consequential thinking by measuring obstacles stated in stories of the means-ends type described earlier. While the obstacle encountered in achieving a goal might in fact be a consequence of an interpersonal nature ("She'll get mad if I come to her house at dinnertime"), it also need not be—"If I go to her house to meet her, she might not be there."

In their work with adolescents, Spivack and Levine (1963) found that spontaneous consequential thinking did relate to behavioral adjustment among teenagers. While latency-period youngsters are capable of thinking this way, it is possible that a spontaneous tendency to weigh the pros and cons of an act does not act as a modulator of behavior until adolescence. Clearly more research with normal and disturbed youngsters in this age group is necessary before definitive conclusions can be drawn.

Causal Thinking

The process of causal thinking, relating one event to another in time, can consist of a spontaneous inclination to think about why an event occurred or the ability to produce a reason if asked specifically for a cause. While both of these processes were investigated in younger children, a slightly different process of causal thinking was of interest in the latency-period youngster.

Social causal thinking, as defined by Muuss (1960*b*), is "an understanding and appreciation of the dynamic, complex and interacting nature of the forces that operate in human behavior. It involves an attitude of flexibility, of seeing things from the point of view of others as well as an awareness of the probabilistic nature of knowledge. A causally oriented person is capable of suspending judgment until sufficient factual information is available; furthermore, he realizes that his behavior has consequences and that there are alternative ways of solving social problems. It is assumed that a person who is aware of the dynamic and causal nature of human behavior is better able to solve his own problems and to meet social situations" (p. 122).

Muuss hypothesized that a socially causally oriented person would display less anxiety and less insecurity because he would have better insight into the dynamics of his behavior and a willingness and/or ability to understand the problems and behavior of others. Muuss further asserts that lack of insight into the dynamics of behavior makes it difficult to react logically to the behavior of others, behavior of others may be misunderstood and perceived as threatening, and such misunderstanding could lead to heightened conflict between the parties involved. Based on this description of causal thinking, it is reasonable to assume that a child who is refused a toy by her sister may consider the next step of the solution in light of her understanding of why her sister said no. If, for example, she perceives her sister as selfish, her next step may be to display anger, hit her, or tell her mother. If, however, the girl perceives her sister as having said no because she just refused her sister a favor, her next act may involve doing something nice for her in order to obtain the toy.

Measuring causal thinking. To measure the child's understanding of the dynamics of human behavior, the social causality test was developed for latency-period children by Ojemann (reported in Ojemann and others, 1955). Eight story stems describing the behavior of children in a story situation were used, each containing three to five true-false items referring to that behavior. For example, in one story, the child is told:

>   Ralph's father has told him that he must not
> play with the boy next door. But when his father is not
> home, Ralph disobeys him and plays with this boy. One
> day his father comes home early and catches him play-
> ing with the boy.

The child is then given three statements and asked if each is
true or false.

(1) Ralph disobeyed his father for no reason at all.
(2) There may be many reasons why Ralph disobeyed
    his father.
(3) If another boy disobeyed his father the same way, his
    reason would be the same as Ralph's.

Correctly identifying the first and third statements as
false and the second as true reveals that a child (1) is aware that
the underlying dynamics of behavior are complex; (2) has ability to assume alternate multiple explanations of behavior—
that different motivations may underlie the same behavior in
different persons and the same underlying motivations may
produce different behavior in different persons; and (3) takes an
attitude that leads to consistent attempts to "see things from the
point of view of others" (Ojemann, 1962).

Causal thinking and behavior.   Muuss (1960a) reports
that children trained to think causally increase their understanding of human dynamics, but that these changes, as well as
changes on paper-and-pencil tests of anxiety and insecurity,
become more noticeable after at least two full years of training.
Larcen and others (1972) found a significant relationship
between causal thinking and overt adjustment measures of
impulsivity and inhibition in their sample of dependent and
neglected children, adjusted youngsters identifying causal
statements significantly more often than those displaying
behavioral aberrance. Both Larcen and colleagues and Muuss
found social causality unrelated to IQ, and Muuss also found
causal appreciation of social behaviors independent of causal
appreciation of physical events (such as what makes fire burn).

The latter adds support to the previously described assumption that social, interpersonal thinking skills should be distinguished from thinking skills concerning events in the impersonal world. Research to date has not ascertained how social causal thinking might function as an ICPS skill independent of alternative solution and consequential thinking.

It is interesting that Muuss found that it took at least two years of training to affect behavioral indices of mental health (albeit paper-and-pencil tests). In four- and five-year-olds, enhanced alternative-solution and consequential thinking improved adjustment in a period of months (Spivack and Shure, 1974), while enhanced causal thinking was unrelated to behavioral improvement. Unfortunately, no research to date has investigated whether training social causal thinking in latency-period children would significantly enhance overt adjustment.

Discussion and Conclusions

Available data suggest that alternative problem solution and means-ends thinking are likely to be important mediators in latency-period children. The well-adjusted ten-year-old is typically able to generate alternative solutions to a problem when he has to and, having selected one solution, spontaneously articulates for himself the sequence of steps needed to carry it out. The processes underlying alternative-solution and means-ends thinking are intrinsically different but complement each other in the child's attempt to define specific ways to think about how to reach an interpersonal goal or how to satisfy a desire. Both thinking processes enable a person to solve a problem. They also share important common properties that underscore their position as ICPS skills within a theory of healthy human functioning.

. Normal youngsters displaying behaviors described as overly impulsive or inhibited and youngsters attending special schools for the disturbed are characteristically less able to think through ways to solve typical interpersonal problems than are youngsters exhibiting healthy, adaptive adjustment. Such youngsters are deficient in the ability to conceptualize separate alternative solutions and step-by-step means to reach a stated goal. Both properties of thought are related to behavioral adjustment independent of verbal productivity, and in general, thought processes of the poorly adjusted tend to be character-ized by thought content dominated by use of physical or verbal force in order to attain a goal. General intellectual functioning relates somewhat to alternative and means-ends thinking skills, but no effect of IQ is sufficient to explain the relationship between ICPS ability and overt behavioral adjustment.

Children trained in alternative-thinking skills improve in behaviors defining ability to adapt to classroom demands, though no attempt has been made to establish a direct link between ICPS improvement and improvement in these behav-iors. However, the similarity of these findings to those found for alternative thinking in four- and five-year-olds suggests that had such a direct link been investigated, alternative and means-ends thinking would probably emerge as significant mediators of behavioral adjustment in latency-period children. Evidence does indicate that, in children this age, thinking of alternatives increases the likelihood that the child will con-tinue to try and not give up in the face of obstacles in a real situ-ation, and increases his sensitivity to the fact that a problem exists that needs resolution.

While thinking processes that enable a person to *attain a goal* are probably skills that play a significant role in the behav-ioral adjustment of the latency-period child, a question remains as to whether spontaneous prior weighing of the pros and cons of an act affects what he does. Available data suggest that in children of this age, consequential thinking may not function as a clear, consistent mediator of behavioral adjust-ment. The extent to which a child understands the causal dynamics of human behavior has been found to relate to behav-ioral adjustment in this age group, but more research substan-tiating this finding is needed before a definitive statement can be made. Unfortunately, training data linking improvement in causal thinking to improvement in overt adjustment are not available. Training data that are available suggest the possibility that more intensive intervention may be needed than with younger children before obstreperous behaviors may be significantly reduced. The length of training needed to create durable increases in problem-solving thinking skills has also not been established.

As is true of younger children (see Chapter Two), role-taking ability does not appear to be as directly linked to overt behavioral adjustment as does ICPS ability, especially alternative and means-ends thinking. Iannotti (1975, personal communication) found that among six- and nine-year-old boys, there was no correlation between measures of role-taking ability and either of his measures of aggression. Further, he found that while a role-taking training program enhanced some measures of role-taking ability, such training did not affect either of his measures of aggressiveness.

Elardo and Cooper (in press) added alternative-solution and consequential thinking to a program designed to train children in role-taking skills. In discussing the development of this program, Elardo and Caldwell (in preparation a, ms. p. 5) speculated that:

> The development of role-taking skills alone will not necessarily guarantee harmonious social interactions among children or between children and adults. In addition, children need techniques and skills for solving the kinds of problems which arise in daily social intercourse. The child who snatches a pencil from another child and the one who says, "May I borrow your pencil" may be equally egocentric, but the latter one has learned a social skill which can generalize to other situations. Thus another major objective [in addition to role-taking skills] of a human relations program for children should be to facilitate the development of interpersonal skills for social problem-solving. Such skills include being able to define and understand a problem, being able to consider alternative solutions to the problem, and being able to understand the possible consequences of each alternative.

While Elardo and Caldwell (in preparation *b*) found that the number of alternative solutions increased as a result of training nine-year-olds, improvement in measured role-taking skills occurred in only one of two groups studied. While Elardo and Caldwell conclude that role-taking skills are not prerequisite to adjustment, and elsewhere suggest that good social adjustment contributes to good role taking (Elardo and Caldwell, 1976), the data also suggest the possibility that it was the problem-solving training more than the role-taking training that led to improvement of four measured classroom behaviors. Chandler (1973) did find that role-taking training increased role-taking skills and decreased antisocial behavior as measured by the number of offenses committed by delinquent boys eleven to thirteen years of age. His training procedures included making video films of the youngsters engaged in a skit of their own creation wherein the "characters," of their own age, were depicting real-life situations. The youngsters then viewed the films so that they could see themselves acting different parts, a procedure designed to improve their role-taking skills. In light of the findings of Elardo and Caldwell, it would be of interest to determine whether the training effects on social cognition and behavior might also have been due to an underlying effect of problem-solving training. Chandler does not describe the content of skits his groups created, but does state that the results of his study "do suggest the utility of attempting to understand delinquent youth in terms of their developmental progress in the acquisition of certain formal, sociocognitive operations necessary for the effective *solution of important human interaction problems*" (p. 332; italics added).

Role-taking data on latency-period youngsters adds plausibility to the interpretation that role taking may be a prerequisite skill to effective problem solving. Ability to see another's perspective, for instance, may enrich and expand one's appreciation of possible consequences, *if* one tends to think of consequences to begin with. As conjectured for younger children, while being able to appreciate the social perspective of another probably enhances the subtlety and range of content of thought manifest in problem-solving thinking, it is ICPS ability that defines the thinking structures more directly mediating actual behavioral adjustment. Research is needed to investigate the details of the relationship between social role taking and ICPS skills before final conclusions can be drawn about this matter.

4

Adolescence

This chapter continues discussion of the importance of interpersonal cognitive problem-solving skills in various age groups, with attention focused specifically on adolescents. While to date the major focus of attention has been upon older and younger age groups, data available on adolescents, even though relatively sparse, is particularly important. Information on adolescents, when examined in conjunction with findings for children and adults, might suggest what interpersonal cognitive problem-solving skills are important in adolescent development as well as suggest the sequence underlying the appearance of interpersonal cognitive problem-solving skills significant in social adjustment.

The two existing primary studies of interpersonal cognitive problem solving in adolescents provide the source material for this chapter (Spivack and Levine, 1963; Platt and others, 1974). These studies have suggested that, in general, adolescents who were having problems of adjustment seem to be deficient in the following interpersonal cognitive problem-solving skills: the ability to generate solutions to interpersonal problem situations, the ability to conceptualize the step-by-step means of reaching goals in specific problem situations, and the ability to see interpersonal situations from the perspectives of other involved individuals. Some adolescents with behavioral difficulties may also be deficient in the ability to spontaneously explore the pros and cons of actions prior to decision making. The complete list of cognitive processes explored to date thus includes: sensitivity to the existence of life problems, the ability to think of alternative solutions to such problems, readiness to view consequences (pros and cons) of acts, social cause-and-effect thinking, means-ends thinking of an interpersonal nature, and the ability to see interpersonal situations from the perspectives of other actors (role taking). Some of these processes have been explored in much greater depth than others.

Means-Ends Thinking

Evidence indicates that one of the most important interpersonal cognitive problem-solving (ICPS) variables is that of *means-ends thinking*. As noted in Chapter Three, this skill involves the ability to orient oneself to and conceptualize the step-by-step means of moving toward a goal. It contains a number of elements, among them careful planning and the insight and forethought to forestall or circumvent potential obstacles. It also involves the recognition that temporal elements are present in particular problem situations and that these elements must be taken into account in planning successfully. An excellent illustration of how an adolescent may employ all of these elements in a particular situation is provided in the following response to a problem situation. The situation involves a young man, Al, faced with the problem of meeting and successfully courting a young lady to whom he is attracted in a restaurant. The respondent who provided this story was instructed to begin the story when Al first notices the girl in the restaurant.

> Al was having lunch when he noticed a beautiful girl sitting at the next table. He wanted to meet her but he was afraid to just walk up to her and say "hello." So he kept going back to the restaurant for several days, hoping to see her again.
> One day they were both standing in line together and Al decided to bump into her and then apologize. He could then introduce himself and ask her if she minded if he joined her for lunch. She said she didn't mind, and they talked about themselves during the meal. He asked her to go to a concert that weekend because they both liked music. She accepted. They dated a lot. Eventually, as their relationship became more serious, they decided to try living together. Then one day Al asked her to marry him. She said yes and they became engaged. They were married three months later.

It is evident that the respondent who provided this story has a richly articulated thought process. He clearly recognizes an obstacle (fear) to reaching his goal, yet continues to go back to the restaurant and finally decides upon a plan (bumping into her) for gaining her attention. He then recognizes the need to introduce himself and to meet with her again (asking her to a concert, dating), as well as the need to get to know each other better (deciding to try living together) before proposing, at the risk of her saying no. Finally, after the intermediate step of engagement, they get married. Throughout the entire story runs the recognition of temporal elements implicit in the problem-solving process.

The above story may be contrasted with the following two:

> That's one fine young girl, Al sat thinking to

himself in the booth. If she would talk I could get an idea of just where she may be at.

Al proposed to this beautiful girl. He then went to church with her and saw the priest. Then, someday, they get married.

Contrasted with the story given by the first subject, both of the latter ones can be seen to be deficient in terms of the clearly articulated, orderly sequence of step-by-step action that the first story reflects.

The measurement of means-ends thinking. The first measurement of means-ends problem-solving cognition was by Spivack and Levine (1963), who studied the relationship of interpersonal problem-solving skills to adjustment in adolescents. The scoring system developed at that time contained the basic elements still used in scoring. Protocols were scored for individual steps in problem solving (means), awareness of potential obstacles, and awareness of the passage of time.

The next use of the means-ends procedure was in a comparison of problem-solving abilities of adult psychiatric inpatients and normal controls (Platt and Spivack, 1970). In this study, the technique was refined and its measurement characteristics were explored. Nine stories were employed. Each story had a beginning in which a need was aroused in the protagonist and an ending in which he had succeeded in satisfying his need. Respondents were asked to provide a middle for each story. Stories dealt primarily with interpersonal themes, although impersonal themes were also represented. Stories dealt with how to become a leader, resolve a difficulty with one's boyfriend or girlfriend, find a lost watch, successfully steal a diamond, gain revenge, make friends, meet and marry a person to whom one is attracted, regain a lost friendship, and "get even" with a friend for a slight. One story, for example, follows in its entirety:

Mr. C. has just moved in that day and didn't know anyone. Mr. C. wanted to have friends in the neighborhood. The story ends with Mr. C. having

many good friends and feeling at home in the neighborhood. You begin the story with Mr. C. in his room
immediately after arriving in the neighborhood.

Two forms were developed for this study, one for males and
another for females, the only difference between the two being
the sex of the protagonist.

Stories were analyzed for four elements. The first of these
was the number and kind of *means.* Examples of means might
include "Mr. C. visited his neighbors in order to become
acquainted," or "Mr. C. tried to be a good neighbor by helping
the other tenants. He did this by holding the elevator doors
open for other tenants, offering to carry packages, and so
forth." The second story element scored was the number of *enumerations* given by the subjects in reaching the goal. Enumerations are different examples of a basic means. Two are evident
in the second means given above—that of being a good neighbor. In this case enumerations would refer to each of the ways,
after the basic means had been given, in which he would be a
good neighbor. *Obstacles,* the third element, refer to events,
situations, and so on, which might prevent the hero from
reaching the goal. An obstacle for the protagonist that would
create difficulties in reaching the goal would be expressed in
language such as, "The neighbors were suspicious of new tenants in general." Finally, any indication of the passage of a specific amount of *time* during the steps taken to reach the goal
was scored as the fourth element. Recognition of the temporal
element in solving this problem might be evidenced by the
statement, "Mr. C. had to work at being a good neighbor *for
about a month* before the first person invited him into his
apartment."

The results showed a significant difference between the
patient and normal groups, with normals giving a greater
number of problem-solving means. Examination of scores on
individual stories also revealed that the significant differences
were not accounted for by any one or only a few stories. The
patient and normal groups also differed with respect to the
number of enumerations of means they provided, with the nor-

mals providing more. Males and females in the two groups did not differ with respect to the numbers of obstacles or with respect to references to the passage of time.

This study also introduced a new measure of means-ends thinking ability. This was the "relevancy score," or percentage of relevant means given in response to the stories. It was obtained by dividing the total number of relevant means given by each person by the total number of relevant means, irrelevant means, and ineffective means. The relevancy score thus shows the extent to which the person responds with relevant and effective solutions to the nine stories used. It was found that the relative proportion of relevant means in total story-directed responses was significantly greater for the normal group for both males and females, although much more so for the females.

In this study, the relationship of the number of means to the number of ineffective (no-means and irrelevant-means) story-directed responses was examined, and it was found that those with middle-range means-ends solution scores tended to have significantly fewer numbers of no-means and irrelevant-means responses than did those having means-ends scores falling in the lower range of scores (high scorers were not included in this analysis because of the relatively infrequent occurrence of no-means and irrelevant responses in their stories). These findings suggested that individuals with lower means scores gave many more ineffective responses as well as simply providing fewer effective means when compared to middle-range scorers, regardless of group membership (patient or normal).

Further information regarding the MEPS, its administration, measurement characteristics, and scoring, may be found in the MEPS Manual (Platt and Spivack, 1975a). It should be noted that the two scores that are primarily used in studies at the present time are the number of relevant means and the relevancy ratio. Enumerations appear to be so highly related to number of relevant means-ends solutions as to effectively represent the same underlying quality of thought. Obstacles and awareness of time seem to be measuring qualities of thought not necessarily related to adjustment, and thus have not been focused upon in most studies to date.

Means-ends thinking and adjustment in adolescents. Examining means-ends cognition, Spivack and Levine (1963) compared a group of adolescent boys at a residential treatment center who were showing poor self-regulation with a matched group of normal adolescents from similar socioeconomic backgrounds. Their finding was that, for four stories combined, the residential treatment group showed a significantly lower number of means.

Platt and others (1974) contrasted means-ends cognition in hospitalized adolescents with that of normal adolescents. The former group consisted of 33 male and female adolescent patients at a private psychiatric hospital. Thirty-one of these adolescents had a diagnosis of either adjustment reaction of adolescence or schizophrenia, latent type. The normal group consisted of 53 male and female high-school sophomores who did not differ from the first group in race, age, or socioeconomic status. While the two groups differed significantly in IQ, this variable was not related to means-ends cognition scores. What did relate to means-ends cognition, however, was adjustment. Both the male and female hospitalized adolescents were deficient, in contrast to the normal subjects, in their ability to generate means-ends cognition.

A third study of means-ends cognition in the age range of late adolescence–early adulthood involved a comparison of heroin addict and nonaddict offenders aged nineteen to twenty-one years (Platt, Scura, and Hannon, 1973). In this study, the addicts demonstrated significantly less means-ends cognition. They also showed a lower relevancy ratio for story elements than did the nonaddict controls. It is interesting to note that the addicts in this study demonstrated poorer means-ends cognition despite the fact that they were significantly older and better educated than the nonaddicts.

The results of the above studies suggest that adolescents demonstrating a variety of behavioral maladjustment (such as poor self-regulation, lack of adjustment to their life situation so as to require institutionalization, or addiction to heroin) exhibit some deficiency in means-ends cognition when compared with equivalent groups not demonstrating such aberrance.

Means-ends cognition and verbal productivity in adolescents. From the earliest studies of means-ends cognition, the concern arose that high means-ends scores might only reflect sheer verbosity on the part of subjects in telling stories; that is, the number of means produced might be dependent upon the length of the stories given rather than any quality of thought process. For instance, in the Spivack and Levine (1963) study, the normal group also had significantly longer stories than the group in the treatment center. Upon failure to find a significant relationship between story length and means-ends scores in either group, it was concluded that number of means was unrelated to story length.

In the Platt and others (1974) study, an analysis aimed at explicating the contribution of motivation or ability to verbalize to means-ends cognition examined the relative frequencies of ineffective and irrelevant story elements given by the patient and control groups. Irrelevant means were defined as responses that described some action on the part of the hero that was instrumental in reaching not the stated goal but some other goal. Ineffective responses were those that (1) failed to specify in sufficient detail how the goal was reached, (2) simply repeated or paraphrased part of the story, or (3) made a value judgment on some aspect of the story. As a result of this analysis, it was found that the adolescent patient group, in contrast to the controls, gave significantly more responses that were scored as ineffective or irrelevant means.Thus, the patient group gave more ineffective or irrelevant responses, while at the same time producing fewer problem-solving means. These results suggested it is unlikely that the obtained difference in means-ends cognition simply reflected differences between the two groups in motivation or verbal productivity. As will be seen in Chapter Five, other analyses carried out with adult samples have produced similar findings, all suggesting that means-ends cognition is *not* a function of the extent to which a person possesses verbal skills or simply gives longer responses.

Means-ends thinking and IQ in adolescents. As has already been indicated, in none of the above studies was means-ends cognition found to be a function of IQ in either the disturbed or control groups. This conclusion is based on the finding, in the Spivack and Levine (1963) study, of no relationship between means-ends cognition scores and total scores on the Wechsler Adult Intelligence Scale (WAIS) for either the normal or emotionally disturbed groups. Similar findings resulted from the Platt and others (1974) study, in which the relationship between means-ends cognition scores and Otis-Lennon IQs was not significant for either the patients or control groups. Finally, Platt and Spivack (1975a) reported that the correlation between means-ends scores and Stanford Achievement Test scores also was insignificant, suggesting that this measure of interpersonal cognitive problem solving was independent of educational achievement.

Modification of the means-ends procedure for the study of emotional problem solving. The work reported thus far was focused on problems arising within the social sphere (for example, making friends, dating, or dealing with peers), chosen to represent typical real-life problems with which people are faced. Problem situations were not defined in terms of the negative affect states (for example, anxiety and depression) that frequently accompany real-life problems. Siegel, Platt, and Peizer (1976) suggested that the ability to cope with one's own negative emotional states or emotional problems should also be necessary for healthy social functioning. Psychologically disturbed adolescents should be deficient in both areas and the ability to solve problems in both areas should be related. The problem situations presented to normal and disturbed groups of adolescents were four usual interpersonal means-ends problem situations and two means-ends stories wherein the protagonist is experiencing and must deal with feelings of anxiety or depression.

Initial means counts for the two measures were significantly different for the two groups, with the patients having fewer means on both tasks. However, when group differences in IQ were taken into account, the patient and control groups were still found to differ on interpersonal problem-solving ability but not on the emotional task. These results suggested that problem solving about how to get rid of unpleasant feelings has much in common with the ability to deal with abstract and largely impersonal tasks of the kind tapped by IQ tests, whereas interpersonal problem solving is more intimately linked to quality of social adjustment. Furthermore, there was no correlation between the ability to conceptualize means to an end when the protagonist had to deal with problems of negative affect and the ability to do so in social situations. This leads to the suggestion that only interpersonal problem-solving ability, and not emotional problem solving, may be necessary for behavioral adjustment.

Alternative Thinking

The ability to generate options in interpersonal situations has been demonstrated in children as early as age four (Shure and Spivack, 1970b). In this age range, as well as in older (fifth grade) children (Shure and Spivack, 1970a; Elardo and Caldwell, in preparation b), poorly adjusted youngsters have been found to demonstrate a deficiency in the ability to generate options when presented with interpersonal problems. This process has also been studied in adolescents (Platt and others, 1974), and similar findings have been obtained.

Measuring alternative thinking. The measurement procedure utilized with adolescents is similar to that used with fifth graders by Shure and Spivack (1970a). To measure capacity to conceptualize alternate solutions to a problem, the subject is told: "Now I am going to tell you some things that happen to a person, and I want you to think of all the things he (she) could do about it. Tell me everything that comes into your head. And don't worry about being right or wrong, because there are no right or wrong answers." A typical problem might be, "John wants to watch his favorite TV program but his friend is watching another program. What can John do so that he can have a turn watching TV?"

A standardized set of probing questions has been

employed to help elicit differing solutions to each problem (for example, "What else do you think he might do?"). In all situations, when the subject has finished but has given only one or two answers, the examiner asks, "Can you think of anything else?" until no new ideas are forthcoming. Four such situations have been used to derive a score, based upon the number of relevant, discrete, alternative solutions generated.

The most frequently given responses to the problem situation described above included the following: "John could ask his friend if he could have a turn," "John could turn the channel himself," "John could compromise with his friend so that he could have a turn"—this might involve taking turns, making a deal, and so on—or "John tried to persuade his friend to let him have a turn by [coercion, logic, and so on]."

Alternative thinking and adjustment. When presented with the above stories, the institutionalized adolescents studied by Platt and others (1974) gave significantly fewer alternatives to the four problem situations than did normal controls. As in the case of the means-ends variable, because of the possible contamination of the obtained group differences by motivation or ability to verbalize, another analysis of the responses was carried out. The results of this analysis indicated that the patient group gave significantly more irrelevant alternative solutions while at the same time producing fewer alternative solutions. It seems unlikely, then, that the differences on this task, as on the means-ends task, simply reflected patient-control differences in motivation or ability to verbalize. Finally, scores on the measure of alternative thinking were not found to relate to the IQ measure used in this study.

Perspective Taking

Successful interpersonal problem solving not only involves the ability to generate the step-by-step means of reaching the goal in specific situations (and to have available alternative problem solutions should the initial route be blocked) but may also be affected by an appreciation of the perspective of others involved in a particular situation. This implies awareness of the fact that others may have different motives and may respond only in terms of their view.

In their study of adolescent problem-solving thinking, Platt and others (1974) included a measure of role-taking somewhat more demanding than the tasks used in previously cited studies of younger children. The procedure used was Feffer and Jahelka's (1968), which involves four situations, each based upon a Thematic Apperception Test (TAT) card. For each, the subject is required to make up an initial TAT story following standard TAT instructions. After the stories are completed, each scene is again presented and the subject is asked to retell the initial story from the viewpoint of each of his characters. Scoring is based upon a modification of Schnall and Feffer's (1970) scoring procedure, designed to indicate the extent to which the subject's stories reflect increasing subtlety of coordination between the various versions. The following examples of two stories given to a TAT card and reflecting a high and low role-taking score, respectively, illustrate this system.

Subject A:

Initial story: "That looks like a confrontation between a father and son. The son looks rather disillusioned, annoyed, perhaps even disgusted. Perhaps because of a relationship with a friend that his father is giving him advice about. The son looks as if he doesn't want advice. The father is trying to understand—perhaps about a decision that the son has to make."

From the father's viewpoint: "He [the father] has sympathy for the difficult position the son is in, and is trying to help him. He is thinking to himself: 'I wish there was something I could do to help him with this problem.' "

From the son's viewpoint: "He appreciates that his father is trying to help him with his problem, but no one else can help him. Whatever is on his mind, he has to solve it himself. He even says this to his father so that he (the father) won't

think that he just doesn't want his advice and
feel badly about it."

Subject B:

Initial story: "That's a son listening to his father. Both
are talking over a problem. Both get to the root of
the problem."

From the son's viewpoint: "The father is telling his son
to stay out of trouble."

From the father's viewpoint: "The son is telling his
father that the problem won't happen again. He
says, 'Let's forget it and go fishing.' "

As is evident, Subject A has gone far beyond pure description of the scene, has taken into account the internal states of
the actors, including motivation and emotion, and furthermore has incorporated into the story the recognition by each
actor of the other's internal states. Finally, the stories are clearly
coordinated. In contrast, Subject B has not gone much further
than description. There is no reference to the internal state of
the actors or any indication of recognition of such states in each
by the other. Clearly this story lacks the richness of the first
story, and its different versions lack the sense of coordination
evident in the first one.

Differences in scores between the adolescent patients and
normals on the perspective-taking task were highly significant,
with the normals demonstrating greater perspective-taking
ability. This finding was consistent with those found with
adults by both Suchotliff (1970) and Platt and Spivack (1973).
Perspective-taking was found to have the lowest relationship to
intelligence of all the measures used with adolescents.

Consequential Thinking

The results presented in Chapter Three indicate that the
tendency to spontaneously conceptualize consequences before
taking action does not relate to behavioral adjustment in pre-
teenagers. Yet it is possible to demonstrate that youngsters at
this age do differ in the degree to which they exhibit such think-

ing, and evidence from other studies suggests that this is a skill in which psychologically disturbed adults are deficient (Platt and Spivack, 1973). Thus, the exact developmental stage at which such consequential thinking begins to contribute to the adjustment process is an open question, on which studies with adolescents may throw light.

Using the procedure outlined for latency-period children, the impulsive and normal adolescents in Spivack and Levine's (1963) study were presented with four situations in which the protagonist was faced with a temptation. For example, in one instance he was tempted to socialize rather than to study. The subject was asked to complete a story, indicating both the tempted protagonist's thoughts prior to a decision and any subsequent actions. Another story, in its entirety, was: "Bill loves to go hunting but he is not allowed to go hunting by himself. One weekend, his parents go on a trip and he remains at home by himself. He has a new shotgun he received recently, and a box of shells. He looks out of the window at the nearby woods, and is tempted to go out hunting." The subject was then instructed to tell everything that goes on in Bill's mind and then tell what happens. The score for this task reflected (1) the extent to which the subject's responses included references to what might happen "if" he carried out one or another course of action, or (2) a weighing of pros and cons of transgressing or not transgressing prior to a decision.

One response given to this story was:

> It would depend on what kind of person Bill is. If he really believes he should obey his parents, he would do so, regardless of what he wanted to do at that time. He probably really wants to go hunting, since he enjoys it a lot, but remembers that his parents trust him, so he wouldn't go. If he were mad at them he might feel differently, since it could be a way of getting even.

Another response was:

> If it was me, I'd really want to get out there and try out that new shotgun. I bet that Bill could get out

there and get in a full day's hunting without anyone else being any the wiser about it. He is just getting ready to get his hunting equipment together when a friend calls him and asks him if he wants to come over and listen to some new records so he does that instead.

The respondent who gave the first story has clearly stated two possible consequences of transgressing. On one hand, he sees a positive outcome in terms of enjoying going hunting but, on the other hand, recognizes that it might result in a loss of his parents' trust in him. It is on this basis that he eventually decides not to transgress. What is particularly interesting about this person's story is that he recognizes that transgression might also be used as a way of getting even with his parents.

In contrast to the story given by the first subject, the second one reflects an absence of considering the consequences of transgressing against his parents' wishes. It should be noted that in this story, whether or not transgression actually took place was not related to prior consideration of the consequences of transgressing. This lack of association was a not uncommon finding.

Stories were scored on a yes-no basis for the presence of consequential thinking, regardless of the quantity of such thinking demonstrated.

In the Spivack and Levine (1963) study, the normal adolescents, when contrasted with impulsive adolescents, were found significantly more likely to mentally preview the various pros, cons, and possible consequences involved in making the decision prior to stating whether or not the protagonist decided to transgress. When Platt and others (1974) compared adolescent psychiatric patients and normal control subjects on this variable, no difference was found between the two groups in terms of ability to conceptualize the consequences of transgression.

Causal Thinking

Causal thinking has been studied in several different ways at different age levels. Among teenagers, causal thinking has been conceptualized as involving the awareness of and tendency to respond in terms of the relationship between present events and prior to possible causal elements in daily living. Thus, when presented with a situation that involves a clearly preeminent emotional state (for example, anger, fear) as well as some other relatively neutral event, such as talking to a friend, the individual with awareness of the cause-and-effect nature of interpersonal events would probably think in terms of what led up to the emotional situation. On the other hand, an individual who does not think in such terms might not even focus on any causal element in the situation, except in a superficial way. It seems reasonable to assume, for instance, that if an individual is presented with the following situation: "Jim feels very mad and he's walking home with his friend," and is asked to describe what Jim is saying to his friend, his response might range from a causal "Did Joe make me mad today! Everything I asked him to do for me, he did wrong" to a noncausal "You're a pain." In the former case, there is a spontaneous tendency to zero in on the cause of the present state of events (that is, Jim's emotional state). In the latter case such a tendency is absent.

In the Platt and others (1974) study of adolescent psychiatric patients and normal high school students, clearly causal and noncausal responses to the four story situations were discernible. In response to the above story, such responses as the following were obtained:

> Harry really made me mad. There was no reason for him to act that way. What do you think I should do? (Causal)
>
> Boy, did I have a rotten day in school. I had a detention, was late for football practice, and my parents are going to be notified. (Causal)
>
> I don't feel like going home today. I'm going to go down to the school yard and play some stickball. (Noncausal)

When the two groups were compared as to the extent to which their responses reflected causal thinking, no difference was found.

Sensitivity to Interpersonal Problems

To cope successfully with an interpersonal problem situation, one must first be aware of its existence. Evidence regarding such an ability in adolescents is sparse, being based on data from a procedure that may not have been sufficiently sensitive. In the Platt and others (1974) study, sensitivity to problems was assessed by asking the subject, "What kinds of problems do you think people have in life?" The intent was to tap the subject's sensitivity to areas of life in which problems may arise. A standardized probing procedure was developed. Scores on this task were based on the number of distinct problem areas conceptualized by the respondent. The major categories into which problems given by respondents fell were: (1) general interpersonal, (2) family, (3) intrapersonal, (4) work, (5) health, (6) goals in life, (7) broad social issues, and (8) maternally oriented problems. No differences between adolescent normals and psychiatric patients were discernible in this study, either with respect to the actual number of responses provided or the number of content categories into which they fell.

Discussion and Conclusions

Most research on interpersonal problem solving has been carried out in populations other than adolescents. More intensive study of interpersonal problem solving in adolescents is, however, important for two reasons. First, it will help us determine the roles played by various problem-solving skills in the adjustment process during an important developmental period. Such understanding would be particularly useful in therapeutic planning for particular individuals or groups of individuals. Second, more complete data on adolescence would abet understanding of the developmental sequence in which specific problem-solving skills appear.

No direct link has yet been established between specific interpersonal cognitive problem-solving skills and adjustment in this age group, in that no studies have manipulated interpersonal cognitive problem-solving skills through training and demonstrated a direct relationship between change in cognition and change in social adjustment. On the other hand, correlational evidence relating interpersonal cognitive problem solving to adjustment in some instances is quite strong, especially considering the fact that the relationships cannot be explained away on the basis of differential verbosity in response to experimental procedures. A direct link between certain interpersonal cognitive problem-solving skills and behavioral adjustment is a reasonable assumption.

Evidence indicates that means-ends thinking is intimately related to adjustment during adolescent years. In attempting to achieve a goal in an interpersonal context, maladjusted groups, when compared with adjusted groups, are less able to conceptualize a step-by-step plan that incorporates details of action, consideration of potential obstacles, and appreciation of a temporal component. Their thoughts focus instead on motives and feelings, or jump to consummation, or introduce irrelevancies. Further, means-ends thinking of relevancy to social adjustment deals with interpersonal problem events, and not problem events of other kinds (for example, feeling depressed). The capacity to think in terms of means-ends is not present in preschool children but emerges and relates to adjustment during middle latency years (Larcen and others, 1972; Shure and Spivack, 1972) and continues as a significant mediator in adolescence.

Though evidence is not as extensive regarding other interpersonal cognitive problem solving processes, it is encouraging and justifies continued study. Maladjusted adolescents conceptualize a narrower range of alternative solutions .to everyday problems than do normals. They respond to a requirement to think about solutions but tend to think of solutions irrelevant to the situation. Thus, the ability to think of possible solutions relates to quality of social adjustment in preschool children (see Chapter Two) and continues its significance through middle childhood years (see Chapter Three) and into adolescence. In contrast to this, the spontaneous tendency to think of consequences (pros and cons of potential action) before decision making may very well only begin to appear during adolescent years as a significant mediator of social adjustment. While the ability to conceptualize alternative consequences of acts has been related to quality of adjustment in preschoolers, the *spontaneous tendency* to think about the pros and cons of what one might do *before* deciding does not relate to level of adjustment among latency-period children (Larcen and others, 1972). It was found related to adjustment in the study done with impulsive adolescents (Spivack and Levine, 1963), but not the study done with institutionalized teenagers (Platt and others, 1974). The possibility arises that such thinking is specifically relevant to behavioral impulsiveness, but only further data will help clarify the apparent inconsistency in findings with adolescents.

Perspective taking was found to be quite significantly related to adjustment among teenagers. Findings using similar though simpler tasks among latency-period children are less impressive (see Chapter Three), suggesting that even simple role-taking ability may make little direct contribution to the level of social adjustment in this age group, though it may perhaps contribute indirectly by enriching the quality of interpersonal cognitive problem-solving thinking. Being able to appreciate and integrate multiple perspectives may very well take on significance with age, to the point where in adolescence it functions in more intimate relationships to social adjustment. This possibility finds support in the study of adults discussed in Chapter Five. It also seems likely that the cognitive requirements of multiple-perspective thinking would exceed the capacity of younger children, especially the requirement that perspectives be reasonably integrated, although this has not been studied.

Current evidence regarding spontaneous causal thinking and sensitivity to the existence of life problems is quite sparse, and does not suggest their operation as mediators of adjustment among adolescents. The possibility exists that causal thinking does play a role in the social adjustment of adolescents that warrants its inclusion as a mediating interpersonal cognitive problem-solving skill, but further thought is required as to how best to conceptualize its operation and thus to measure it. For instance, it may be that the spontaneous thought of causes does not significantly contribute to adjustment among adolescents, but that the adolescent adjustment groups might differ in ability to generate alternative causes in a given situation. Similar comments might be made regarding sensitivity to the existence of problems as an interpersonal cognitive problem-solving skill among adolescents. The current evidence indicates that ability to think of categories of human problems is not a skill relevant to adolescent adjustment. It is possible, on the other hand, that adolescents differing in adjustment level might differ in their sensitivity to problems that may arise between two people in a particular situation or between the adolescent and other people.

Adulthood

Previous chapters have laid out a picture of similarities and differences in interpersonal cognitive problem solving in various age groups from preschool years through adolescence. Data relating interpersonal cognitive problem solving to adjustment in adults suggest answers to certain developmental questions and further highlight the issue of process versus content in interpersonal cognitive problem-solving thinking. A new issue is also touched upon: the ability to *recognize* appropriate means in contrast to ability to *generate* such means. Finally, studies have identified possible parameters underlying the relationships among interpersonal cognitive problem-solving skills, and the relationship of interpersonal problem-solving skills to other capacities that have been of interest to psychologists for many years.

Means-Ends Thinking

Research on interpersonal cognitive problem solving in adults has been focused mainly on the means-ends variable. Initial research strategy was to assess measures of possible interpersonal cognitive problem-solving skills in adults, and then to focus on the variable(s) most significant in mediating adjustment. Means-ends thinking has emerged as the most significant skill. Early studies suggested it was clearly related to adjustment status. The relationship of means-ends thinking to adjustment is only minimally, if at all, confounded by IQ, creativity, or productivity. The means-ends thinking variable has also yielded up qualitative as well as quantitative data of interest in studying interpersonal cognitive problem-solving thinking, and a factor analysis (Platt and Spivack, 1975b) of the individual stories composing the MEPS instrument has indicated that they were all measuring the same underlying dimension.

Relationship to social adjustment. The significance of means-ends thinking appears to change little from adolescence to adulthood, in that there persists a clear relationship of this variable to adjustment status. In both age groups, there is also evidence to indicate that degree of means-ends cognition is directly related to adjustment level within patient groups.

The first in the series of studies of means-ends thinking in adults involved a comparison of psychiatric patients, in treatment in an intensive-care short-term inpatient facility, with a nonpatient group. Most of the patients were schizophrenic. To assess interpersonal cognitive problem solving, these subjects were administered the Means-Ends Problem-Solving (MEPS) problem situations individually, and their performance was compared with that of hospital employees with similar age and educational characteristics.

Stories were scored in the same manner as for adolescents. This included examination for numbers of *means* given by the subject in order to reach the story goal, *enumerations* of means, *obstacles* that might prevent the hero or heroine from reaching that goal, and indications of the passage of a specific amount of *time* before reaching the goal. Story elements unrelated to the *stated* problem situation received no score. Relevant means were defined as any instrumental acts that enabled the hero or heroine to move toward the goal stated in the story or to overcome obstacles preventing him or her from doing so. If a response involved some action on the part of the main character that would be instrumental in reaching a goal other than the one stated, the response was scored as an *irrelevant means*. A *no-means* score was used to identify responses that failed to specify in sufficient detail how the goal was reached, merely repeated or paraphrased part of the problem situation, or made a value judgment regarding some aspect of the situation.

Typical responses by patients and controls are presented below. The hypothetical problem situation was:

> H. loved his girlfriend very much, but they had many arguments. One day she left him. H. wanted things to be better. The story ends with everything fine between him and his girlfriend. You begin the story with his girlfriend leaving him after an argument.

One subject provided the following story in response:

> After H.'s girlfriend had left, H. got to thinking, while he was alone, of all the good things he and his girl had done. Out loud he thought, "It just doesn't make sense that if we love each other, why let things that could easily be avoided, with a better understanding, break up our romance?" H. had finally come to an answer, in which he decided to call his girl right away and explain to her his feelings on the situation. He explained everything thoroughly and honestly and not at all to his surprise his girl had agreed to do the same.

This story contains three scorable means. The first is introspection or thinking about how to solve the problem, and the second is calling the girl to explain his feelings. The third was his explanation of his feelings in the conversation.

In contrast, the following story given by another subject contains no effective means:

> That was their worst argument. Three weeks pass. Now they do not argue anymore. They each are satisfied with their new situation sexually, emotionally, mentally, financially, etc. Each is going with someone else.

This story does, however, contain an irrelevant means of "solving" the problem—that is, finding someone else. This response is irrelevant because, while it may solve the problem of a breakup in a relationship, it does not address the goal as stated: everything being fine between them again.

The comparison of the patient and control groups revealed a number of findings. A significantly greater total number of means was given by the normal group for all nine stories. Each story contributed to differences between groups. Scores were not related to diagnostic category, with one exception; patients with a manic-depressive diagnosis tended to have higher scores than schizophrenics, although this tendency did not reach significance. Patients had a lower mean relevancy ratio, reflecting a significantly smaller proportion of relevant means among all story-directed responses. Normals gave significantly more enumerations of means than did patients, although there were no differences between the groups with respect to the story elements of obstacles and time.

To insure that the above findings were not an artifact of the sheer length of stories given by each group, the relationship among numbers of means, no-means, and irrelevant means of high and low thirds of scorers was examined. High numbers of means were found to be related to the presence of low numbers of irrelevant and no-means responses, and low numbers of means to high number of ineffectual responses. Thus, just having a large number of elements in one's story did not necessarily result in a high means score, just as a brief response did not necessarily result in a low number of means.

Further data comparing psychiatric with nonpatient groups have been provided by Platt and Spivack (1973) and Platt and others (1975). In the former study, acutely ill inpatients in a private psychiatric hospital were compared with a control group drawn from among hospital employees at the same institution who were equivalent in age, education, and marital status. Psychiatric patients were again found to be deficient in means-ends cognition, both with respect to number of means present in their stories and the percentage of relevant means. In this study, IQ was obtained for both groups and found not to affect group differences in number of means and the relevancy ratio.

The Platt and Spivack (1973) study also examined capacity for means-ends thinking when confronted with an unpleasant affect (depression, anxiety, or fear, for example). On this variable there was a strong initial difference between the patient and control groups, with evidence of greater emotional problem-solving ability on the part of the normals. When the effects of IQ were controlled for, however, this difference disappeared, reflecting the strong relationship of problem solving (relative to specific feelings) to intelligence, a finding parallel to that reported in the previous chapter for adolescents. This variable also showed a moderate and statistically significant relationship to interpersonal problem solving, but only for the patient group. This finding parallels that for adolescents.

A second study (Platt and others, 1975) compared acutely ill, predominantly psychotic middle-class psychiatric patients with normal individuals, again drawn from among hospital employees. Once again, patients were found to be deficient in their means-ends cognition.

Means-ends cognition: within-group relationship to adjustment. The studies of means-ends cognition described above all involved criterion group comparisons. Means-ends thinking, if meaningfully related to successful adaptation to the environment, should not only be capable of discriminating between groups of individuals demonstrating markedly different levels of adjustment but should also differentiate within such groups of individuals. Two studies have related means-ends cognition to adjustment level within patient groups.

In one study (Platt and Spivack, 1972*b*) means-ends cognition was related to prehospitalization social competence as determined on the basis of the Zigler-Phillips (1962) scale. Social competence on this scale is defined as having successfully met the social demands made upon the individual at various levels of maturation. This scale is based on biographic data and has been widely used as an index of adaptation prior to illness. Scores are based on the level of adequacy achieved by the patient in six areas of development: age at first psychiatric admission, education, intelligence, occupation, employment history, and marital status. Biographical data were obtained from hospital records for a sample of acutely ill patients on the inpatient and outpatient services of a community mental health center. The results indicated that both the number of means provided and relevancy ratios were inversely related to level of premorbid social maturity achieved, suggesting that failure to successfully meet real-life demands was most frequent in patients most deficient in cognitive means-ends capacity.

An interesting incidental finding in this study was that the means-ends scores of patients with either primary or secondary diagnoses of organic origin (excluded from the primary analyses) were frequently higher than for those with nonorganic illness. It may well be that a deficiency in means-ends cognition (or any other aspect of interpersonal problem-solving thinking) is not as important in determining the psychiatric status of these patients to the degree that it is with nonorganics. Psychiatric symptomatology *may* more directly reflect nervous system involvement than a history of interpersonal failure.

Because of the rather global nature of the Zigler-Phillips scale and its focus upon characteristics of the individual *prior* to the onset of illness, another attempt to more precisely delineate the relationships between interpersonal problem-solving cognition and extent of psychopathology was undertaken.

Platt and Siegel (in press) contrasted groups of relatively good and poor problem solvers among patients, as identified by the MEPS, on the MMPI. The first step in this comparison was to compare high and low MEPS scorers, using the indices of extent of psychopathology developed by Haertzen and Hill (1959). The findings indicated a greater prevalence of peaks on the Paranoia or Schizophrenia scales of the MMPI, as well as a greater incidence of high schores on the F-scale among males who obtained low means-ends scores. Lowest means-ends thinking capacity typified patients exhibiting the most confused, bizarre, or disordered thinking. No differences were obtained between females who obtained relatively high and low scores on the MEPS.

While group MMPI profiles were similar in both high- and low-scoring males, with both group profiles interpretable as schizophrenic, males scoring very low on the MEPS responded on the MMPI with greater immaturity, antisocial ideation, and confused and unusual thought and a greater degree of withdrawal from social contacts and responsibilities than males with higher MEPS scores. For females, however, the high- and low-scoring groups did not differ significantly on any of the clinical scales, although the validity-scale scores suggested greater defensiveness in the low-scoring female groups.

Since, among males at least, the low MEPS groups seemed to be more clearly psychotic than the high MEPS group, the data were further analyzed by means of the Goldberg Index, a measure of neurosis-psychosis. As expected, the low-scoring male group was more clearly psychotic than the high-scoring one, which was more clearly neurotic.

These results suggest that male patients higher in social problem-solving ability not only are more likely to have been more socially competent prior to the onset of illness but also show less psychopathological impairment than male patients low in interpersonal problem-solving ability. In addition, the finding of a significant difference between the high and low male MEPS groups on the Goldberg Index links interpersonal problem solving to the neurotic-psychotic dimension, with psychotics clearly demonstrating a greater deficiency in inter-personal problem-solving thinking.

Means-ends thinking: the content of thought. Another group of studies have had as their point of focus the *content* of thinking generated in response to the MEPS procedure. It was hoped that such exploration of content would throw further light on the process of problem solving.

In one study, Platt and Spivack (1974) raised the issue of whether psychiatric patients and nonpatients differ in *kinds* of means they provide, as well as in number. As a first step, the overall distribution of story content for each story for the patient and nonpatient groups was compared. It was found that, for all but one MEPS situation, the two groups tended to have a different distribution of response content categories. While the responses of both the patients and controls fell into the same categories overall, the relative distribution of re-sponses in these categories was different. For example, in one story, concerned with becoming a neighborhood leader, the major difference between the patient and normal groups was that normals were more likely to think of and mention "offer-ing plans or ideas," while patients were more likely to be con-cerned with the mechanics of nomination and election.

On examination of these results, it became clear that the differences between the two groups followed a pattern. Nor-mals were more likely to include in their stories an element suggesting that for them the thought *to think* comes to mind before thoughts of overt action. In contrast, patients tended to give responses reflecting concern with the taking of immediate and concrete action. This was evident in a story in which the protagonist had stolen a diamond. In this instance "planning how to carry out the theft" was given by almost three times as many normals as patients. In another story, dealing• with regaining friends, almost four times as many of the normals as patients gave the response, "looking within oneself to find out what's wrong," or a similar response reflecting introspection. This finding was present throughout almost all of the stories.

Another question regarding content has been whether

the *kinds* of means generated as part of an overall plan differ as a function of the particular subcultural group to which one belongs. For instance, in a situation where one wants to meet someone of the opposite sex in order to establish a relationship, parts of the overall plan might include meeting, dating, falling in love, or buying gifts, none of which in itself solves the problem of forming a relationship. The question raised was whether there might be differences in such content as a function of one's particular cultural background, even though there might be no difference in the overall quantity of means-ends cognition generated. Would blacks coming from a low-income inner-city environment conceptualize kinds of means different from those of a group of Middle-American whites? For this comparison the responses of a normal female group employed in an earlier study of patients were compared with those of a group of female students at two beautician schools in a small West Virginia city. No differences in the content of the means emerged, even though one of these groups differed in content (for example, the thought *to think*) on all but one story from the disturbed group, which came from the same inner-city area.

Another issue studied has been whether level of sophistication about or knowledge of how to solve interpersonal problems would relate to choice of means to solve interpersonal problems. Siegel, Platt, and Spivack (1974) reasoned that if trained mental health professionals made similar judgments as nonprofessionals regarding the relative effectiveness and social appropriateness of means to an end in problem situations, this would further support the emphasis heretofore given to the process of generating problem-solving thinking in contrast to the specific thought content.

Two groups distinctly differing in sophistication about mental health matters, as inferred from level of educational preparation and area of employment, were compared. The sophisticated group was composed of mental health professionals (five Ph.D.s, one M.A. clinical psychologist, two B.A. psychology research associates), and the nonprofessional group was composed of seven clerks and secretaries in a hospital records department. Years of education were distinctly different for the two groups—18.8 years for the professionals and 12.8 for the nonprofessionals. A third intermediate group consisted of thirteen undergraduate college students. Each person was asked to rank-order the most commonly given means responses to each of eight interpersonal problem situations on the basis of their effectiveness and social appropriateness in solving the problem. On seven of the eight problem situations, as well as on two story situations dealing with noninterpersonal problem issues, there was substantial agreement among all three groups as to what constitutes relatively effective and socially appropriate solutions to problems.

On the basis of these findings, it seems reasonable to conclude that, regardless of variety in social background and level of sophistication about mental health matters, normal adults tend to share a common frame of reference about what constitutes effective and socially appropriate means of reaching goals in interpersonal problem situations and that psychiatric patients probably share this frame of reference, even though they are less prone to generate the idea of making up a plan in response to a problem and may give some different priorities at various times to different means. For example, both patients and normals, when presented with all possible means in a problem situation in which the protagonist had the goal of becoming a leader, agreed that "offering plans on how to improve the community" would be the most effective and socially appropriate one. When required to spontaneously generate such means, however, most patients were concerned with the mechanics of nomination and election and rarely with offering plans. Among normals, on the other hand, the means of offering plans or ideas was given most frequently.

Means-ends cognition: the issue of recognition vs. generation of thought. Another study shed further light on the roles played by the recognition and generation processes in successful problem solving. In this study, Platt, Siegel, and Spivack (1975) raised the question of whether psychiatric patients and normals share the same frame of reference with respect to what constitutes effective and socially appropriate means of solving various interpersonal problems, and how this social sense relates to capacity to generate means-ends thought.

The initial procedure used was the same as in the Siegel, Platt, and Spivack (1974) study, except that, in addition, reasons for choosing or not choosing a particular course of action were requested, rankings were obtained of the relative perceived importance of each problem situation, and two of the MEPS situations were presented in the usual manner so as to obtain a measure of the ability to generate problem-solving means.

When the ranked order of effectiveness of the means provided by the psychiatric-patient and normal groups was compared, almost complete congruence was found. Patients and nonpatients agreed as to the relative effectiveness of the means in dealing with the interpersonal problem situations provided. This finding indicated that patients can distinguish the more from the less likely means of solving interpersonal problems if a choice is provided them. At the same time, however, response to the MEPS procedure indicated that these same patients were significantly less able to generate means of resolving interpersonal problem situations. Patients can recognize a good means of solving a problem when presented with it, but cannot generate effective means on their own. Further, neither within the patient group nor within the nonpatient group was ability to recognize appropriate means of solving interpersonal problems correlated with ability to generate appropriate means.

Finally, members of the two groups were asked why they had picked particular means as either the best or worst ways of dealing with a particular problem. Analyses indicated that, on almost all stories, patients and controls differed significantly in terms of ability to provide a valid reason for choosing a particular course of action over another. Normals provided a significantly greater proportion of valid explanations for ranking the means as they did.

The findings clearly indicate that while psychiatric patients are deficient in contrast to normals in their ability to generate means of solving interpersonal problem situations, they do *not* differ from normals in their ability to recognize the relative effectiveness of means of solving such problems when the means are presented for their inspection. Neither patients when contrasted with controls nor normals differing in educational level or degree of expertise in mental health matters differ in this regard. This suggests a common, culturally given frame of reference for all these groups. Furthermore, the ability to generate means and the ability to recognize their relative effectiveness are unrelated skills. The capacity to generate problem-solving thinking is the issue. The fact that patients are deficient with respect to the generation of means of solving interpersonal problems has been clearly documented in earlier studies of both adolescents (Platt and others, 1974) and adults (Platt and Spivack, 1972a, 1973), and is consistent with Spivack and Shure's (1974) suggestion that the underlying element in successful problem solving might be the *spontaneous capacity to generate possibilities* when confronted with interpersonal problems. Being able to articulate a related and sequential set of steps that may solve a problem (means-ends thinking) is one important facet of this capacity.

Recognition of effective means is unrelated to the generation of such means, and patients and normals do not differ in the ability to recognize effective means. It is clear that the ability to distinguish effective from ineffective means when presented with them does not contribute as much to mental health as does the capacity to generate effective means. The ability to generate would seem to reflect significant mediational processes. Moreover, patients are less able to provide a "valid" reason for choosing a particular means of solving a problem and are less likely to think of generating a plan when one is appropriate. A psychologically disturbed person may recognize an appropriate problem solution when presented with it, but be unable to think further about and through the problem situation.

Means-ends cognition and paper-and-pencil measures of personality. MEPS scores have been found to possess little or no relationship to scores on such paper-and-pencil measures of personal adjustment as the Personal Adjustment Scale of the

Adjective Check List and the Personal Adjustment, Social Adjustment, and Total Adjustment Scales of the California Test of Personality. As expected, the correlations are usually positive but low, and of borderline significance (Platt and Spivack, 1975a). These findings are difficult to explain, particularly since MEPS scores have been found to relate to measures of extent of psychopathology in psychiatric populations (compare Platt and Spivack, 1972; Platt and Siegel, in press). Possible explanations may reside in the very nature of the self-report, paper-and-pencil instruments that were used, in some unique characteristic(s) of the sample on which the data were collected, such as a limited range of adjustment scores, or in other factors.

Not only is means-ends cognition seemingly unrelated to such paper-and-pencil measures of adjustment, but MEPS scores have been found to be unrelated to such personality traits and predispositions as anomie, social self-esteem, extroversion, locus of control, future time perspective, and Murray's needs as measured by the Adjective Check List (Platt and Spivack, 1975a). These findings suggest that in looking for the significance of ICPS skills for adjustment, it will be a less than fruitful endeavor to look for dynamics in terms of personal traits or characteristic need states of the individual. It would seem that means-ends and related thinking skills define means of coping separate from motive states or general predisposition in interpersonal relations that define styles of relating (for example, dominance, extroversion, and so on). Perhaps the most useful line of research in this area might be one that attempts to identify those specific abilities within the cognitive domain which, in their interaction with motivational and other variables, determine level of social adjustment.

Means-ends cognition and measures of IQ and creativity. In adults as in younger groups, ICPS skills appear to be relatively independent of conventional measures of IQ and of measures of academic achievement and creativity as well. Among the various measures that have been examined in this regard are the California Test of Mental Maturity (language, nonlanguage, and total score scales), the Revised Beta, the Quick Test of Intelligence, the Otis-Lennon Test of Intelligence, the Scholastic Aptitude Test (verbal and quantitative scores), and the Stanford Achievement Test. The general finding in these studies has been that the relationship between ICPS and these measures is a borderline one.

Measures of creativity and abstract thinking, such as the Survey of Spatial Relations Ability Test, Preference for Visual Complexity-Simplicity, or the Remote Associates Test have also been found to be unrelated to means-ends cognition. Here, the average correlations approach zero. These latter results tend to confirm the assertion that *interpersonal* problem-solving thinking must be considered as a domain separate from creativity and related abilities. It is not the same as general ability to think abstractly, nor does it only reflect tolerance of imbalance, or openness of mind as a general quality. Rather, it appears to be specific to thinking competence in the interpersonal domain.

Studies of Other Interpersonal
Cognitive Problem-Solving Variables

As was indicated above, most interpersonal cognitive problem-solving research with adults has involved means-ends thinking. However, some data are available that deal with other cognitive-skill domains that have been discussed earlier in connection with younger age groups. These data derived from a study by Platt and Spivack (1973) that compared psychiatric-patient and nonpatient groups on a number of cognitive variables. This section will discuss findings in the following areas: (1) sensitivity to problems, (2) conceptualizing alternative solutions to problems, (3) multiple perspective taking, and (4) consequential and causal thinking regarding logical stages in problem solving.

Sensitivity to problems. Sensitivity to problems was assessed in a fashion similar to that used with adolescents (see Chapter Four). Individuals were asked to articulate as many of the problems facing the average man in everyday life as they could. The findings did not indicate any overall difference between the patient and normal groups. The suggestion is that the abstract ability to conceive of categories of problems does not relate to adjustment.

Alternative-solution thinking. The alternative-thinking task used was similar to the one already described in Chapters Four and Five. This task required the individual to provide optional problem solutions in response to interpersonal problems involving a peer. Typical of the problem situations designed to elicit alternative thinking was: "Victor wants people to listen to him, but no one ever does. What can Victor do to get listened to?" The respondent was asked to think of all the things the hero could do about this problem and advised not to worry about whether his responses were right or wrong since there were no right or wrong answers. Typical alternatives provided for this story were: "Victor can try and find new people to talk to" or "He can try to talk about a different subject than he used to talk about."

Results indicated that the patient group generated significantly fewer solution alternatives than did the normal group. However, this difference did not remain, once the influence of IQ was taken into account statistically. This measure of alternative-solution thinking was highly related to IQ in both the patient and normal groups. It would appear that, among adults, the ability to simply generate solutions to problems does not play as significant a role in adjustment as it does in younger age groups.

Multiple perspective taking. The extent to which an individual recognizes and can integrate the fact that different people may have different motives and thus may respond differently in a given situation has already been shown to be of importance in adolescents (see Chapter Four). Multiple perspective taking was also examined in adults with the use of a procedure introduced by Feffer and Jahelka (1968) that involves retelling stories given in response to TAT cards from the point of view of each character.

The findings indicated that the normals demonstrated

greater perspective taking and that this variable was not consistently related to intelligence. Interestingly, perspective taking was highly related to interpersonal means-ends thinking.

Consequential and causal thinking. Consequential thinking was measured with the story-telling procedure designed to assess the degree to which the individual considers pros and cons before deciding whether or not to transgress. Causal thinking was defined as the extent to which an individual spontaneously thinks in terms of the possible causal elements involved in a current problem situation. Both measures have been described earlier (see Chapter Four).

Analysis of results comparing the psychiatric patients and normal adults on consequential thinking indicated no difference between the two groups in the likelihood of considering the possibility of transgressing. Also, there was no difference between them in terms of whether or not they saw transgression as actually occurring. There was a significant difference between the two groups in that aspect of cognition of most interest—whether or not they considered and weighed the possible consequences of transgressing before deciding whether to transgress. The normal adults were more likely to spontaneously conceptualize the pros and cons of a particular course of action before embarking on it. This tendency was not related to IQ.

A similar pattern was obtained for causal thinking. Normals were significantly more likely to think spontaneously in terms of prior causes and the relationship between past and present events than were psychiatric patients, and this quality of thinking was not related to IQ. For the first time, in adults, there emerged a clear indication that spontaneous consideration of prior causes is a possible determinant of adjustment.

These findings with adults are similar in most respects to those described earlier with reference to adolescents. The sample of adult psychiatric patients was found to be deficient in a number of interpersonal cognitive problem-solving skills when contrasted with normal individuals. The patients generated fewer optional courses of action in problem situations and were less able to conceptualize the steps involved in reaching specified goals in interpersonal problem situations. They were less able than normals to see problem situations from the perspectives of other involved persons and to integrate these perspectives. The patients were less able to relate present events in daily living to their prior causal elements, and they were also less prone to spontaneously conceptualize the pros and cons of action before taking action. The pattern of findings points to specific deficiencies, not a general performance deficit in pathological groups or deficiencies ascribable to the depressing effect of psychopathology on IQ. All of these findings underline a common element differentiating adults who differ in adjustment—the *spontaneous generation* of thought related to solving problems that arise in the interpersonal sphere.

Interrelationships and Structure of Interpersonal Cognitive Problem-Solving Skills

The findings presented above do not suggest how the various elements of interpersonal cognitive problem solving are related to each other except in the most general terms. To determine the underlying structure of the interpersonal problem-solving variables that have been studied, data resulting from the comparisons of adult psychiatric patients and nonpatients were subjected to a factor analysis. Data from the five interpersonal cognitive problem-solving measures and the multiple-perspective-taking task were included in this analysis. The six variables were: sensitivity to problems, optional solution thinking, interpersonal means-ends thinking, prior consideration of consequences, spontaneous causal thinking, and multiple perspective taking. The factor analyses were carried out separately for the patient and normal groups, since it was not known to what extent interpersonal cognitive problem solving in these two groups shared a common factorial structure.

Table 3 presents the intercorrelations among the six skills. Those for the normals appear to the right of the diagonal and those for the patients to the left. The pattern of intercorrelations indicates that, while certain of the skills do relate to

Table 3

Interrelationships Among Five ICPS Skills and Multiple
Perspective Taking in Normal-Adult (N=47) and
Psychiatric-Patient (N=105) Groups

	(1)	(2)	(3)	(4)	(5)	(6)
(1) Problem recognition		.39	-.05	-.02	.21	.05
(2) Alternative thinking	.45		.14	-.12	.34	.12
(3) Means-ends cognition	.16	.25		-.06	.38	.04
(4) Causality	.01	.18	.15		-.02	.24
(5) Perspective taking	.15	.30	.52	.32		.17
(6) Consequences	.06	.19	.10	.06	.16	

Note: Intercorrelations for normals appear to the right of
the diagonal, those for patients to the left.

each other, others do not, suggesting that the amount of overlap among the six variables is insufficient to permit considering
them as identical in meaning.

The factor analyses yielded similar factors for both the
patient and the normal groups, and these are presented in
Table 4. Three ICPS parameters emerged, accounting for much
of the variance in the data. Factor I, labeled "simple generation," consisted of the abilities to generate different categories
of human problems and to conceptualize alternative problem
solutions. This factor accounted for 25 percent of the variance in both groups and suggested an underlying cognitive
dimension that taps capacity to generate in a relatively simple
demand situation.

Factor II, labeled "complex coordination and integration," included interpersonal means-ends thinking and multiple perspective taking and accounted for 24 percent of the variance in the normal group. The third factor in the normal
group, labeled "spontaneous sequential thinking," consisted
of causal thinking and consideration of consequences and
accounted for 21 percent of the variance. The factor structure
for the patient group was similar for the last two parameters,
accounting for similar amounts of variance.

As can be seen from the factor loadings presented in
Table 4, each of the variables contributing to any one factor

Table 4

Factorial Structure (Rotated) of Interpersonal Cognitive Problem Solving in Adult Psychiatric Patients and Controls

Factor	Normal Adults (N=47)			Adult Psychiatric Patients (N=105)		
	ICPS Variables Loading on This Factor	Factor Loading	% Variance Factor Accounts for	ICPS Variables Loading on This Factor	Factor Loading	% Variance Factor Accounts for
Simple generation	Sensitivity to problems	.85	25%	Sensitivity to problems	.89	25%
	Alternative thinking	.74		Alternative thinking	.76	
Complex coordination and integration	Means-ends thinking	.89	24%	Means-ends thinking	.71	28%
	Perspective taking	.73		Perspective taking	.82	
Spontaneous sequential thinking	Causal thinking	.80	21%	Causal thinking	.66	17%
	Considering consequences	.77		Considering consequences	.99	
Total variance accounted for			70%			70%

loaded highly on that factor. Also, with the exception of causal thinking, which loaded together with consideration of consequences for normals but with interpersonal means-ends cognition and perspective taking for patients, the two underlying structures are identical.

Considering the almost perfect replication of findings, it seems relatively safe to assert that ICPS thinking among adults is not a unidimensional process. While a common underlying property may be the generation of problem-solving thought, problem situations that demand the simple generation of problem types or solutions do not require the same thought processes that accompany responses to situations calling for connection of events in time, or causal thinking. Further, other processes appear to be called into play when the situation calls for more complicated problem solving wherein planning is demanded, where there is a subtle interplay of social action and reaction, and where the situation requires an orderly integration of issues in one's mind.

Discussion and Conclusions

Studies of interpersonal cognitive problem solving in adults suggest continuity but not complete congruence with respect to the relationship between interpersonal cognitive problem solving and adjustment in adolescence. As in adolescents, means-ends thinking in adults is strongly related to adjustment status. This skill, which seems to emerge during the middle latency period, is consistently more evident in groups of individuals displaying higher levels of adjustment. Paradoxically, however, while it also relates to adjustment level within groups of psychiatric patients, it does not do so within normal groups, when adjustment is measured by paper-and-pencil instruments. The reasons for this latter finding are unclear at present.

Studies of means-ends cognition also suggest that the *content* of means-ends thinking—not merely the quantity of it—is related to level of adjustment. Even though the same categories of means of solving interpersonal problems are conceptualized by both normal and patient groups, apparently the two groups tend to call on different categories of such means in particular situations. In this regard, normals are much more likely to use means involving the thinking process in contrast to those involving the taking of immediate and direct action. Significantly, the actual selection of means is independent of membership in a particular subcultural group, and judgments about their relative effectiveness and social appropriateness are independent of level of sophistication about mental health matters. Perhaps most significant to an understanding of the process of means-ends thinking is the finding that psychiatric patients *recognize* effective and socially appropriate means of solving interpersonal problems but are deficient in ability to *generate* means-ends thought when called on to do so.

Another significant finding with adults is that the ability to think spontaneously of causes and consequences is clearly related to adjustment status. As was indicated in Chapter Four, the role played by causal and consequential thinking in the adolescent years is not clear. Yet in adulthood there is unambiguous evidence to suggest that these skills are important in relation to adjustment.

As was the case for adolescents, multiple perspective taking is related to adjustment status in the adult years, although perhaps not as strongly as for adolescents. This variable is also found to be highly related to means-ends cognition in adults. The latter finding helps us to better appreciate the nature of means-ends thinking, which may require the rather sophisticated capacity to take into account different perspectives at the same point in time.

One of the most surprising findings in the studies of interpersonal cognitive problem solving in adults is that alternative thinking, or the simple generation of solutions, seems to take on a less significant role in the adjustment process. For the first time, in this age group, strong group differences between patients and nonpatients on this variable are seen to be lost when IQ is taken into account. It is not clear why there is a strong relationship between IQ and simple tasks such as this one while, at the same time, such a relationship does not exist between IQ and more complex interpersonal tasks such as means-ends thinking and multiple perspective taking. It appears that for adults, however, underlying the generation of solutions to interpersonal problems is the more general intellectual ability tapped by IQ tests.

Finally, there is evidence indicating that, while the ability to generate thought may be a common element in all interpersonal cognitive problem-solving skills, all the processes studied are not highly related to each other. Rather, in both patients and normals, ICPS skills seem to fall into groups with three underlying qualities: the simple generation of interpersonal thought, the coordination and integration of complex interpersonal situations, and the spontaneous ability to think sequentially about interpersonal affairs.

Role of Family and Childrearing Practices in Development of Interpersonal Problem Solving

⧣⧣⧣⧣⧣⧣⧣⧣⧣⧣⧣⧣⧣⧣⧣⧤⧤⧤⧤⧤⧤⧤⧤⧤⧤⧤⧤⧤

With the exception of the studies to be reported in this chapter, there has been no research to date specifically relating family or individual parental behaviors to the ICPS development of the child. This is due in large part to the fact that theorizing about and measurement of ICPS ability is only of recent vintage. However, the paucity of studies in the area of parenting and interpersonal cognition is still surprising, considering the vast literature that has accrued in recent years dealing with early cognitive development in children, the existence of a traditional area of study relating childrearing to personality

124

development, and intensive interest over the past decade or more among clinicians in family life and family psycho- pathology.

The Family and Interpersonal Problem Solving

There is good reason to expect there would be a direct relationship between certain family and/or parent childrear- ing variables and ICPS ability. Evidence that ICPS ability is quite teachable in four- to six-year-old children indicates that these processes are not internal structures that unfold as the developing child grows, irrespective of social experience (see Chapter Two). If a teacher can alter ICPS ability in preschool children over a three-month period, it seems safe to assume that an adult in an intimate parental role must have a signifi- cant impact on the evolution of this ability. Further, the social nature of the processes themselves suggests that the social sys- tem within which the child grows must play a significant if not the primary role in their development. It seems plausible to as- sume that these ways of thinking are largely learned, the ques- tion remaining as to what parameters of family or parental influences may be most relevant.

Some evidence and theory exists that focuses on the family as a problem-solving unit (see Aldous and others, 1971). Strauss (1968) hypothesized that families from different social classes differ in the ability of the family group "to deal with the kinds of novel and problematic situations characteristic of a rapidly changing urban-industrial society" (p. 417). Strauss examined actual problem-solving behavior in a laboratory situation among middle-class and working-class families con- sisting of mother, father, and twelve-year-old offspring in Bombay, San Juan, and Minneapolis. Observation and mea- surement of family group behavior revealed that, in compari- son with middle-class families, lower-class family members functioned more in isolation from one another, shared infor- mation less often through words, and were less prone to act out a potential solution to other family members. Across cultures, the lower-class families were more restricted in the range of solutions that were tried out and in the amount of verbal and nonverbal communication within the family. Further, the number of action options displayed was correlated with the quality of problem solving that resulted.

Stylistic differences in the way in which families from different backgrounds deal with their children and their children's problems have been discussed by Hertzig, Birch, Thomas, and Mendez (1968). The authors noted differences in how preschool children from American middle-class and Puerto Rican working-class families react to problems, having first eliminated from consideration the issues of intelligence, deprivation, family size, and living conditions as possible explanations. The Puerto Rican group of children were found less prone to offer work or performance responses when given a cognitive task, or to shift from nonwork to work behaviors; they verbalized less and responded with action or gesture more; they responded with more irrelevant verbal substitution when they failed; they introduced fewer verbalizations indirectly related to the task; and they produced more work in response to "performance" than "verbal" demand tasks. The investigators concluded that the issue was not the possession of language but rather the *use* to which language was put in response to a cognitive problem. They reasoned that the use to which language is put probably relates to childrearing practices and family lifestyles. Middle-class American families were found to be more task-oriented and task-completion-oriented than the working-class Puerto Rican families and more businesslike regarding the concepts of time and scheduling, rules and structure. Middle-class American parents were more prone to push their children to master self-care in eating, dressing, and toilet training, and the home atmosphere was organized to produce regular and systematic improvements in skill. In all these matters, the Puerto Rican family was less businesslike, more socially oriented than task-oriented, and less insistent on pushing for grownup behavior. In a parallel comparison, middle-class verbalization was seen to be more focused on clear articulation of the task to be done and making sure directions were understood and carried out, while verbalization in the Puerto

Rican homes was more social and affective. In middle-class families, toys were "educational" and considered important to learning, but among Puerto Rican parents they were considered mainly for amusement and left to the whim of the child. If the child needed help with something, the middle-class mother would be inclined to encourage mastery and direct the child to problem-solve by himself. The Puerto Rican mother would be more likely to solve the problem for the child.

Minuchin, Chamberlain, and Grambard (1967) have studied how a disorganized family below the poverty level that includes a disturbed and delinquent adolescent will behave when problems arise within the family. They noted a marked deficit in communication through words if, for example, an issue of rules arose in the family or there was an expressed need on the part of a family member. The child learned that "power" resides not in the logic of argument but only in the intensity of sound and action. Family talk was full of interruption and yelling, and never were topics focused upon, questions elaborated, nor information gathered in an organized fashion. In communication between child and adult, the child learned to focus almost exclusively on who the adult *was*, to the relative exclusion of the content of the communication. There was a tendency for problems not to be resolved.

Reiss (1971) has evolved a theoretical system within which total families may be categorized, each of the three family categories having implications for how effectively a family unit responds to problems confronting it. The "environment-sensitive" (normal) family sees the problem as "out there," logically searches for solutions, and is open to cues about the problem and its possible solutions from both inside and outside the family. As a consequence, conclusions are not reached too quickly, and the process is characterized by a sharing of experience with a sense that consensus is possible. In contrast to such a family, the "consensus-sensitive" family approaches a problem as a potential threat to its solidarity. The family is not open to all external cues. Members are quick to surrender their individual ideas, and dissent is not tolerated because the family goal is always to maintain a close and uninterrupted agreement at all times. As a consequence, the family reaches hastily forged consensus too quickly and may even need to create and maintain a sense of agreement even to the point of illusion. Reiss views the schizophrenic family as an extreme example of the consensus-sensitive type, and has provided some evidence to this effect (see Reiss, 1967; 1968; 1969). Others have reported upon the overcontrol of ideas in schizophrenic families (Mishler and Waxler, 1968), the extreme mutual involvement and entanglements of family members (for example, Scott and Askworth, 1967; Hoover, 1965), and the boundaries that contain schizophrenic family members in a closed social system (Friedman and others, 1965).

The third family type Reiss calls the "interpersonal distance-sensitive" family. Confronted with problems, family members approach problem analysis and solution as simply a means by which each can show independence from the family. Each member has a private universe of laws and values, and each functions alone on the assumption that nothing he or she does can be useful to or evaluated by others. Members are isolated. As a consequence, there is no sense of sharing in problem solving, and family solutions are uncoordinated affairs. Family members may be in constant conflict, preoccupied with their own satisfaction and point of view, with little if any sense of emotional connection. Reiss sees families of delinquents as fitting this category.

Reiss's theories are relevant here not only in their obvious implications for family problem solving but also because he sees members of families that fall into these categories as probably exhibiting certain qualities of individual cognitive functioning. Unfortunately for present purposes, Reiss articulates this level of functioning in terms of cognitive and perceptual "styles" as formulated in the work of Witkin (1962) and Gardiner and others (1959), but his ideas are suggestive relative to ICPS. For example, he sees effective problem-solving families as consisting of members who are good "field articulators," who are ready to see problem situations as complex and open for exploration. The suggestion is that family members would see many possible solutions and consequences. He also sees families who can tolerate not coming to a conclusion quickly as consisting of members who can "tolerate unrealistic experiences" and who are able to set aside preconceived notions. One expects such family members would be sensitive to interpersonal problems and generate many ideas about them. Reiss is not specific in hypothesizing how or even whether family style may determine individual cognitive styles, although he speculates that the interaction between family and individual functioning "may be particularly true for children whose emerging capacity to articulate stimulus fields may be a direct product of such family experience" (p. 17).

Childrearing and Problem Solving

The fact that certain parameters of childrearing or parent-child interaction may influence the child's cognitive development has been well documented, at least insofar as abstract (that is, impersonal) intellectual development is concerned. Hess and Shipman (1965) studied the interaction of mother and child to assess how a mother assists her child in handling an intellectual task, and how differences reflect a more general cultural deprivation. In noting differences, Hess and Shipman refer both to style of approach and to more specific qualities of the mother-child interaction:

> One of the features of the behavior of the working-class mothers and children is a tendency to act without taking sufficient time for reflection and planning. In a sense one might call this impulsive behavior —not by acting out unconscious or forbidden impulses but in a type of activity in which a particular act seems not to be related to the act that preceded it or to its consequences [p. 884].

and later:

> The effect of restricted speech and a status orientation is to foreclose the need for reflective weighing of alternatives and consequences; the use of an elaborate

code, with its orientation to persons and to consequences (including future) tends to produce cognitive
styles more easily adapted to problem-solving and
reflection [p. 885].

The work of Bee and her colleagues (Bee, 1971) has cor-
roborated the significance of maternal behaviors in the development of the young child's cognitive abilities. Comparing the
behavior of lower-class and middle-class mothers in both an
unstructured waiting-room and a structured child-task situation, it was noted that the lower-class mother was less attentive
and also, when attending to her child, would more often tell the
child what to do or disapprove of what he was doing.

The middle class mother guided the child's
action with a kind of "Socratic" questioning; she was
active, but not intrusive; she participated in the problem, but encouraged the child to do the task himself
insofar as possible. In contrast, the style most typical of
the lower class mother markedly reduced the scope of
independent action available to the child, and did not
focus his attention on the basic features of the problem
[p. 195].

Analysis of the language used by the mothers revealed
further differences. Middle-class mothers, when compared
with lower-class mothers, used longer and more complex sentences, relatively more adjectives, and fewer personal referents,
all associated with a more elaborate linguistic code. Bee notes
that the more restrictive form of language used by lower-class
mothers in the presence of the child may not only limit what
the child attends to "but perhaps more importantly, insofar as
language serves as a mediator in complex problem-solving,
restrict the type of mediational concepts available to the child."

In reviewing the literature on early cognitive development, Gray and Miller (1967) refer to the work of Hess and
Shipman and their colleagues, concluding:

Impoverishment of meaning in the family communication and control system means fewer available

alternatives for consideration and choice. Unavailability of behavioral alternatives and a restricting parent-child relationship militate against adequate cognitive growth. Interaction patterns which rely on status rules rather than attention to the characteristics of the specific situation, and where behavior fails to be mediated by verbal cues, tend to produce a child who relates to authority rather than rationale. A strong case for the pivotal point a mother plays in early cognitive development as an instrumental source of stimulation is made by such studies [p. 483].

Chilman (1966) has reviewed the childrearing literature in an attempt to summarize the childrearing patterns reportedly characteristic of families with emotionally healthy offspring. Results suggested such families are (1) sensitive to causes in their child's behavior, considering reasons *why* things occur, (2) open and free in verbal communication, with control manifest largely through verbal communication (in contrast to physical means), (3) unrepressive and unpunitive in response to child's questions about sexual behavior, and (4) flexible and open to new experiences. The overall flavor suggests an orientation that supports and guides problem solving about personal matters, that limits arousal of inhibiting anxiety, that educates through verbal exchange, and that encourages open-mindedness. Consonant with these findings is the conclusion of Bloom (1964), after considering developmentally various facets of stability and change in human characteristics. Bloom concludes that apparent influences in cognitive development are: opportunities for the child to have certain kinds of enjoyable contact with parental figures, including opportunities to solve problems; encouragement to think clearly; and encouragement to attack problems flexibly and while considering outcomes.

What may happen to cognitive problem-solving functioning over the long run when certain parental styles are manifest is also suggested in two longitudinal studies reported by Weinstock (1967a, 1967b). In one study (Weinstock, 1967b), data derived from a thirty-year longitudinal assessment procedure. Weinstock examined adult cognitive defense styles through extensive structured interview data. Cognitive defenses were classified as differing in degree to which denial or a style of avoidance was manifest by the adult, in contrast to styles of a more intellectual or cognitively sophisticated nature. Weinstock found that adults who in their early childhood were raised in lower-class homes (generally characterized by more punitive and less verbally articulating childrearing practices) were more prone to use denial defenses, thirty years later, than adults raised in families of higher social class. The latter manifest more cognitively differentiated and "intellectual" defenses, defenses less prone to distort the total problem situation and thus more prone to allow of realistic solution. In his second study, Weinstock related early family and childrearing information to defense mechanisms manifest in adolescence. He discovered that the use of more primitive denial and repressive mechanisms in adolescence related to the use of similar mechanisms on the part of the parent when the child was quite young. Weinstock proposes that these defensive means of dealing with personal problems reflect an "identification" or imitative modeling of parental behavior on the part of the child.

Weinstock's studies are relevant here because defensive styles define ways of thinking in response to interpersonal problems. In the face of a problem, effective solution requires exploration of the situation and its various parameters. A "no-think" strategy of denial or repression directly militates against problem solving. The qualities of childrearing conducive to developing defensive (rather than effective) strategies closely approximate many of those related to eventual lack of emotional well-being (see Chilman, 1966).

Two studies have examined the relationship between parental behavior and qualities of a child's problem-solving thinking style more specifically than the studies already mentioned. Interested in flexibility of thinking among lower-class fifth-grade boys, Busse (1967) observed maternal and paternal style of teaching sons how to solve intellectual problems and also measured more general parental childrearing attitudes. In the actual teaching situation, mothers of boys who were flexible thinkers gave fewer commands as to what to do and gave an appropriate amount of guidance. Their fathers manipulated materials in teaching these boys as judiciously as the mothers gave instruction (not too little and not too much), but also tended to use more verbal communication and exhibited more warmth in the interchange. Again, a better problem-solving approach in the child was related to parental behavior that is not overbearing, that guides the child in the problem, and (at least with fathers) also involves verbalization and positive human contact. The results relating general childrearing attitudes to the child's thinking flexibility indicated differences, depending upon the sex of the parent. None of the maternal correlations were significant. Flexible thinking in boys was related to absence in the father of rigid and absolute standard-setting, presence of paternal feeling of having power and involvement in and out of the home, a moderate (though not excessive) involvement with the boy, and a moderate attitude toward physical aggression. The results complement those of other studies, suggesting the positive effects of unrepressive childrearing for cognitive development and also suggesting a differential role of mother and father, perhaps as a function of sex of child.

A study of Bearison and Cassel (1975) is unique in the literature insofar as it relates a particular parental childrearing style to a cognitive process in the young child that has direct bearing upon interpersonal problem solving. Bearison and Cassel differentiated mothers on the basis of degree to which they were oriented toward and appealed to human needs, thoughts, and feelings when engaged in controlling or regulating their child. This "person-oriented" appeal was compared with a "position-oriented" approach, wherein the mother appeals to rules or merely demands conformity. Children were evaluated to assess the degree to which they were sensitive to the perspective of the listener when communicating. Results indicated that children of predominantly person-oriented mothers showed greater evidence of sensitivity to the perspective of the other person during communication than children with predominantly position-oriented mothers. The authors interpret their findings as having meaning beyond specific instructional interchanges between parent and child. They propose that what is operating becomes generally manifest in childrearing. What are important, relative to the child's development, are the events in the home "which are raised to a level of verbal elaboration and inquiry" (p. 36).

The evidence and theory to date relating family, childrearing, and interpersonal cognitive problem-solving development provide a variegated landscape, replete with suggestive evidence but sparse nevertheless. The consistencies would indicate that there are styles in family methods of coping with problems and that some methods are probably more effective than others, both for immediate success in problem solving and for the raising of reasonably healthy children. Probably, families characterized as tolerant of varied personal viewpoints, that encourage verbalization about and into interpersonal issues and problems, that are not too authoritarian, and that share some degree of task orientation provide an optimal environment for the operation of good ICPS functioning among their members and support childrearing practices conducive to the development of ICPS abilities in young children. This chain of relationships has remained unstudied as a totality. The childrearing component of this totality has received the most attention. The evidence points to the quality of verbal interaction between adult and child during the solution of real problems as most relevant, perhaps reflecting broader familial characteristics or the internal ICPS ability of the parenting adult.

To conclude from the evidence that oppressive and nonverbal childrearing has deleterious effects, while probably true, still leaves unanswered the question of how exactly to act and what to say with children in problem situations so as to enhance ICPS ability. The data of Bearison and Cassel highlight the wisdom of focusing on human issues, in particular "inner" states of experience. Data from a number of studies imply that it is good to get the child to verbally explore and articulate without adult domination but that the child may also need guidance or suggestions that he may imitate or choose to think about during the problem-solving process. In line with this, Margolin (1974) concludes, after reviewing sociocultural elements in early childhood education:

> Some writers on family studies would like to see families treating their children's problems in a specific verbalized fashion so that children will begin to learn how to solve their own problems in a constructive context. Rather than giving the child the answers to a complicated set of events, such as when the child tries to make a decision as to whether he should or should not participate in a specific school function, parents can help the child think through reasons for his decisions. This would give the child a conceptualization of the problem and a broader view of it with his own specific problem as the central issue. Children also learn philosophic views in this context, and these principles can be applied to solving later problems with greater feeling of security in the process.
>
> Problem solving when defined and dealt with in the family setting can facilitate children's ways of dealing with their own world. They can learn to perceive the advantages and disadvantages that can result from even a single answer. A kind of transaction with society results, and the child learns that he is accepting the pleasant along with the unpleasant as a result of the choice that he himself made. The consequences might have been anticipated correctly or not, but at least they were considered before making a decision. An active involvement for one's experiences in life becomes more than an incidental pattern. Greater self-consciousness in decision-making is heightened.
>
> More research is needed on the way children make decisions and the effects of family background on that process [p. 390].

Maternal ICPS Ability and Childrearing Style, in Relation to the Child's ICPS Ability and Behavioral Adjustment

Spivack and Shure (1975) examined the childrearing style of mothers in problem situations with their young children, to relate childrearing style to the mother's own ICPS ability with adults, and to further assess the relationship of the mother's ICPS ability and childrearing style to the child's own ICPS ability and behavioral adjustment. For reasons outlined above, it seemed reasonable to expect that certain qualities in the mother's verbal interaction with her child in a problem situation should relate to the child's evolved ICPS ability, which in turn affects his behavioral adjustment. Similarly, it was assumed that the mother's own ICPS ability would manifest itself in her handling of her own child in the problem situation. Ideally, data would suggest that mother's ICPS ability affects her childrearing, which in turn affects the child's ICPS ability and consequent behavioral adjustment.

Subjects. Subjects were 94 black inner-city mothers and their four-year-olds, 48 boys and 46 girls. All children (average age, 4.4) attended the Philadelphia Get Set Day-Care program.

Maternal measures. Each mother was interviewed for about two hours, the session divided into two sections. The first section consisted of a semistructured set of questions aimed at eliciting the childrearing style a mother uses in handling actual problems the child brings to or creates for her. The second section tested the mother's own ICPS ability.

In eliciting how a mother handles typical problems with her child, the interview was introduced in the following way:

> This is a study we're doing as a part of our work at Hahnemann, in cooperation with the Get Set Program. This is what we'll be doing. We'll be spending about two hours together. We'll be doing a number of things and I'll explain them along the way. You'll probably enjoy it.
>
> One thing we want to do is talk about the little problems that turn up in bringing up four-year-olds. Having talked with many mothers and children, we've discovered that all four-year-olds sometimes cause little problems for their mothers. For example, they might do some things they shouldn't do, or they might fight with their brothers and sisters, or they may want something they can't have, or a mother wants her child to do something and the child won't do it. Can you tell me what

> problems like these have recently come up with [name
> of child]?
>
> I'm interested in knowing what the problem
> was, what happened, and what was said or done. We
> want to be able to see it like a movie; you know, he says
> or does something, then you say or do something, then
> he does or says something. We want to know everything
> that happened, OK? Now let's start with the first
> problem.

Each mother was carefully questioned so that no interaction between the mother and child would be omitted. General
phrases such as "he was angry" were probed: "What did he do
or say that made you know he was angry?"

After the mother had completed relating the dialogues of
her own stated problem situations, a set of hypothetical problem situations were presented to her.

> Well, now I'd like to present some problems to
> you that we've made up and I'd like to ask you about
> them. Tell me everything that happens in the same way
> you did before, OK?

Each mother was given six hypothetical problems in
story form. The stories depicted: (1) the child refusing to drink
his milk (or eat something mother desires him to eat); (2) the
child getting upset because he cannot have something he sees
while shopping with mother (for example, candy); (3) the child
snatching a toy from a friend; (4) the child breaking or damag-
ing property; (5) the child telling mother he was hit by another
child; (6) the child taking something that belongs to someone
else without asking permission (for example, from a store).

After the mother finished telling about these problem
situations, she was then asked if they reminded her of any
others that had not been mentioned earlier. The average length
of time for this part of the interview was one hour.

A scale was devised to score the reported extent to which
a mother helped her child articulate a problem, see possible
solutions and their consequences, and guided or encouraged

the child to explore these in his own mind. The scale was derived from careful analysis of a large number of responses. Each interaction incident was scored on a scale from 0 to 20. Scores were based on such questions as:

(1) Does the mother typically tell the child what to do (that is, solve problems for him), or does she guide him in solving his own problem through verbal and nonverbal cues?

(2) To what degree does the mother encourage the child to verbalize about the problems?

(3) Does the mother seem to discourage the child's bringing problems to her or discourage verbal interchange during any problem situation?

(4) Does the mother tend to seek out the "why" in the child's behavior and pay attention to his reactions?

(5) Does the mother tend to point out the consequences of what the child does?

(6) Does the mother tend to discuss with the child different ways of handling such situations?

(7) To what extent does the mother resolve problems with her child by calling upon her own authority— "Because I said so"—as opposed to judgments based on the reasonableness of a decision?

At the high end of the scale was a statement such as "Think about what you're going to do—hit him back, let him beat you up or what"—whereas at the low end was, "Hit him back and I don't want to hear any more about it." A statement such as, "Tell me what happened," eliciting the child's view of the problem, was scored higher than a statement like, "Stop sulking, don't be a baby." Even simple solutions offered to the child—"Hit him back" or "Go tell the teacher"—were scored higher than a mother's solving the problem independently of and without interacting with the child (for example, the mother reports she talked to the teacher about a child who hit her child). Mother's offering an explanation, such as "If you dirty the walls it's harder for me to keep your room clean," was scored higher than "You know better than to mark the walls."

Interscorer reliability, based on the protocols of 22 mothers, yielded a rho coefficient of .90.

Following the interview, each mother was administered three stories from the MEPS test (see Chapter Four) to assess her means-ends ICPS ability. The ability of mothers to generate alternative solutions to typical adult problems was measured by an adaptation of the procedure described in Chapter Four. The interviewer said:

> Now I'm going to tell you some things that happen to a person. The idea of what we're going to do now is to think of all the things the person could do about the problem she has in the story. Tell me everything that comes into your mind. And don't worry about being right or wrong because there are no right or wrong answers, okay? Now, I'm going to tell you the story and you tell me as many things as you can think of.

The first problem the mother was given was:

> Jane wants to watch her favorite TV program but her friend Alice is watching another program. What can Jane do so she can have a chance to watch her program?

Using standardized probing techniques, each mother was encouraged to name as many different ways she could think of. Three problems were given, the second depicting a woman having accidentally thrown out her sister's valuable watch, with her sister now being mad at her, and the third describing a situation wherein a woman is trying to get her friend to go to the movies with her, but her friend doesn't want to go.

A mother's score was the total number of different, relevant solutions offered for all three stories. For example, in the first story, "Jane could do her friend a favor," "Jane could tell her friend she's wanted on the phone and then switch channels," and "Jane could tell her friend she has to watch it for school" were all scored as different, relevant solutions. Interscorer reliability of the total score of 20 mothers yielded a Pearson correlation of .94.

Two measures of *consequential thinking* were employed. One procedure does not demand a consequential response (No-demand consequences) but analyzes whether, in the process of responding to a hypothetical temptation situation, the person spontaneously introduces consequences in the form of considering pros and cons to transgressing before deciding what to do (see Spivack and Levine, 1963; and Chapter Ten). Instructions were:

> Now we have a new kind of story. I'll tell you the story and you think of what goes on in the person's mind and what might happen in the story.

In story 1, mothers were given:

> Mrs. Brown finds a beautiful pair of earrings on the floor of a hallway at work. When she picks them up she looks around and notices that there is no one else in the hallway. She could really use the earrings. She is tempted to keep them.

Three such stories were given. The second story depicted a woman, having been given money by a vacationing neighbor to pay for a rug, tempted to use the money in an emergency that turns up. The third story described a woman very angry with her friend and tempted to tell her off. For the total of all three stories, a mother's score consisted of the number of times she considered the pros and/or cons of transgressing or venting anger.

The *alternative consequences* procedure required that each mother simply name all the things that might happen as a result of story plots provided her. The mother was told:

> Now, I'm going to tell you another story. This time, list the consequences. Tell me all the

things you can think of that might happen.
Ruth and a close friend have made
plans to go somewhere together. They
have both looked forward to going to this
for a long time. At the last moment, some
things turn up and Ruth realizes she can't
go. She calls her friend and tells her she
won't be able to go.
Tell me all the things you can think of that
might happen next, or what might be said or done.

A second story depicted a woman borrowing a punch
bowl from her neighbor, without asking. A score consisted of
the total number of different, relevant consequences given to
the two stories (Shure and Spivack, 1975a). Interscorer reliability yielded a correlation coefficient of .97.

Child measures. Each child was administered the Preschool Interpersonal Problem-Solving Test (PIPS) of alternative thinking, the What Happens Next Game (WHNG) to
assess consequential thinking, and the Sensitivity to Interpersonal Problems Test (SIP). Details of administration and scoring are provided by Shure and Spivack (1975a).

Each child's overt behavioral adjustment in school was
measured through classroom ratings by the teacher, employing
the Hahnemann Pre-School Behavior Scale (HPSB). (See
Spivack and Shure, 1974.) The scale allows of classification of
the child into a normal, impulsive, or inhibited behavior
category.

Results are presented and discussed in four sections:

1. Relationship of child's ICPS ability to behavioral
adjustment classification. An analysis of variance revealed that
the child's ability to conceptualize alternative solutions to an
interpersonal problem, as well as the child's consequential
thinking ability, related to the criterion measure of overt classroom behavioral adjustment at the .01 level, for both boys and
girls (see Table 5).

Looking at the means in Table 6, it is clear that adjusted
youngsters showed superior ICPS skills relative to those judged
either as impulsive or as inhibited, replicating previous find-

Table 5

Summary of Analyses of Variance for Three Measures of
Child's ICPS Skills

Measures	Source	df	MS	F	p
Alternate	Behavior adjustment group* (A)	1*	88.27	17.11	.01
solutions	Sex (B)	1	.41	.08	ns
(PIPS)	A x B	1	.25	.05	ns
	Error (within)	90	5.16		
Consequential	Behavior adjustment group* (A)	1*	56.19	10.95	.01
thinking	Sex (B)	1	1.18	.23	ns
(WHNG)	A x B	1	3.47	.68	ns
	Error (within)	89	5.13		
Sensitivity	Behavior adjustment group* (A)	1*	2.00	1.10	ns
to problems	Sex (B)	1	3.04	1.67	ns
(SIP)	A x B	1	1.42	.78	ns
	Error (within)	89	1.82		

*Due to the small number of inhibited boys, impulsive and inhibited Ss were combined

ings (see Chapter Two). The child's sensitivity to problems, however, did not relate to overall behavioral adjustment, although there was a definite trend indicating that the inhibited children tended to obtain low scores.

2. Interrelationship of mother's ICPS skills and the relationship of these to mother's childrearing style. As seen in Table 7, significant intercorrelations between mother's ICPS skills were noted for both mothers of boys and mothers of girls, indicating that adult thinking skills are, in general, correlated functions (see also Chapter Five). However, a clearly significant relationship between a mother's ICPS ability and her conceptualized childrearing style when handling actual problems with her child occurred only among mothers of girls. This relationship was evident between mother's means-ends thinking and childrearing style scores ($r = .53$, $p < .01$).

3. Relationship of mother's childrearing style and ICPS skills to child's ICPS skills. Table 8 shows that mother's childrearing style significantly related to two of three ICPS skills of daughters (alternate solutions and sensitivity), with a positive trend in the case of consequential thinking. Such was not the

Table 6

**Means and SDs of Three Measures of Child's ICPS Skills
by Behavioral Adjustment Group and by Sex**

Behavioral Adjustment Group

Measures	*Adjusted*			*Impulsive*			*Inhibited*			*Total*		
	X̄	SD	N	X̄	SD	N	X̄	SD	N	X̄	SD	N
PIPS solutions												
Boys	5.73	2.32	30	3.92	1.89	14	4.25	2.87	4	5.00	2.42	48
Girls	5.63	2.50	27	4.00	1.58	9	3.10	1.79	10	4.85	2.43	46
Total	5.68	2.38	57	3.78	1.88	23	3.64	2.21	14	4.91	2.42	94
Consequences												
Boys	5.83	2.39	30	4.50	1.70	14	3.16	1.50	4	5.27	2.25	48
Girls	6.15	2.47	26	5.11	1.62	9	3.90	2.64	10	5.44	2.50	45
Total	5.98	2.42	56	4.74	1.66	23	3.86	2.32	14	5.35	2.36	93
Sensitivity												
Boys	1.83	1.49	30	1.79	1.31	14	1.50	1.29	4	1.79	1.40	48
Girls	1.65	1.29	26	1.33	1.32	9	1.00	1.25	10	1.44	1.29	45
Total	1.75	1.39	56	1.61	1.31	23	1.14	1.23	14	1.62	1.35	93

Table 7

Intercorrelation of ICPS Skills and Childrearing Style for Mothers of Boys (N=48) and Mothers of Girls (N=46)

Measures	Consequences Alternatives Mothers of		Consequences No-Demand Mothers of		Means-Ends Mothers of		Childrearing Style Mothers of	
	Boys	Girls	Boys	Girls	Boys	Girls	Boys	Girls
Alternative solutions	.65*	.57*	.56*	.31†	.37*	.29†	.07	.25
Consequences (alternatives)			.42*	.33†	.22	.31†	.29†	.18
Consequences (no-demand)					.49*	.17	.26	.17
Means-ends thinking							.14	.53*

*p < .01
†p < .05

Table 8

**Relationship of Mother's Childrearing Style and ICPS Skills
to Child's ICPS Skills**

| | Child's ICPS Skills | | | | | |
| | PIPS Solutions | | Consequences | | Sensitivity | |
Mothers' Measures	Boys (N=48)	Girls (N=46)	Boys (N=48)	Girls (N=45)	Boys (N=48)	Girls (N=45)
Childrearing style	.20	.33*	.01	.24	.06	.36*
Alternative solutions	-.14	.32*	-.08	.30*	.05	-.05
Consequences (alternative)	-.07	.09	-.06	.09	.05	-.05
Consequences (no-demand)	-.01	.22	-.21	-.01	-.04	-.09
Means-ends	.00	.35*	-.17	.07	-.28	.34*

*p < .05

case between mothers and their sons. Table 8 also indicates that mother's means-ends thinking skill significantly related to the same two ICPS skills of daughters, as did childrearing style, alternative solutions and sensitivity to interpersonal problems.

Given that mothers (of daughters) who had greater means-ends thinking skills also had higher childrearing scores, and given that both of these maternal measures related to the child's alternative solution and sensitivity scores, the next question was whether maternal ICPS ability or childrearing style would relate to daughter's ICPS ability independent of the functioning of the other. To determine this, partial correlations were calculated between maternal and daughter ICPS ability, partialling out childrearing scores. In all cases, the previous significant relationships fell below the level of significance. Similarly, the correlations between maternal childrearing and daughter's ICPS skills were calculated, partialling out the effect of maternal ICPS (means-ends) skill. Again, the previously significant relationship fell below the level of significance. In contrast, the correlation between maternal ICPS and childrearing scores remained significant, even after partialling out daughter's ICPS scores (for example, between MEPS and childrearing, partialling out PIPS = .47).

These results suggest an intimate relationship between the operation of the mother's means-ends thinking and child-rearing style in problem-focused situations with her four-year-old daughter. They further suggest that certain maternal qualities of thought, as manifest both in adult and in childrearing interactions, play a significant role in determining the ICPS ability of young daughters.

4. Relationship of mother's childrearing style and ICPS skills to child's behavioral adjustment. Having already established that the child's alternative-solution and consequences scores significantly related to behavioral adjustment, the question now was to determine the role played by childrearing style and the mother's ICPS ability in the relationship between the child's ICPS skills and behavioral adjustment. Because mother's ICPS skills and childrearing style related to child's ICPS skills among mothers and their daughters, but not among mothers and their sons, these analyses involved only data from mothers and their daughters.

Table 9 shows that a mother's childrearing style score significantly related to the child's behavioral adjustment, but her ICPS skills did not. The means in Table 9 reveal that the mother's childrearing style score was lower among impulsive and inhibited girls than among girls judged to be behaviorally adjusted. That is, mothers of impulsive and inhibited girls tended to use more of a commanding or telling-the-child-what-to-do style of handling problems than a style encouraging the child to think out the problem and its solutions and consequences.

Analysis of covariance was performed to determine the strength of relationship between the child's ICPS ability and behavioral adjustment and whether that relationship was actually due to the common relationship of both to childrearing style. Results indicated that, with childrearing style controlled, there was still a significant relationship between the child's ICPS skills and behavioral adjustment (F = 4.57; df = 1,43; $p <.05$).

The results suggest that the effect of the mother's thinking skills on the child's behavioral adjustment is not a direct

Table 9

Means, SDs, and F-Ratios of Mothers' ICPS Skills for Adjusted, Impulsive, and Inhibited Girls

	Adjusted (N=27)		Child Behavior Impulsive (N=9)		Inhibited (N=10)			
Mothers' Measures	$\overline{X}$	SD	$\overline{X}$	SD	$\overline{X}$	SD	df	F
Childrearing style	20.78	8.83	13.67	3.50	13.10	3.45	2,43	5.91*
Alternative solutions	13.96	4.06	11.33	3.20	11.40	2.55	2,43	2.84
Consequences (alternative)	7.59	4.30	6.67	3.71	6.10	2.13	2,43	.62
Consequences (no-demand)	6.00	2.72	4.89	2.47	4.90	1.97	2,43	1.06
Means-ends	5.78	2.04	4.78	1.64	4.50	1.51	2,43	1.07

*p < .01

one. A mother's ICPS ability is manifest in how she interacts with her child in problem situations, and it is in such interaction that influence on the child takes place. Further, while maternal influence on the daughter's behavioral adjustment may occur through more than one channel, one significant channel is the mediating ICPS ability of the child.

That the foregoing data are reliable has been confirmed by a subsequent study replicating the procedures with a new though similar group of mothers and children and adding some new measures that help refine certain relationships (Shure and Spivack, 1975a). The results of this second study revealed the same strong relationships between the child's ICPS ability, especially alternative thinking, and behavioral adjustment. The same sex differences also emerged, indicating an intimate and causally connected link between maternal ICPS ability, maternal childrearing style, daughters' ICPS ability, and daughters' subsequent behavioral adjustment. In combination, data from both studies indicate that a mother's childrearing style in handling real problems with a daughter plays a key role in the child's evolving capacity to problem-solve and subsequently handle real problems with others. A problem-solving style of maternal childrearing in actual situations is a function of the capacity of the mother to conceptualize ways of solving typical problems between a mother and child. This conceptual skill reflects in part a more general capacity of the mother to solve problems of an interpersonal nature.

Discussion and Conclusions

The findings reported above support already accumulated data across age groups indicating an intimate relationship between ICPS ability and overt behavioral adjustment in children of both sexes. Childrearing effects upon behavior are mediated in large part through ICPS skills. It is not surprising, then, that enhancement of these cognitive skills would improve behavioral adjustment.

When one explores the possible childrearing precursors

of development of ICPS skills, clear sex differences emerge. These differences are not in level of maternal ICPS ability between mothers of girls and boys or in levels of ability between daughters and sons. The difference lies in the *relationships* among cognitive processes and between cognitive processes and overt behavioral adjustment in the mother-daughter and mother-son relationship. With mothers and daughters, there is an intimate relationship between the mother's ICPS ability in handling adult problems and her thinking when confronted with problems involving her daughter. Her problem-solving thinking ability is brought to bear in the way she conceptualizes childrearing problems and actually responds to her daughter, the latter in turn affecting the daughter's evolving ICPS ability. This influence is observable in the daughter's behavior. The effect of mother on daughter is not situation-specific (for example, operative only at home) but transfers to other settings.

Such an integrated set of likely causes and effects does not emerge in the relationship between mother and son. In this dyad, there appears to be little if any relationship between the mother's ICPS skills and her response when actually confronted with her son in a problem situation, and no relationship between her own thinking and behavior in this situation and her son's evolving ICPS ability. All of this is true despite the fact that, in sons as well as in daughters, ICPS ability significantly relates to overt behavioral adjustment, and despite evidence (see Chapter Two) that indicates that mothers are able to teach ICPS skills equally well to sons and daughters when participating in a special training program. Further, sons and daughters do not differ in level of ICPS ability. Sons do evolve these skills but apparently not at their mothers' knee. Goldberg and Lewis (1969) have shown that mothers react differently to daughters and sons in the earliest months of infancy, one area of difference being the extent to which mothers verbalize to their newborn offspring.

Margolin and Patterson (1975) point to evidence indicating that parents may be more apt to take the disciplinarian role with a like-sex child and that children have a view consonant with this; they also provide evidence that fathers are more likely to provide positive reactions to their sons than to their daughters. Epstein and Radin (1975) have also demonstrated that fathers play a different role in their relationships with their preschool sons and daughters, resulting in effects on the cognitive performance of sons but not daughters. These sex differences in childrearing are consistent with the findings reported by Busse (1967), insofar as Busse's data indicated that paternal factors may in some areas of development play a more significant role in the development of sons' thinking ability than maternal factors. It is unwarranted to compare these studies in detail, since the Busse families had both mothers and fathers in the home and the present sample of mothers largely represented the mother-directed type of home that characterizes a center-city poverty area. Nevertheless, experience with such homes suggests there usually are male adults in the home, or at least other forms of male influence that have an impact on the growing boy and probably affect his developing thinking skills.

The present results highlight certain qualities in childrearing that may enhance the evolution of ICPS ability. These would be manifest in a problem situation but very likely characterize parental functioning on other occasions as well. One quality is that of *extracting from the child his own thinking*. In some instances the parent extracts the child's point of view about the problem situation (for example, "Tell me what happened"; "How hard did he hit you?"; "What does that mean when you say . . . ?"; "Do you think that was a good idea?"; "Who do you think was to blame?"). In other instances the parent extracts the causes of things in the child's eyes (for example, "Why did he hit you?"; "Did you do anything first?"; "What did you do so that he cried?"). In still other instances the parent extracts the child's thoughts about his own and others' feeling reactions (for example, "How does that make you (or him) feel?"; "How do you think I feel when you do that?"; "Were you sad?"). In all such inquiries the parent elicits interest in and patience with the child's thoughts and suggestions and, through them, encourages the child to *generate* problem-relevant thought. No value judgment is made, and the parent makes no attempt to influence or alter the content of what the child is thinking.

Another quality of parenting that seems to abet the development of ICPS ability in young children is the *willingness and ability of the parent to act as a catalyst, model, or guide in the child's attempts at problem solving in social situations.* The parent may do this by suggesting possibilities (for example, "Maybe he was mad because you said that?"; "Is it possible that he wouldn't play with you because . . . ?"). The parent may suggest possible solutions (though not insisting on any one, as, for example, in "Why can't you both share the toy?" or "Why don't you write on the paper instead of the wall?"), or express a consequence ("I don't like you when you do that; . . . it makes me mad" or "If you hit him, he may not want to be your friend"). The parent expresses his reasons for acting as he does ("I can't buy you that because I don't have the money" or "If you dirty the walls it's harder for me to keep your room clean").

A third quality is *parental support when the child manifests ICPS skills and makes decisions based upon them* (for example, "That's a good idea!"; "O.K., let's do that"; "Why don't you try doing that?"; "You had a lot of good ideas there; which one do you want to do?"). This is not to suggest that this quality implies a license for the child to do anything he wishes, but suggests rather a parental approach that reinforces decision making based on choices the child can generate and/or appreciate (for example, "You can't have candy now, but you can choose between _____ or _____").

In contrast to these qualities, there is a wide range of specific behaviors that would seem to discourage the generation of ICPS thinking in children. In the present study, mothers of low ICPS daughters reported ignoring the child when the child came to her with a problem or verbally attacking the child for being unhappy (for example, "Don't be a baby") or being troublesome (for example, "Keep quiet and stop crying. Can't you see I'm busy!"). At times she solved the problem for the child without the child's participation. This did not always indicate rejection of the child. In one instance, for example, a mother went to school to talk with the teacher about a problem involving her child. What she did not do was engage the child in the process with her or explain what she was doing or why. Mothers of low-ICPS daughters require the child to solve the problem in the mother's way, with no exploration of what the child might think (for example, "Give the toy back"; "Stop crying and go out and hit him back"; "Eat your food"). At best such mothers command the child to solve a problem a certain way, adding a simple explanation but affording no opportunity for verbal interchange (for example, "You can't stay up because you have school tomorrow" or "Eat it because it's good for you"). In each of these discrete acts, the parent does not extract thought from the child, and at times even acts indifferent to or even discourages problem-solving thought on the part of the child. If the child offers an alternative thought, it may be devalued as irrelevant to what will happen (for example, "I don't care what you say . . ." or "That's no reason to do that" or "That's the silliest thing I ever heard").

　　　The present findings suggest that a general form of child-rearing interaction is important in the evolution of both interpersonal and impersonal problem solving in children. It involves a verbal-conceptual orientation and a willingness on the part of the parent to become engaged with the child as a guide and model in the problem-solving process. The issue is not mere quantity of words but whether language is used to articulate the elements important in solving problems, and whether thinking becomes the medium in reasonable problem solution. It is unlikely, for instance, that an interpersonal problem for a child in the area of social rejection will be handled well by a parent who himself is so troubled by feelings of rejection that he must avoid talk about this topic or must rush to a quick solution to avoid continued discomfort. It is also unlikely that such a parent, because of his own anxiety and need to avoid the topic, has ever evolved an articulate language system in the area with which to converse with the child. The intimate relationship between an avoidant and repressive defensive style and a sparse and unarticulated language style has been well documented by Levine and Spivack (1964). It is also unlikely that childrearing styles that appeal to rules and authority relations, in contrast to human feelings and "inner" causes and effects, will be conducive to the evolution of ICPS ability in children. It is by no means an accident that the "authoritarian personality" is associated with a repressive cognitive style and that authoritarian early childrearing results in an adult apt to fall back on avoidant, denying, and repressive psychological defense mechanisms.

It is now possible to return to the family as a social system and pinpoint likely qualities of most direct relevance to the development of ICPS ability in offspring. It seems likely that families that defensively cut themselves off from input outside of the family, or preclude from personal discussions a variety of possibilities or options in order to maintain a oneness of mind or myth of solidarity, fail to provide a setting conducive to appropriate childrearing for ICPS ability. It also seems likely that a family system wherein members are isolated from one another, emotionally as well as verbally, will not foster the development of ICPS ability.

It is not likely that a family system that accentuates power relationships, to the relative exclusion of human feelings, will support the development of ICPS ability. In elaborating likely issues that may determine the effectiveness of family problem solving, Turner (1970) also pinpoints the issue of power. He asserts that an important determinant in the effectiveness of family problem solving is the extent to which members contribute a range of alternatives wider than what one individual could supply, and that such contribution will only be made when authority is not used suppressively by those in power against those with less authority. This would seem to hold whether problems concern collaborative activities in which all household members share (for example, summer vacations, household maintenance) or instances in which the family functions as a regulatory or coordinating agency regarding individual members (for example, scheduling of meals, use of automobiles).

Individual families may also differ in ways that are relevant to the development of ICPS ability. The data suggest that conducive families would be prone to value their children's ideas about the social world and encourage the expression of these ideas as part of family interchange. Implied here is a family style that is child-centered in the sense that even "childish" views are solicited about interpersonal events that occur as part of family life. The child is seen as warranting an explanation about what happens to him and others, and family members share their ideas with the growing child. A family problem is explored to gain an appreciation of its parameters and to compare possible avenues of solution and their pros and cons, and it is resolved by some action. As children get older, discussion in the family begins to involve exploration into details of a particular approach to a problem, examining it as a total plan of action. Discussion might touch on the step-by-step aspects of the plan, possible obstacles that might arise, and the timing of action. Much remains unknown about when in early childhood the different facets of ICPS ability may be profitably taught. The most favorable family climate, however, probably accentuates these qualities throughout the life-span, and children progressively perceive and understand them as time progresses.

Aldous (1971) has proposed a framework for the analysis of family problem solving that highlights the strengths and weaknesses of the family as a problem-solving group, as compared with ad hoc groups that do not share a common history, obligations, and emotional commitment. Of interest here is that Aldous's framework highlights new ways in which family styles may differ from one another, ways that would affect family problem solving and the problem-solving capacity of offspring that are worthy of future study. All families share a history, and experience a centripetal, cohesive force for self-maintenance. This quality, when it leads to shared experience and knowledge (through good communication), should abet problem solving, just as a warm emotional tone supports the persistence of family members in their efforts to solve a problem. This same quality, when excessive, however, may hamper the search for new solutions if the generation of new ideas is viewed as a challenge to shared norms, threatens to cause conflict, or raises any risk of family breakup. Specific affective relationships within the family may function the same way, not only because new solutions may lead to new behaviors that can threaten a particular relationship, but because change in any one relationship may affect the balance of relationships within a total family.

All families also have power and status roles built in, with potential positive and negative effects. An established and accepted power and leadership role can abet problem solving by coordinating problem-solving efforts and keeping the group's attention focused on the problem. If, on the other hand, the power role is used suppressively and intimidates others in the family (especially children), participation in problem solving is absent. New ideas are not generated, and children (and others in low status roles) evolve no commitment to solutions or sense of control over events. Family heads, insecure in their roles, will be loath to use information offered by others, and children quickly learn that what they believe and say makes no difference. Referring to such family heads, Aldous comments:

> Their fear of competitors also may lead them to guard the information sources and problem solving skills jealously. Indeed, this fear of competition can grow out of the kind of inadequate socialization for problem solving the parents experienced as children that they in turn are passing on to their children [p. 276].

Intrafamily threats that may hamper problem solving may also work in reverse direction. Owing to the emotional bonds and parental needs in families, children may exercise a form of power through intimidation that can hamper the problem solving of parents and the total family. It is in and through children that parents often seek self-fulfillment, and this ascription of significance may lead to unrealistic appraisal of a child's contribution to a problem situation.

Families may also differ in their problem solving as a function of their economic and educational resources. Families with adequate resources may be free of the burdens of daily living to the extent that they may consciously choose, define, and allot time to the solution of problems. Less fortunate families may have to evolve the capacity to face rather than solve problems. While a certain form of strength may be suggested in this capacity to face problems, family problem-solving capacity will only emerge and the family persist in the effort when the family has defined the problem itself. It may very well be that the sense of hopelessness and the fatalistic attitude that characterize the life of poverty derive not only from actual limited options but also from a limited capacity to respond to problems when they arise.

Future Directions
and Theoretical
Issues

Our purpose at this point is not to review but rather to discuss results and examine where work outlined in previous chapters leads us in terms of possible future steps and theoretical considerations. First, it would seem reasonably safe to conclude that there is a domain of interpersonal cognitive problem-solving thinking composed of thought processes that mediate levels of social adjustment across a broad age range. These thought processes are in relatively close interface with overt behavior, and it is suggested that they significantly influence how effectively individuals handle interpersonal problem situations. How well these processes operate has been shown not only to differentiate normal and maladjusted groups of people but also to differentiate individuals within normal and aberrant groups who differ in levels of adjustment.

It has also been reasonably well established that the ICPS domain of thought must be considered and examined aside from the ability to cope with abstract, impersonal problems. Repeatedly, and across age groups, ICPS performance has been shown to relate only modestly or not at all to established measures of intelligence and to relate to and affect social adjustment independent of abstract intellectual ability. Training programs that enhance interpersonal problem-solving thinking have no effect upon IQ scores, and individuals differing widely in IQ have been shown to benefit from training. Nor are ICPS skills a mere reflection of verbal ability or propensity to verbalize in experimental situations or in real life. Individuals may be quite competent in interpersonal thinking and only modestly so in handling abstract problems, and vice versa. To this extent at least, the evidence suggests that the area of social intelligence might warrant some reexamination, especially with respect to thought *processes* in contrast to content. Whereas social intelligence or competence has been viewed in terms of knowing what to do in social situations or as the ability to understand the thoughts, feelings, and intentions of others, it might be well to shift focus to the individual's capacity to *generate* certain classes of thought when confronted with interpersonal problems. Social intelligence might be more profitably defined in terms of the processes called forth in social contexts rather than the products (that is, content knowledge) that may emerge as a result of increased maturity and social awareness.

The Generation of Problem-Solving Thought

The domain of ICPS focuses attention on the capacity of people to generate certain ways of thinking in problem situations. We may all be able to recognize an effective way of handling a social problem situation when we see it or even to appreciate that a particular way of handling it is better than another. Our combined life experience builds up a shared reservoir of likely and less-likely methods of coping that we may call on, at times in an almost mechanical fashion and without thought as to rationale. In contrast to these mental operations, however, ICPS ability is the ability to generate in one's mind certain thinking processes when confronted with a problem situation, out of which may emerge a "best" solution after consideration of a variety of factors. Not only has a solution emerged but the problem solver is aware of his reasons and his rationales, and has weighed pros and cons, because he has engaged in a process. While in the short run it may be the "right" answer that is at issue in a given situation, in the long run the issue for social adjustment is the ability of the person to generate the kind of thinking in a given situation that increases his chances of coming up with the best solution for him. The significance of this distinction may seem self-evident and without serious implications for intervention. In fact the distinction has quite significant implications, if one is determining the goals of any intervention or educational program and especially if one is considering what role to play in attempting to help another person with an interpersonal problem. A focus on the "right" answer or conclusion focuses attention on the content of thought—the end product itself—and suggests that the role of a helper is to teach or supply solutions. A focus upon generation of thought puts attention upon how a person is thinking out a problem, and the role of the helper is to extract such thought processes or act as a catalyst to and guide through problem-solving thinking.

A final word is necessary about this issue of thought content versus process, lest it appear that the present stance is that *what* a person thinks is irrelevant to social adjustment. Three bits of data may help at this point. In the study of Spivack and Levine (1963) it was discovered that, when confronted with a hypothetical temptation situation, normal adolescents thought of the idea of transgressing as often as did impulsive adolescents. The difference was that normals more often anticipated pros and cons of a variety of possible actions, both conforming and transgressing. Platt and Spivack (1973) have reported the same results in their study of adult normals and patients. Shure and Spivack (1975a) found no relationship, among young children, between an ability to conceptualize forceful and aggressive solutions and an actual display of aggressive and impulsive behavior. Only the capacity of the child to generate *different* kinds of solutions, including forceful and aggressive ones, related to likelihood of an overt show of impulsive-aggressive behavior. And Platt and others (1975) noted that patients and normals do not differ in their judgments about the relative effectiveness of different means to solve a problem when a list of means was presented to them for comparative judgment. What patients could not do was generate processes of thought, one element of which is the ability to generate means to solve a problem. The conclusion to be drawn is that if effective decision-making in interpersonal affairs is to occur, the individual must be able to produce for his own perusal and evaluation all the possible courses (that is, content) open to him. He must be able to generate thought about them, he must weigh them, he must balance likely advantages and disadvantages. The more options a person generates, the more likely an effective solution is to emerge, because effectiveness depends at least in part upon an available display of reasonable options that may be weighed and evaluated. To think of a course of action is not necessarily to act upon it, except when no other course can be thought of, means and consequences are unexplored, or perhaps certain external forces become manifest that press for premature action.

The Thinking Implicit in ICPS Skills

Within this ICPS domain, certain processes emerge as particularly important, while the status of others remains somewhat in doubt. It would seem worthwhile to explore and analyze these processes for what they may suggest about how people think in problem situations. Alternative-solution thinking is a significant component of ICPS. It reflects a capacity to generate options. Individuals who do not exhibit effective generation of options have been found to generate irrelevant thoughts or thoughts that do not stay with and apply to the problem at hand. Thinking may shift from the problem at hand to a related problem, or the person may shift from thinking of options to concentrating on only one facet of the problem to the exclusion of other important elements. Does this reflect an inability to control thought or maintain a focused attention on one issue to the exclusion of competing others? Does generating many possible solutions to a problem signify tolerance for "openness" and indecision, or an ability to temporarily withhold judgment? Or is there, underlying this process, an operating appreciation of the fact that there may be many possible solutions to an interpersonal problem, all of which may have some legitimacy and thus justify consideration?

Many similar possibilities arise if one considers the ability to generate optional consequences to a particular solution. Here, too, the process suggests a capacity to suspend final judgment while keeping one's eye on the essential problem at issue. Consequential thought, however, also introduces a temporal element, especially when the measure is the spontaneous tendency to consider consequences. Here the process involves a hypothetical "if this—then that might . . . later on." The thought processes imply time-binding and for this reason may be limited by the capacity to make the future operative in the present. The extent to which one extends himself in time into the future should limit the number and variety of consequences considered. The number and variety of consequences conceptualized by a person focused on the here and now should certainly be more limited than those of a person who extends his thoughts into the future. Consequential thought is also hypothetical, in the sense that a person often says to himself, "If I do this, then that *might* happen." Spontaneous consideration of consequences introduces the world of the possible as well as the future and suggests rather sophisticated cognitive demands. This is supported by developmental evidence discussed further on.

Certain elements composing poor means-ends thought

are best revealed in stories wherein verbalization is high but scores reveal low ability. In such instances, rather than focusing on step-by-step means of moving toward problem resolution, thought fixates on events and feelings that define and are associated with the resolution of the problem. There is thought of how good it will feel when the goal is reached and elaboration on what having achieved the goal will be like. If the person "gets even," thoughts describe the pleasure in revenge. If loneliness is the problem, thoughts jump ahead to how good it will feel to have friends. Thought may also fixate on the emotions surrounding the problem (for example, the need state or motivating wish). If revenge is the motive, thought focuses on the anger and rage felt on the occasion. In the case of loneliness, thought focuses on feelings of unhappiness or the circumstances defining the loneliness. In contrast, successful means-ends thought implies a capacity to limit and temporize the emotions associated with desire and anticipated gratification, and at the same time to employ these as guides in creating a plan of action. This capacity to keep the beginning (wish) and end (consummation) in mind as guideposts is further suggested by the fact that faulty means-ends thinking is often characterized by a plan that loses direction and becomes irrelevant to reaching the goal, takes on a new goal halfway through, or becomes so vague as to lose obvious connection with final resolution of the problem. Good means-ends thought is also characterized by a sophisticated use and appreciation of people. This fact probably explains the intricate relationship found to exist between multiple perspective taking and means-ends thinking. The well planned resolution of an interpersonal problem most often involves other people, with anticipation of how they might react and, if so, what might be done to anticipate such an obstacle or take advantage of the other person's needs or point of view.

Means-ends thought implies an appreciation of the necessity to think, to have a plan, to think out what to do. Stories of high means-ends individuals frequently include such a statement: "So Joe decided he'd better plan out what to do," or "So she thought it out, and decided. . . ." This form of statement may very well set the stage for creating the plan to follow. Means-ends thought suggests an appreciation of a temporal element, either explicitly recognized or implicitly manifest in thinking, that places one step after another in a time line. Poor plans, resulting in low means-ends scores, are often character-ized by a lack of logical development in a plan. Gaps appear, indicating a break in the continuity of thought and reflecting a lack of appreciation of the fact that events occur in logical con-nection to one another through time.

Finally, it is important to note that with means-ends thinking, as with alternative-solution thinking, it is the pro-cess and not content of thought that should be highlighted. Individuals with widely disparate cultural backgrounds and psychological sophistication generate similar means. What characterizes good problem-solvers is their ability to plan the sequence of potential acts, anticipate what may happen along the way, and, in the process, not lose sight of where they are going and for what reason.

Much less is known about the nature of causal thinking at the present time, despite the very extensive work of Oje-mann, Muuss, and their colleagues over the past thirty years. The reason is that the work of these investigators, while employing the term *causal thinking*, has in fact focused on a much broader array of thought processes than simple causality. They have attempted to measure and train in the appreciation of human dynamics—pointing out, for example, that human motives are involved in social relationships, that motives, or causes, are complex and must be appreciated as such, and that people differ in their social motivations.

Returning to the more limited definition of causal think-ing, the suggestion is that the significant elements composing spontaneous causal thinking are the ability to see the sequence of events involving people, combined with a temporal orienta-tion that binds the present to the past. Sequential thinking is an element suggested by the adult factor analyses, wherein spontaneous causal and consequential thinking defined a sepa-rate factor, both processes requiring that prior and subsequent events be sequentially connected. The binding of the present with the past would appear to require significant maturity, perhaps consistent with the theorizing of Erik Erikson on the processes involved in ego identity that become highlighted during and after adolescence. One facet of this total process is the coordination of and sense of continuity with the past that emerges and requires integration in the total personality. Current evidence suggests that spontaneous causal thinking emerges as a significant ICPS skill only in adulthood. These data at least match, in suggesting the significance of the quality of *looking back* into human behavior when one explores causal thinking.

While the issue of sensitivity to interpersonal problems warrants continued study, it is necessary perhaps to reconsider how to define it and thus how best to measure it across the age span in relation to social adjustment. One may settle on a definition which asserts that sensitivity is a readiness to pick up cues indicative of possible interpersonal difficulty. Having employed such a definition and measured this skill among young children, the authors suggest that this ability reflects specific readiness to see interpersonal problems and not problems in general. The value of being sensitive to social cues is supported by the fact that socially withdrawn children tend to be uniquely deficient in this skill. Its low relationship to overt behavioral adjustment, yet significant relationship to alternative-solution and consequential thinking, suggests that such sensitivity may be an important antecedent event to conceptualizing solutions and consequences, but in itself only indirectly related to final behavioral success. This formulation makes sense, but requires confirmation at all age levels.

Sensitivity may also be defined as readiness to respond with possible solutions in an interpersonal problem situation. This threshold for responding type measure was employed by McClure (1975) with nine- and ten-year-old children. The problem with this definition and measure is that McClure found threshold of response to be determined by the number of alternative solutions generated (and offered) by the child. Sensitivity thus measured may also reflect the availability of solutions and thus add no new dimension to the ICPS domain. On the other hand, McClure's results suggest the possibility that sensitivity to the presence of an interpersonal problem may, at least in part, be determined by problem-solving competence. Put conversely, the person who is insensitive (or acts insensitively) may be (or act) that way because he knows he does not have the ability (or available solutions) to cope successfully.

Still a third approach at definition presents itself. Sensitivity may be viewed as a readiness to see an interpersonal problem as existing between oneself and someone else. Such a definition implies not only sensitivity to social cues in others, but sensitivity to those inner cues (for example, feelings, tensions) that clue a person into recognizing that all is not well with himself. Rothenberg (1970) found willingness to face uncomfortable feelings and concern about one's relationships with others to be positively related to appreciation of the feelings of others. It remains to be demonstrated whether such sensitivity relates to actual social adjustment. Results of studies with adolescents and adults indicate that the ability to enumerate the typical kinds of problems people have is not a fruitful approach to definition and measurement, suggesting that any useful conception of sensitivity must account for more subtle perceptual and perhaps emotional issues, and not merely ability to intellectually enumerate human problems.

A final word about the thinking implicit in ICPS skills. There is no reason to believe that the processes involved when a person sees and deals with problems are as ordered in time as they seem to be when we are describing them. As in many other areas of study, when the processes under investigation are not directly observable in operation, the methods of measurement, analysis, and theorizing may do great injury to the reality of the functions studied. We do not know whether a problem sensed leads to enumeration of alternative possible solutions, followed by appraisal of possible consequences of each, and so forth. Commonsense experience suggests the contrary. The actual process probably involves jumping back and forth between a solution and its possible consequences, jumping back to another solution, and even reassessing and perhaps redefining the problem itself. Some of these steps may take only an instant, while others may be mulled over for days. Some aspects may occur only on the fringe of consciousness, as when one possible solution is discarded because it does not "feel" right. Seeing an affront as unintentional rather than intentional may completely alter feelings and lead to major shifts in a plan to deal with a grievance. The likelihood that the process of solving interpersonal problems will follow an uneven and shifting course need not, however, discourage investigation of the elements likely to compose the process. Rather, it suggests the need to design new forms of study that can pursue ICPS thinking as it emerges and proceeds in real life situations.

Developmental Issues

Understanding of the developmental implications of ICPS research is complicated by the fact that in some cases processes have been measured by different procedures at different age levels and the fact there are major gaps in information. A few overall trends have emerged, however, suggesting the relative significance of different ICPS skills for social adjustment at different age levels.

Among preschool children, the most significant ICPS skill is that of being able to generate alternative solutions to problems, followed by the ability to generate alternative consequences to given solutions. There is evidence that children so young do differ in their sensitivity to or readiness to report interpersonal problems, although its significance for adjustment level is not well established.

The ability to generate alternative solutions to problems remains a dominant ICPS skill in the middle childhood years, but this skill is joined by means-ends thinking. It is not known whether ability to generate alternative consequences is still a significant issue, but evidence indicates that the spontaneous prior consideration of possible consequences (pros and cons) in a dilemma situation is not yet a significant quality affecting social adjustment. Neither simple causal thinking, as measured by the ability to deal with why problems occur, or sensitivity-to-problems thinking has been studied in this age group.

Adolescence marks an age when means-ends thinking

appears as the most significant process affecting social adjustment. The generation of alternative problem solutions is still an issue, and the spontaneous consideration of consequential pros and cons in problem situations begins to take on significance for social adjustment. However, the spontaneous tendency to consider causes has not yet emerged as significant in social adjustment. Simple causal and sensitivity-to-problems thinking have not been studied in this age group.

In adulthood, the simple ability to generate alternative solutions to interpersonal problems loses some of its power to differentiate adjusted from maladjusted groups. Instead, more complex and demanding processes must be examined before discrimination is possible. Means-ends thinking emerges as a central ICPS skill. Accompanying this, however, are the tendencies to spontaneously conceptualize consequential pros and cons relating to possible future acts, and to spontaneously consider the prior causes of interpersonal problem events. Processes significant in determining adult social adjustment thus include skill at planning step-by-step means to carry out any particular solution, in combination with the tendency to look both forward and backward in time as part of the process of evaluating and understanding the nature of interpersonal problem situations and what might best be done about them. Among adults there is a quality of *sequential* thinking, as reflected in causal and consequential thought, that bears upon adjustive capacity, which accompanies the ability to conceptualize *complex well-planned action* in the arena of human affairs.

One can only conjecture at this point about the cognitive skills prerequisite and complementary to ICPS functioning. Certainly an ICPS skill can only emerge as significant for social adjustment in an age group that has the cognitive wherewithal to exhibit the skill. Four-year-old children, for instance, are not capable of the foresight reflected in means-ends thinking. It is also probably quite rare for any child this age to give prior consideration to the pros and cons of alternative courses of action.

On the other hand, an ICPS skill may bear no significance for adjustment in an age group that is not *expected* to exhibit that skill, even if many children in that age group are capable of the thinking required. The present temporal orientation of a young child might make spontaneous consideration of causes in human affairs irrelevant to most of his social tasks. Presence of such a skill might make him more sensitive in his responsiveness, but its relative absence might not cause him to fail in the typical social interactions with which he is expected to cope. The suggestion is that any ICPS skill is relevant to social adjustment only when the social demands of the age group require the use of such skills to deal effectively with these age-relevant social tasks.

It seems reasonable to assume that, as the growing person acquires sensitivity to social cues, appreciation of the variety of differing views held by others, and appreciation that others may think and feel differently, and learns to integrate multiple person perspectives, the subtlety and range of thought content manifest in problem-solving thinking will increase. Sensitivity to social cues should enhance sensitivity to possible problem encounters. Awareness of others' feelings should enrich the quality and quantity of consequences conceived, just as our awareness that others think and feel differently should help substantially to refine the choices we make among options in solving a problem involving other people. Being able to integrate multiple perspectives makes means-ends planning more subtle and sophisticated.

The implication is that, as those complementary cognitive skills evolve, they will abet effective interpersonal problem solving. The hypothesis being offered is that *the effect of these developing processes on the quality of social adjustment will be felt through the manifestation of ICPS skills that provide the structure for interpersonal problem solving.* A child who is more aware than another child of how others feel will probably succeed better in his social relationships because he will better handle problems that come up. He is more likely to get what he wants from his peers because solutions will be generated that are more in tune with his social setting. He will appreciate a more subtle range of emotional consequences that may deter him or tell him when to move ahead if he is challenged. A teenager who sees another's perspective can weigh this into his prior consideration of pros and cons before taking action. The suggestion being made is that ICPS skills define the cognitive contexts wherein a variety of social cognitive capacities become operative. ICPS skills become the vehicles through which the variety of such capacities make their effects felt in actual or potential problem situations.

The Relationship of ICPS Skills to
Other Variables and Circumstances

The data relating one or another ICPS skill to tests of personality are scattered and suggest no clear overall pattern. Platt and Spivack (1975) have correlated means-ends (MEPS) scores in a variety of older adolescent and adult groups with measures of mood, personality traits, and social adjustment as tapped by paper-and-pencil tests. Findings have been insignificant. Among nine- to ten-year-olds, ability to generate alternative problem solutions has been found correlated with belief in inner control over circumstances, and training that enhanced such thinking increased the belief in inner control (Larcen and others, 1974; McClure, 1975). McClure (1975) has reported that increase in alternative-solution thinking was associated with greater persistence when faced with actual failure to solve a problem. Coche (1976) has reported that training ICPS skills in psychiatric patients led to decreased scores on MMPI scales measuring depressive affect and social deviancy, while increasing frequency of choice of positive statements about the self on an adjective check list measure.

The absence of findings among older individuals between tested means-ends thinking and personality and mood tests is difficult to interpret. Relationships between tested alternative-solution thinking and a variety of tested, rated, and actual behaviors among preadolescents form a somewhat consistent and reasonable picture. Essentially, the evidence suggests that at this age level the better problem-solver feels a greater sense of control over what happens to him and persists when confronted with failure in problem solving by suggesting new alternatives. The findings of Coche are also consistent, suggesting that enhanced ICPS ability may result in increased self-esteem and sense of mastery, decreased depressive affect, and increase in socially adaptive behavior.

Clearly a more organized and concerted effort to study such relationships should add to our understanding of the implications of ICPS thinking for general personality functioning. It would seem reasonable to expect that enhanced interpersonal problem-solving ability would lead to an increase in self-confidence with others, an increase in the sense of inner control over events, and a decreased likelihood of feeling depressed and anxious. Increased ability to problem-solve should enhance the capacity to wait or tolerate tension in a problem situation, as well as increase frustration tolerance when initial attempts to handle interpersonal problems fail.

Little is known about the relationship of ICPS functioning to current diagnostic nomenclature. It has been noted that, among young children, inhibited-withdrawn children are the most deficient in ICPS ability, consistently more cognitively deficient than impulsive-impatient and normal children. Among adult psychiatric patients, schizophrenic groups have demonstrated least ICPS ability, and unpublished data of the authors indicate that within this group long-term chronic patients are particularly deficient. Consistent with this overall picture, psychiatric patients exhibiting more neurotic than psychotic test patterns achieve higher problem-solving scores (Platt and Siegel, in press), and schizophrenics with better premorbid histories achieve higher scores than those whose histories are marked by failure to successfully achieve the usual educational, marital, and vocational goals set by society (Platt and Spivack, 1972b).

Beyond data relating ICPS to general dimensions of psychopathology, no data are available relating ICPS skills to particular clinical types. The possibility exists that certain neurotic types might reveal characteristic profiles of ICPS skills. For example, one might expect the obsessive-compulsive person to exhibit high scores on alternative-solution thinking and prior consequential consideration of pros and cons before action yet do relatively poorly in generating a means-ends plan. In contrast, one might expect a typical hysterical type to exhibit a more consistent and low level of ICPS skills. Of perhaps even greater interest than such matching would be exploration of ICPS profile types as a form of cognitive diagnosis. The purpose would be to seek out which ICPS skill is most deficient as a way of identifying an area of thought requiring specific remedial action.

Finally, nothing is known of those circumstances that may at any given time determine how well ICPS thinking is manifest. One would expect that a situation of intense emotion or threat would narrow the range of solutions a person would be able to generate, that an excessively high drive state might so focus thought upon consummation as to make means-ends thinking impossible, and that intense internal or external pressure for a quick decision might often lead to errors of judgment on the basis of unexplored and thus unanticipated consequences. It also seems reasonable to hypothesize that social settings that emphasize power relations and authoritarian social patterns will inhibit the easy exploration of alternative problem solutions by individuals involved, and that groups that place a heavy emphasis on consensus will discourage alternative-solution thinking (which may threaten group solidarity) and heighten sensitivity to consequences (lest a solution lead to estrangement from the group). Learning environments most conducive to the exercise of ICPS skills will be characterized by a nonjudgmental and encouraging attitude about problems and their solutions, a tendency to guide toward thoughts of multiple solutions and consequences—an approach that emphasizes and rewards the process of exploring problem-solving sequences of thought rather than "correct" outcomes—and a tendency to encourage taking action on a chosen solution.

Enhancement of Interpersonal Cognitive Problem-Solving Skills

ⅹⅹⅹⅹⅹⅹⅹⅹⅹⅹⅹⅹⅹⅹⅹⅹⅹⅹⅹⅹⅹⅹⅹ

A number of training programs have evolved out of the research work that has identified specific ICPS abilities. Others have developed programs of intervention to teach social skills or decision making and reported on them in the literature, but these programs usually deal with similar issues from a very different perspective or have a different goal in mind. Most often these programs teach specific social behaviors assumed to underlie successful social adjustment, such as how to ask questions, how to invite someone to a party, or how to listen to another person, or deal with decision making about life issues

that may or may not be specially concerned with social adjustment (for example, Gelatt and others, 1972). Unlike these programs, the training programs that have developed out of
research with ICPS all share a common goal of teaching or
enhancing directly one or more interpersonal cognitive
problem-solving skills, with the assumption that, once these
are enhanced, there will follow alteration in overt social behaviors toward more successful interpersonal adjustment. In some
instances the development of these training programs has
incorporated a before-and-after experimental design to demonstrate not only enhancement of the trained ICPS skills but also
improvement in overt behavioral adjustment.

The programs deriving from ICPS research all focus on
interpersonal problem solving. It is necessary to reemphasize
this, considering the long history of study of impersonal problem solving and attempts to create educational programs to
enhance critical thinking, creativity, and reasoning. There is
no reason to assume that knowledge of how a person
approaches abstract tasks will tell us anything about how that
same person may solve a social problem he actually encounters.
Similarly, there is no evidence that a program to enhance critical thinking with math or spatial problems or causal thinking
involving physical (for example, scientific) events will enhance
the quality of social relationships.

The settings in which these ICPS programs were developed and intended for use include the schoolroom, home, hospital, and clinic. Some are intended for children, others for
adults. Usually the recipients are seen in groups, although two
programs have employed a one-to-one arrangement. Despite
this variety, all of the programs share a common approach and
set of assumptions. All assume that a direct educational
approach to certain key cognitive processes can strengthen
adjustive capacity. This is not meant to suggest that the goal is
to keep the training impersonal or purely intellectual. In some
instances what goes on in a group might be quite personal and
full of emotional undertones. The response under such circumstances, however, is not necessarily to pursue the underlying
motive or feeling through discussion, but through questions

and guided dialogue to keep attention focused on the cognitive processes to be learned, even while employing a real problem situation. In this sense, the approach is generally more structured than the usual forms of psychotherapy and more focused in the sense of having a specific preplanned point of interest and attack.

A related simi'arity among these programs is their educational focus. Orthodox psychotherapies are predicated on the assumption that social maladjustments derive from inner conflicts in motive and/or misconceptions about self and others, which in turn lead to unsuccessful social relationships and unpleasant feelings. To the extent that this is true, a legitimate approach would be to seek out the nature of these conflicts and misconceptions and to help the person to see them, so that he or she can begin to act in different ways. The assumption in such psychotherapies is that the person already has the ability to see options, to appraise consequences, to lay out in his mind a plan of action, and so forth, but is not manifesting it in significant areas of life because of his inner conflicts and misconceptions. The approach underlying the programs to be described here implies that, for many people, this assumption of latent cognitive ability is not safe to make. Many adults may suffer from social maladjustment and associated anxiety and depression because they have never learned to think in ways that lead to successful interpersonal problem solving. Further, the programs for young children are predicated on evidence that if one can help young children learn necessary ICPS skills early in life, it will decrease chances of subsequent inner distortions and social maladjustment (see Spivack and Shure, 1974). Clearly there is room for and good reason to employ both approaches, the balance in large part depending upon the needs of the recipient of one's intervention.

The educational focus of the present approach makes it similar in certain respects to some of the behavior therapies and training programs, especially those that emphasize cognitive modification (for example, Mahoney, 1974). Both approaches see cognitive processes as important guides and mediators of behavioral adjustment. Thought not only "houses" our motives, but points the way toward self-controlled action. The present approach differs from the behavior therapies in placing emphasis on certain specific cognitive skills, especially the capacity of the person to *generate* certain types of thought when confronted with an interpersonal problem. Whereas most behavior therapies focus on modifying *what* someone might think or say, the present approach attempts to influence *how* the person thinks. The concern in training, for example, is less with what option a person might generate in a situation than with his tending to generate options. While a person's having a plan of action to deal with a problem is important, this approach focuses particularly on how articulated the plan is, whether it includes anticipated future problems, and how such problems may be handled. Again, there may be room for emphasis both on content and on process. The content of a solution to a problem may be as important, for some purposes, as the fact that a person could generate it himself. The issue at this moment is that programs to enhance ICPS ability have taken on the mission of educating the recipient to generate certain ways of thinking on his own, with the assumption that being able to do this increases the likelihood that in any given situation he will think his way through to his own satisfaction.

Another quality of programs that have emerged from the study of ICPS ability is their structuredness. In most instances the designers of the program have produced "scripts" to be followed, "lessons" in sequence, or at least well-defined rules to follow in applying the program. This has made them easy for others to follow, to assess, and to use. Generally, the designers accept individual variations and script departures to permit adaptability to specific settings. Usually, the programs have been designed for specific categories of recipient, on the basis of age and/or type of maladjustment.

Work in the area of ICPS ability is still in its relative infancy. The variety of programs that have been designed to date, however, speaks for the adaptability of the concepts and perhaps also for the validity of the underlying theoretical position.

♈♈♈♈♈♈♈♈♈♈♈ 8 ♉♉♉♉♉♉♉♉♉♉♉

Preventive Early Intervention Program for Kindergarten Children

♈♈♈♈♈♈♈♈♈♈♈♈♈♈ ♉♉♉♉♉♉♉♉♉♉♉♉♉♉

A curriculum entitled *A Mental Health Program for Kindergarten Children* (Shure and Spivack, 1974a) is designed for use by teachers and others who work with five-year-olds in a group atmosphere. It is an upgraded adaptation of an earlier nursery-school program developed by Shure and Spivack (see Shure, Spivack, and Gordon, 1972; Spivack and Shure, 1974).

It has significantly enhanced the problem-solving thinking of children who are behaving normally and enhanced the thinking and normalized the behavior of children who before

177

training tended to be impatient and impulsive or withdrawn and timid. The impatient children have been characterized as unable to wait, prone to becoming emotionally upset, and socially aggressive. Withdrawn children have been described as overly inhibited or controlled insofar as display of feelings is concerned, overly timid, and displaying less than normal amounts of aggressiveness and self-assertiveness.

Follow-up study of normal children exposed to the nursery program has demonstrated that one year later they are less likely to begin to show behavioral difficulties than similar normal children not exposed to the program, and the same is true of those receiving training in the kindergarten year. The program also significantly reduces impatient-impulsive behaviors and withdrawn-timid behaviors, as the learning process enhances ICPS ability.

The program is a carefully sequenced series of lessons in the form of games that the teacher or group worker plays with the children. In addition to the formal games and dialogues presented in this script, there is a general problem-solving approach that the adult can incorporate and is encouraged to use throughout the day as real problems arise. The formal part of the program takes about twenty minutes per day, over a period of three months. Teachers find little difficulty in incorporating it into their usual day, and the children usually enjoy the games. The adult works with children in small groups of about ten. It is best when a group consists of some talkative and some quiet children. It is feasible for an average kindergarten teacher with a class of thirty children to break the class up into three groups, work with each group every second or third day, and complete work with the entire class well within a school year.

In an introduction for the user, specific suggestions are made regarding how the children might be seated on chairs or on the floor, where quieter children might be placed, how the children's names should be used in the script, what to do if the children get restless, and how the teacher can use the script without having to memorize anything. The materials needed to operate the program are listed, along with the addresses of the manufacturers or publishers. These include pictures, hand puppets, storybooks, and assorted plastic animal trinkets and toys. It is noted that many of these may be replaced by similar materials already available, and some can be made quite easily if budgets are limited.

The program script is composed of thirty-five games that build up selected prerequisite thinking skills in the child, followed by twelve interpersonal problem situations to which the group is guided to respond in terms of (1) problem solutions, (2) consequential thinking, and (3) pairing of specific solution with consequence. Interspersed between problems are stories and other experiences to maintain interest. Review lessons are interspersed with the learning of new material, and material learned earlier is always incorporated into lessons that teach new material.

The major elements of the formal script are outlined below to convey the essence of the program. The concepts are basically the same as those in the original nursery version, though different in most of the content and level of sophistication. Additional concepts will be noted.

Language, Listening, and Paying Attention

The program assumes that certain very basic language concepts are necessary to understand in order to achieve the end result of seeing alternative solutions to a problem and their consequences, as well as appreciating the meaning of the problem. Solving an interpersonal problem includes deciding on solution A *or* B or A *and* B, as well as A but *not* B. If one is to think in terms of causes or consequences, one must be able to employ *if–then* statements (*"If* I say 'please,' *then* he might give me the [toy]"*).

The initial twelve games concentrate on the use of such prerequisite language skills as a *tool* for thinking of alternatives and the negation *(not)*. The words *same* and *different* are practiced in order that the child be able to name different new alternatives to a problem. Some of the games simultaneously focus upon listening and paying attention, a first step in the ability to take in bits of information for consideration before deciding what to do.

All of the games during this and subsequent stages of training employ other people and often the names of children in the group. An example from the eighth day of the program may communicate the flavor of a typical lesson.

> *And* or *not*
>
> *Distribute picture cards so that children are holding two different cards.*
>
> Stephanie, you are holding a picture of a rabbit *and* a picture of a dog.
>
> Robert, you are holding pictures of a cow *and* a _____. *Let child respond.*
>
> Good, you are holding pictures of a cow *and* a cat.
>
> Darren, are you holding pictures of a horse *and* a cow OR are you holding pictures of a zebra *and* a dog? *Let child respond.*
>
> Yes, you are holding pictures of a zebra *and* a dog.
>
> Sandra, you are *not* holding a picture of a _____.
>
> *If child does not respond or says what she is holding, say, "You are* not *holding a picture of a horse, you are* not *holding a picture of a* _____?" *If she still does not respond, ask another child what Sandra is* not *holding.*
>
> If I point to Stephen, then I am *not* pointing to _____. *Let children react.*
>
> Who else am I *not* pointing to? *Let group respond.*
>
> If I am tapping my knee, can you show me something I am *not* doing? *Group responds.*
>
> Good, Rochelle, I am *not* stamping my foot.

To teach the words *same* and *different,* one of the best-liked games from the nursery script is repeated in the kindergarten script, the idea of it being to involve the children in motion. The teacher begins by raising her hand, lowering it and raising her hand again. She then explains that she just did the *same* thing. The teacher then taps her knee, explaining that tapping her knee is *different* from raising her hand. During this game the children engage in several different body motions, some being the same as the teacher's or child leader's and some being different.

Incorporating the words *same* and *different*, the children focus on other people in a game on the thirteenth day of the program.

> *Give children trinkets from packets. Make sure that two children have toys that are the same.*
>
> Close your eyes. *Give them each a trinket.* Okay, now open your eyes. *Ask each child to name the trinket he has.*
>
> Is a comb the *same* as a mirror?
>
> No, a comb is *not* the *same* as a mirror. A comb is *different* from a mirror.
>
> Johnny, you have a *(say what he has)*. Who has something that is the *same* as Johnny? *Children answer.*
>
> *If a child with the same trinket does not answer, ask,* "Peter, do you have a comb? Yes or no?" *Let child say yes.* "Is what you have the *same* or *different* from what Johnny has? Yes, you have something that is the *same* as what Johnny has."
>
> *Repeat with each child, sometimes asking who has something that is the* same as _____, *sometimes asking who has something that is* different *from* _____, *and sometimes using the phrase* "not the same as."
>
> Ann, what do you have?
>
> Who has something that is *different* from what Ann has? *Child responds.*
>
> Steven, what do you have? *Steven responds.*
>
> Who has something that is *not* the *same* as what Steven has? *Group responds.*

These key language concepts are woven into games that the adult and children play together during this first stage of the program and all subsequent lessons as well. The games get the children to participate verbally and at times physically to maintain interest and involvement.

Identifying Emotions

The next game associates the words *sad, happy,* and *mad* with the usual signs (crying, laughing) that indicate each emotion. The teacher also uses pictures and through questioning of the child elicits whether a crying child is feeling happy, sad, or mad. It is assumed that in order to consider people's emotions in deciding what to do in a problem situation, it is first necessary to identify them and label them reliably.

Multiple Attributes

The purpose of this game is to encourage beginning awareness that there is more than one element about a person at any one time which may have to be considered before taking action. An example would be: "This boy is in the library *and* he is reading a book *and* he is [*child responds*]. What else can we say about this boy?"

Information Gathering

Utilizing skills learned in the preceding lessons, the goal is to stimulate thinking of ways to find out how others feel and to teach that not everyone feels the same way for the same reasons and that the same person feels different ways at different times. Attending to others' feelings and preferences is considered important in later problem-solving ability, including consequential thinking. Through teacher demonstrations and games, attention is focused on how we use our eyes to see with and our ears to hear with and the idea that we find out how people feel by watching and listening.

Subsequent games to teach information gathering stress individual choice, with the notion that a child cannot assume that because he likes something someone else will like it too. For example, a doll that makes one child happy will not always make another happy, or one child's not liking something does not mean that another person will not like it. An important feature of these games is guidance in how to find out what other people like. Much emphasis is placed upon the practice of asking others what they like or do not like, or how they feel. Each child in the group is asked, for example, to tell whether he or she would choose to go on a ride on a train or a boat. After each child responds, the children are guided to comment that some picked the *same* thing and some picked *different* things. A child may be asked how he might find out what another child would like to do. The point is made that different people often choose different things and that is all right.

Emotional Awareness

Games in this area go beyond the ability to identify emotions, with the thought that problem solving requires one to be sensitive to others' feelings and how they react on the basis of them. How to understand and influence others' emotions is stressed ("Let's pretend we know that Rachel has a doll to play with, and Sandra snatched it away from her. How would that make Rachel feel?"). During these games the words for different emotions are stressed once again. Different children are asked how they would feel if someone took their truck away, or someone gave them a doll, or someone pushed them off the slide.

An excerpt from one of the lessons may help communicate the flavor of the games:

> Now this is just a game. *Have each child hold a toy previously used from trinket box.* Peter, you snatch Kevin's toy from him.
>
> Kevin, how do you feel about that? *Kevin responds.*
>
> Peter, now let him have it back.
>
> Now how do you feel, Kevin? *After child answers, repeat with other pairs.*
>
> *Use a picture of a firetruck.* Larry, how would going for a ride on this firetruck make you feel? *Let child respond.*

Let's pretend that a man came and drove the truck away and you could NOT have a ride. How would you feel now? *Same child responds.*

Now let's pretend he came back and said, "Okay, now you can go for a ride." How would that make you feel? *Same child responds.*

Use a picture of a ball. How do you think Steven might feel if we let him play with this ball? *Group answers.*

Maybe he would feel happy and *maybe* he would *not* feel happy. Let's find out. How can we find out? *Encourage children to ask.*

Let's pretend someone came along and threw the ball out the window so Steven could *not* play with it anymore. Now how do you think Steven might feel?

He *might* feel sad *or* he *might* feel *mad.* How can we find out? *Encourage children to ask.*

After about six weeks a puppet story, "Allie the Alligator," is repeated because it is popular with the nursery youngsters. It includes much of the material on emotion. The first part of the story finds the main character (Allie) very sad because he cannot run and play in the same games as do other alligators. In the puppet dialogue it emerges that he cannot run fast but he can swim. The second part of the story introduces a problem situation between Allie and a friend, stressing three points:

(1) One cannot assume that because an individual likes to do something he will like to do it *all* of the time. The same individual likes different things at different times (Allie does not like to swim all of the time).

(2) One must gather information or risk coming to the wrong conclusion (Allie's friend thought Allie did not want to go swimming because Allie did not like him, whereas in fact Allie was only tired of swimming at the moment).

(3) It is often important to find out what the other person likes in order to solve an interpersonal problem.

Several similar puppet stories were added to the kindergarten script.

Additional Language Concepts

As in the nursery script, *why-because* connectives and the concept of *might-maybe* are emphasized, as are two new ones, those of *before-after* and *now-later*. These, together with language concepts taught earlier, serve as precursors to the final problem-solving skills to be learned. These words can be used to foster such thoughts as: "I can play with that toy *later,* not now," or "I can wait till *after* you're finished," or "If you won't play with me *now,* maybe you'll play with me *later."*

An excerpt from the thirty-first day of the program illustrates a typical lesson: The concepts *before-after* and *now-later* are viewed in the context of everyday events that have obvious temporal elements.

Today we're going to talk about the words *before* and *after.*

I got out of bed this morning. *After* I got out of bed, I brushed my teeth. I got out of bed *before* I brushed my teeth. I brushed my teeth *after* I got out of bed. Did I get out of bed before *or* after I brushed my teeth? *Let group respond.*

Yes, I got out of bed *before* I brushed my teeth. Did I brush my teeth *before or after* I got out of bed? *Group responds.*

Yes, I brushed my teeth *after* I got out of bed.

Johnny, did you come to school today *before or after* you got out of bed this morning? *Let child respond.*

Yes, you came to school *after* you got out of bed this morning.

Now we're going to talk about the words *now*

and *later. Clap hands. Now* I am clapping my hands
(keep clapping). I am clapping my hands *now. Now* I
am stamping my foot. Did I clap my hands *before* or
after I stamped my foot?
   *The game continues in the same vein for several
different motions.*

Though introduced earlier in the script, particular
emphasis is now placed on the language concepts *why-because*
and *might-maybe.*

Why-because connectives are crucial to appreciation of
the cause-and-effect relationships implicit in motives and the
reasons for what has already happened, and for the consequences of one's behavior ("Johnny hit Jimmy because Jimmy
hit him first"). Beginning on the thirty-third day, the children
are guided to think of a variety of "becauses" for one child in a
picture to be happy or sad. The children are encouraged to look
beyond the obvious and most noticeable clues: "Look at the
whole picture for reasons why the girl might have fallen off her
bike."

The concepts *might* and *maybe* become important
because preceding causes may be no more certain than succeeding consequences. In the weighing of consequences, it becomes
important to consider the likelihood that one event *might* happen, or that *maybe* the other person will feel mad. The fact of
uncertainty is also important to the issue of alternatives, specifically the importance of thinking of alternative solutions
and consequences because no one solution may lead to a desired
consequence in a given situation. Having an alternative in
mind may be quite adaptive.

Emotional Causality

Emotional or social causality is a new concept added to
the kindergarten script. Emphasis here is on asking why a
child in a picture might be feeling happy, sad, or mad, and
what another child might have done or said to make him feel
that way. These games incorporate previously learned con-

cepts. For example, a picture is shown of two boys, one depicted as angry. After the children identify the child's anger, the teacher follows with: "This boy *might* be mad *because* _____"
After one reason is given, the teacher asks for lots of *"different becauses."* She may guide the children with statements such as *"Maybe* this boy [*pointing to other boy in picture*] did (or said) something to make him feel mad. Can anyone think of something this boy might have done or said that made the boy mad?" To encourage the habit of thinking of more than one thing (necessary for later problem solving), the teacher follows with: "Yes, that's one thing; can anyone think of something different he might have done (or said)?"

Beginning Consequences

Just prior to work with actual interpersonal problem situations, a beginning is made with simple consequences. Employing pictures that depict children carrying out acts that have obvious consequences, discussion is focused on why the child's act may or may not be a good idea, and: "What might happen next?" In one picture, where children are standing in front of a swing, the questions raised are: "Is that a good place for the boys to play or *not* a good place? Why is it *not* a good place?" "If the swing hit them, how might they feel?" Other games make up problem situations, and the question is: "What might happen next in the story?" In these stories, consequences are sought in terms of what children might do and feel and what other children might do or say in response: "Let's pretend Susan pushed Karen, and Karen did not want to be pushed."

Problem Solving

The remainder of the formal training program, approximately one-third of the program, is composed of twelve interpersonal problem situations divided into three parts: (1) those seeking solutions only; (2) those seeking consequences only; and (3) those pairing specific solutions with consequences. The problem situations are presented in visual form by the teacher and the problem explained clearly.

The goal of the first four scenes is to elicit from the group of children alternative solutions to the problem situation. The scenes are of a girl who wants her brother to let her push the grocery cart; a boy who wants to sit on a man's lap; a girl who wants a chance to use scissors and a pencil another child is using; and a boy who wants to get a girl to stop crying. The children are encouraged to generate solutions. The emphasis is on "What else could I do?" The teacher emphasizes that the idea of the game is to think of a lot of different ways, and she writes the ideas of the children down on a blackboard as they generate them. (The fact that the children cannot read does not dampen the enthusiasm they feel when their ideas are recorded. Rather, it serves as a motivating technique—"Let's fill up the whole board!") No value judgment is placed on any relevant solution. "Hit him" is accepted as relevant along with "ask please." The children are told that the idea is to fill up the board with *different* solutions. If the solution offered by a child seems irrelevant, he is asked: "Why is that a good idea?" or "Tell me a little more about that."

The goal of the next four scenes is to guide the children to offer alternative possible consequences of an act of one child in a depicted scene (a child pushes another, a child will not help another clean up blocks they have both been playing with, and so on). The teacher, in presenting these scenes, focuses on what might happen next "if . . . ?" All possible consequences are written on the blackboard as before, with the comment, "Let's fill up the whole board!" The teacher aids the group by asking: "How might the girl feel if . . . ?" or "What might he do if . . . ?" or "What might she say if . . . ?" After a particular solution and all its possible consequences are recorded, the teacher then elicits from the children whether they think the *solution* to the problem is a good one. The reasons given, pro and con, must be based upon the consequences listed. This affords an opportunity for each child to evaluate solutions on the basis of possible consequences.

The goal of the final four story scenes is to encourage the

children to offer a solution to a problem, follow it up with a consequence, return to the same problem for a second solution and its possible consequence, and so forth. The purpose is to offer experience in linking pairs of solutions and consequences as a supplement to the weighing of pros and cons, as the children decide which solutions were good ones and which were not. At no point in this section does the teacher ever suggest a particular solution or consequence. The purpose is to guide the child to think for himself, "What can I do?" or "What might happen if I do that?" or "What else can I do?" Thus the child learns to decide on and evaluate his own ideas, with guidance but not direction from the teacher.

During this final problem-solving phase, the teacher is instructed to employ the dialoguing methods with the children as problems actually arise in the group. For example, if a child takes a chair belonging to another child and gets hit for it, the attacker might be asked how the other boy feels about being hit and what else might he do or say to get his chair back. The child who took the chair might be asked why he wanted the chair. If he said "I can't see," he might be encouraged to think of other things he might do to see better. Throughout this process, the emphasis is upon encouraging the children to think of what they are doing about a problem, why, and how they feel about it; along with that, they relate the consequences of what they do to the feelings and behavior of others. It is not the quality of any particular solution that is at issue but the fact that the child is manifesting a problem-solving style of thought.

9

Treatment Program
for Hyperactive
Children

Camp and Bash (1975) have designed a program entitled *Think Aloud*. Despite the fact that this program is still in its early development, its relevance to present interests justifies inclusion. It is an individually administered program for children between the ages of six and eight who are manifesting hyperactive, poorly self-controlled behaviors. The program script borrows heavily from the early preschool and kindergarten curricula of Shure and Spivack described above, combining procedures and at times actual lessons from these two programs

190

with the self-instructional methods studied and described by Meichenbaum and Goodman (1971).

Like the Shure and Spivack materials, the *Think Aloud Program* is a carefully designed and sequenced daily script consisting of lessons and games planned to consume about twenty-five minutes per day over a period of six weeks. Specific instructions are provided the user in how to proceed and how to use the materials needed (pictures, stories, puppets, and so forth). Some lessons are clearly reminiscent of purely self-instructional procedures aimed at aiding the child in developing an inner dialogue that will help him problem-solve. Other lessons focus exclusively on the teaching of ICPS skills, and still others cleverly combine the two. As one proceeds through the materials, previously learned skills and word concepts are integrated into new learning material to abet development of more adequate functioning.

As with the Shure and Spivack programs, the terminal lessons and goals of the program are aimed at helping these children evolve a style of thought that includes a capacity to elicit alternative solutions to interpersonal problems, to consider possible consequences, and to decide upon a plan of action as a function of these abilities. Implicit in these is the goal of making the child more reflective (less impulsive) in style. The program borrows the notions of prerequisite linguistic concepts needed in the evaluation of ICPS ability and necessary intermediate learning about how to identify feelings and the language and thinking of social causality.

The *Think Aloud Program* differs from the Shure and Spivack programs in placing great emphasis upon the modeling and reinforcing of self-instruction and/or self-interrogation on the part of the child during learning and somewhat less emphasis on the idea of eliciting from the child his own thoughts. A major theme of the Shure and Spivack programs is for the adult never to offer the child a solution or consequence but rather to "cue him in" through guiding questions, so as to stimulate his own thinking along these lines. In many instances, the *Think Aloud Program* has the teacher model what to think and say and, in some instances, actually teach the child what categories of solution he should employ in problem solving. Another difference is that, while the *Think Aloud Program* at times employs impersonal tasks, the Shure and Spivack programs employ only interpersonal tasks and stimuli.

Pre-Problem-Solving Phase

The first fourteen or so days of training are aimed at (1) teaching the child self-instructional habits, (2) encouraging a reflective, planned approach to a problem, (3) teaching of the prerequisite word concepts *same-different, if-then, not, might,* and *why-because,* and (4) an introduction to emotional causality and consequences (that is, what might happen next).

The first five days of lessons focus exclusively on teaching the child to model (copy) what the adult does and says and to practice some of the specific self-instructional skills used throughout much of the remainder of the program. Initially the child is given an impersonal problem and shown how to think out loud such questions as: "What's my problem?" and "What am I supposed to do?" and "What's my plan?" and "How do I do it?" Cue cards are used to assist the child in remembering these rules, and the adult prompts wherever necessary. If a task is to color inside the line of a picture, the internal dialogue might include: "Go slow—be careful—stay inside the lines." If the task is a puzzle, he might be encouraged to say: "OK, here I go. I'm looking at the pieces. Let me find a piece that looks like something I know. Oh, here's a foot. A foot usually goes at the bottom so I'll put it down here." While modeling, the adult might even make an "impulsive" mistake and say out loud: "This one! Oh, oh, slow down. I don't know what that piece is. Be careful. What's a different piece I could use?"

Perceptual comparison tasks are also employed, quite similar to those used in research on the reflectiveness-impulsiveness dimension first described by Jerome Kagan. For instance, the child has to search for a picture within an array of pictures, with the purpose of selecting the one that looks exactly like a standard. The adult models a careful, planned approach with overt verbalization. Following this, the child is asked to do the same thing (for example, "I'll plan ahead," "I'll look carefully at this picture so I know what to look for, then I'll look at all four pictures"). A companion game is one wherein the child listens to a group of words and rings a bell when he hears the "standard" word.

The sixth through eighth lessons focus on appreciation of the word concepts *if-then, not, same-different, might,* and *why-because.* Some of these lessons incorporate teaching about how one uses one's eyes and ears to acquire information about the emotional style of another person. For example, pictures are placed in front of the child and involved in the problem with requests and queries such as:

"Show me a child who is smiling."
"Show me a girl who is *not* crying."
"*If* this girl is crying, *then* she is *not* laughing."
"*If* this girl feels happy and this boy feels sad, *then* they do *not* feel the *same* way. They feel *different* ways."
"How can you tell the girl feels happy? You can see with your eyes."

Games also involve auditory cues signifying emotional states to highlight how we may learn about others by listening carefully.

The *why-because* games begin with "whys" about simple states: "I'm very hungry"—"Why?"—"Because I haven't had my lunch"; then they progress through interpersonal situations. The ninth day focuses on emotional causality. The "whys" focus on why a person may be mad, or sad, the task being to discover different possible "becauses."

The tenth and eleventh days touch on initial elements of consequential thinking. In the "What might happen next?" games the child is presented with a situation in school wherein he was not listening and is asked what might happen. This line of questioning is pursued through chaining of responses with: " . . . and what might happen now if you said that?" "What would happen next? What might she do or say?" During these days, the lessons also introduce a trail-making problem that the teacher first models and then asks the child to do. The task requires the person to move a pencil slowly through the trail from one number to the next, without lifting the pencil or going in the wrong direction. The emphasis is on looking ahead, planning what to do before doing it, and remaining calm. The tasks gradually become more like the typical mazes wherein only the beginning and end points are specified. Self-instruction aloud is an essential ingredient.

Beginning consequences emerge on the eleventh day. Situations are presented in picture form—for example, a girl is pulling a cat's tail—and the child is asked: "Is that a good idea?" Questions explore how the cat might feel, and the "because" of it: "Why is pulling the cat's tail not a good idea?" and "What might happen next?" Other scenes include boys playing where they should not and a girl reaching for cookies in a rather precarious fashion.

Subsequent prerequisite lessons touch upon inductive reasoning and the concept of fairness and review previous themes dealing with self-instructional techniques and word concepts. The inductive reasoning lesson employs adult modeling (verbalizing aloud) when attempting to solve a task such as: "What is brown, made of paper, and used to carry groceries?" The lesson provides examples of such questions, varying in difficulty, from which the adult may choose. After the adult has modeled, the child is given a number of such problems (at an appropriate difficulty level). During this process, the adult slowly lessens his supervision by attending to other business. The purpose of this "fading" is to enable the child to instruct himself in the absence of close attention of the model.

The final pre-problem-solving game involves situations in which the child makes judgments about the "fairness" of a series of events between two people: "Let's pretend that you have Wally the Wolf (puppet) and I have Dilly the Duck (puppet). You have this toy that Dilly wants. So Dilly grabs it." (Dilly actually grabs at Wally.) "Is that fair?" This question may be followed with "Why not?" or "How does he feel?" or "What would be a fair thing for him to say or do?" or "What *different* thing might happen if he . . . ?" or any number of such inquiries.

Problem-Solving Phase

Beginning on the fifteenth lesson and through to the end, lessons concentrate on interpersonal problem solving: (1) alternative solutions to problems, (2) alternative consequences to a given solution to a problem, and (3) the pairing of individual solutions and consequences. During the initial lesson, the adult models aloud an internal dialogue about what a boy might do in order to get a girl to let him feed the hamsters. The adult first enumerates all the different things the boy.might *do:* "He could give her something . . . potato chips, if she will let him feed the hamsters." "He could grab the food from her." "He could tell the teacher." The adult then models some different things he might say: "Can we share?" "Can I feed the hamsters?" "You feed the white one and I'll feed the black one." The adult employs five types of solution: ask, give something, tell someone, or trick or hurt the girl. New problems are presented the child. The child is to state the nature of the problem out loud and then attempt to talk to himself as did the adult. During this process the adult may contribute a category of solution the child may have missed and even remind the child that there are five categories of ways to handle such problems (that is, get what you want). This technique departs from that of Shure and Spivack, who make a point never to directly suggest a particular solution or category of solution. The problems presented to the child include wanting to sit on mother's lap while the baby is there, wanting to use scissors another child is using, and a scene where a child's friend flies an airplane to him in class against the rules.

The adult introduces the lessons dealing with consequential thinking by modeling the thinking of someone who is generating different consequences. The situation presented is one in which a child solves a problem by pushing another child. As the child listens, the teacher provides alternative consequences and records them.

I have to think of what might happen next if
Mickey pushes Lucy. What's our plan? I know I have to
plan for this problem. We can think of what *Lucy*
might *do* next. Then we can think of all the things *Lucy*
might *say* after Mickey pushes her. Okay, what's one
thing that might happen next if Mickey pushes Lucy?

Depending on the child's responses, the teacher elicits
consequences in much the same way as in the Shure and
Spivack programs. The child is then asked to respond to this
situation with whether or not he thinks it a good idea for
Mickey to push Lucy, to think of a different thing Mickey
might do to get Lucy to play with him, and to supply what
might happen next and whether he thinks that solution is a
good idea. The entire procedure described above is then
repeated during a subsequent lesson in the following situations: a girl wants her brother to look at her truck, but he is
watching television; a boy wants the baby to stop crying; a
friend chases you down the hall against the rules.

The final lessons revolve around four problems: (1) in
gym the child gets handed an old bean bag to toss; (2) a boy
tries to cut into the line at the drinking fountain; (3) a girl grabs
the paper of a friend and he tells the child to give it back; (4) the
child is talking when the teacher gives directions for a math
paper. Puppets are used for interest's sake. For each situation,
the adult asks the child to repeat the problem and then asks
what the child might do, what might happen next if he did
that, and then to say whether he thinks his solution was a good
idea. The pairs of solutions and consequences are recorded by
the adult, and then the child is asked for one other different
solution and its likely consequence.

Program for
Mothers of
Young Children

ᘏᘏᘏᘏᘏᘏᘏᘏᘏᘏᘏᘏᘏᘏᕷᕷᕷᕷᕷᕷᕷᕷᕷᕷᕷᕷᕷᕷ

A program entitled *Problem-Solving Techniques in Childrearing* (Shure and Spivack, 1975*d*) resulted from adaptation and reevaluation of the program described in Chapter Eight. This program can be used directly by mothers or can be included as a relevant training program for mothers within an educational or mental health setting, for prevention and early intervention purposes.

Just as teachers can become successful mediators of ICPS skills through the use of specific training techniques, the present program has demonstrated that mothers can also learn to

197

transmit ICPS skills to their children. Before-and-after research evaluation has indicated that use of the program by the child's own mother not only improves ICPS skills in the child but improves the behavior of impulsive and inhibited youngsters in school, as observed by teachers unaware of the training procedures and goals. It has also been demonstrated that children who improve the most in ICPS skills have mothers who (as a function of training) adopt a problem-solving style of communication when handling real problems that occur with their children at home (see Chapter Seven).

In addition to carefully sequenced lessons designed for participation by the child, two procedures are included for direct participation by the mothers. The first consists of exercises for the mother to think about that have direct relevance to the games she plays with her child. The second consists of exercises designed to enhance the mother's thinking ability to solve typical mother-child problems, as well as problem-solving techniques she can incorporate informally into her handling of actual problems that arise with her child during the day. These exercises for participation by mothers are interspersed throughout the formal program script and are noted below at the points at which they occur.

For that portion of the script designed for child participation, the mother works with her child at home for about twenty minutes per day, over a period of approximately three months. Mothers find it useful to establish a regular time of day for the games such as just after dinner or right before bedtime, though flexibility is desirable when occasion demands it. The games have been designed so the mother can work with one child or more than one child. Mothers have reported interest and enthusiasm by their children up to about the age of eight, although it was designed for the four-year-old level.

Instructions to mothers include suggestions to stimulate and maintain interest, including the possibility that an older child might occasionally read the script, thus helping to teach the younger child. The importance of insuring that the younger child respond often is emphasized, so that the older children do not dominate and drown out the four-year-old.

The parent program script is composed of twenty-five games that build up selected prerequisite thinking skills in the child, followed by twelve interpersonal problem situations to which the child responds by offering: (1) solutions to the stated problems, (2) potential consequences to solutions stated by the child, and (3) pairing of one specific solution with one specific consequence. Stories and simple role-playing games are interspersed throughout the final problem-solving section to maintain interest.

Although, for the most part, the concepts are the same as the previous Shure and Spivack scripts, differences in content and examples of specific readaptation for use with one child are described below, as are exercises designed for specific participation by the mother.

Language, Listening, and Paying Attention

The first seven games focus on basic word concepts needed to establish an association for their later use in problem solving. So that the child can later decide what and what *not* to do, and whether something is or is *not* a good idea, one early game the mother plays simply teaches the meaning of the word itself, saying something like, "I am your mother. I am *not* a tree. Let's think of lots of things I am not." Then the mother asks her child to tell what he *is*, and lots of things he is *not*. In teaching the words *same* and *different*, so that the child can later think of different ideas (solution thinking) and different things that "might happen if . . ." (consequential thinking), the most popular games from earlier scripts are repeated. The mother might say: "I am tapping my knee. Can you do the *same* thing?" "Now, can you think of something *different* to do?" [*Child responds.*] "Yes, patting your head is *different* from tapping your knee."

An important word to associate with problem-solving thinking is the word *or*, so that the child can learn to think, "I can do _____ *or* _____." An example of a game on the fifth day of the program illustrates the teaching of basic word concepts. Large poster cut-out dolls provide a substitute for real children, a necessary adaptation for mothers playing this game with a single child.

> *Point to a boy doll.* Am I pointing to a boy *or* am I pointing to a girl? *Let child answer.*
> Good, I am pointing to a boy.
> *Point to a girl doll.* Am I pointing to a boy *or* am I pointing to a girl? *Let child answer.*
> Is your name (Child #1) *or* is your name Albert? *Let child answer.* Yes, your name is _____. Your name is *not* Albert. *Repeat with Child #2, etc.*
> *Lay the dolls on the floor and place a crayon on top of three of them.*
> *Some* of these children have a crayon and *some* do *not* have a crayon.
> *(Child #1),* point to a doll where there is *not* a crayon.
> Point to a doll where there *is* a crayon.

Identifying Emotions

Games that teach the child to identify and label emotions are included as a first step in recognizing the feelings of oneself and others when confronted with a problem situation.

It is at this point in the script that the first exercise for the mother to think about is inserted. The purpose of the first exercise is to stimulate the mother's own thinking about ways people feel, including her child, and is strategically placed at that point in the script where the mother first begins teaching these concepts to her child. Each mother is encouraged to think about what her child does or says that makes her feel a certain way—happy, sad, or angry. She is also encouraged to think about the reverse—what she could do or say that might make her child experience these feelings. Thus the mother not only focuses on emotional reactions but focuses on them from more than one point of view, a cognitive skill she will be transmitting to her child as the program progresses.

Multiple Attributes

Through use of the word *and,* the child learns to consider more than one aspect of a situation at a time, with emphasis on people and interpersonal relations—"This policeman is standing *and* he is talking to a child *and* [*child answers*]."

Information Gathering—How Can We Tell?

After the mother teaches her child how to find out about how other people feel (by listening, by watching, by asking) and to recognize that people feel differently at different times, a second exercise for the mother to think about is inserted. Questions raised include: (1) How can you tell that your child is feeling the way you think he is? How else can you tell? (2) How can you find out how your child is really feeling? (3) How can you guide your child to find out how *you* are feeling? Mothers are then encouraged to think of specific examples of times when their children felt happy, sad, or angry and asked to recall how they could tell. If a mother were to say, "I could tell he was sad because he was crying," she would then be asked if she could think of anything he *said* that also indicated how he felt. Such exercises stimulate the mother to think about more than one way to learn how someone feels and to develop a greater sensitivity to the feelings of others, elements of thinking she has just taught to her child.

Information Gathering—Do You Like?

These games stress (1) individual choice, (2) ways of finding out what other people like, and (3) that different people might like different things. In these games, family face puppets are introduced so that a mother can play these games with one child (the puppets serving as a substitute for other real children). For example, the mother asks her child whether he would choose a dog or a cat to play with. After the child makes his choice—say, the dog—the mother places a puppet face over her own face and, in the character voice of the puppet, says, "Hi, I'm Terry. I would choose the dog. You chose the dog. Did we choose the *same* thing or something *different?*" After the child answers, the mother picks up another puppet and, in a new voice, says, "Hi, I'm Nancy. I choose the cat. You chose the dog. Did we choose the *same* thing or something *different?*" The mother then points out that different people choose different things. The game is repeated with other animals, forms of transportation, and places to be. Also included in these games are questions to the child about how he found out what the puppet characters (or other children in the group) would choose. By pointing to her ears, the mother guides the child to recognize that one way to find out is to hear (listen to) what someone chooses, and the child also learns that still another way to find out is by asking.

An exercise for the mother to think about is inserted at this point in the script. The purpose here is for the mother to appreciate that different people like different things and that there are ways in which she can discover other people's preferences (including her child's). For example, the mother is asked to think about a TV show she likes and whether she knows anyone who does *not* like that TV show. With regard to her own child, she is asked to think about how she can find what her child likes and does not like. She is guided by such questions as: "Can you think of a time when you found out by *hearing* what your child said . . . by *watching* what your child did . . . by *asking* him?" In each instance the mother is asked to describe the situation. (If group training meetings are held, the mothers play these games with each other, just as they play them with their children.)

The mother then returns to games she plays with her child, guiding him to think of his own ways to make another person (or puppet character) happy and to find out what the other person (or puppet character) thinks of his idea.

Emotional Awareness

This part of the script stresses how to understand and influence others' emotions. For mothers playing with one child, puppets are used as a substitute for other children. For example, the mother holds up the puppet (Terry) and follows with:

> Let's make up a story. Let's pretend we know
> that Terry likes cookies. If you let him have a cookie,
> would that make Terry happy?

After the child answers, the puppet is asked if he would be happy if the child gave him a cookie. Terry answers yes.

Then the mother asks how Terry might feel "if you would *not* let him have a cookie." After the child answers, Terry says, "Yes, that would make me mad (or sad)." The purpose is to get the child to think through the influence of specific actions on others' feelings.

Why-because connectives are utilized to stimulate cause-and-effect thinking in problem situations—"He grabbed the toy *because* I grabbed it first." Through pictures and puppet stories the child is asked to think of why specific events occur and then to think of lots of "different becauses."

After completion of games that stress how the child can find out how other people feel, Exercise No. 4 guides the mother to think about *how to find out* facts and feelings when her child has a problem. For example, a child tells his mother that another child hit him. She is then presented with a series of questions to think about (or discuss). Questions are raised around such issues as: (1) how she can find out the facts as her child sees them; (2) how her child feels as he tells her someone hit him; (3) how the mother can tell what her child's feelings are; (4) what the child did when he was hit and why; (5) how the mother reacted to the situation and why she did or said what she did in the situation. After the mother gives these questions some thought, two sample dialogues between a mother and child are presented.

Example 1

CHILD: Mommy, Tommy hit me.
MOTHER: Hit him back.
CHILD: But, I'm afraid.
MOTHER: You've got to learn to defend yourself.
CHILD: Okay, Mommy.

Example 2

CHILD: Mommy, Tommy hit me.
MOTHER: Why did he hit you?
CHILD: (crying) I don't know.
MOTHER: I see it made you sad. What were you and
             Tommy doing when he hit you?
CHILD: Playing.
MOTHER: When he hit you, what did you do next?
CHILD: Nothing.
MOTHER: Why did you do nothing?
CHILD: I kicked him.
MOTHER: Before or after he hit you?
CHILD: After.
MOTHER: Okay, you kicked him. I see.
CHILD: Mommy, I called him a dummy.
MOTHER: When?
CHILD: Before.
MOTHER: Is that why he hit you?
CHILD: Yea!

The mother is then asked the following:

Now let's think about these dialogues.
  1. In what way are the dialogues in Example 1 dif-
     ferent from Example 2?
  2. Which mother was more effective? Why?
  3. What facts were in the story that the first mother
     may have never found out that the second
     mother did find out?
  4. How did the second mother find them out?
  5. What else might you say to find out your child's
     feelings?

The second mother got her child's point of view and encouraged him to think about the facts. Her questions were not threatening and her child was not afraid to tell her he hit first.

This exercise serves as an introduction to dialoguing techniques the mother can use in handling actual problem situations that arise, after she teaches her child problem-solving thinking skills.

Beginning Consequences

At about the twenty-third day of the program, the children are introduced to the first games that guide consequential thinking. The words *might, maybe, why,* and *because* are highlighted, and previously learned emotional feelings (happy, sad, mad) become thought of as important consequences of an act performed in a problem situation. For example, a mother says to her child, "Let's pretend you scribbled on your brother's [or the puppet Terry's] painting and he did not like that. How might your brother [or Terry] feel about that?" After the child answers, the mother follows with, "Why might he feel that way? Because _____." After the child answers the mother then asks, "What might happen next in the story? What might your brother [or Terry] do or say next?"

After two more puppet stories designed to reinforce previously learned concepts, another exercise for the mother to think about appears. Its purpose is to get the mother to begin thinking of alternative ways of dealing with problem situations that her child may bring to or create for her, as well as what consequences her actions may have on her child's thinking and behavior. First the mother rereads Example 1 and Example 2 above. She then thinks about what the first mother might do or say when her child tells her someone hit him/her. In preparation for teaching her child how to think of alternative solutions to a problem, the mother then thinks of different things the first mother could do or say in the problem situation presented. For each idea the mother thinks of, she is asked to think of several possible consequences that might occur—that is, different possible things the child might do or say if her ideas were carried out.

Problem Solving

The problem-solving section is divided in the same manner and serves the same purpose as that described for the kindergarten script: (1) alternative solutions, (2) alternative consequences, and (3) solution-consequences pairing. The problems differ in content, and use is made of the puppets, especially when working with an individual child when no siblings or friends happen to be there. Beginning on about the thirtieth day of the program, the child is shown pictures depicting an interpersonal problem, the first four designed to elicit alternative solutions from the child. One example will communicate the flavor of a typical session. Using a picture depicting a child and her mother in a grocery store, the mother presents a hypothetical problem appropriate to the content of the picture.

> *Problem 2.* Girl wants mother to buy her a box of cookies.
>
>> 1. Solutions Game:
>>
>> This girl [*point to picture*] wants her mommy to buy her a box of cookies.
>>
>> What does this girl want her mommy to do?
>>
>> This girl wants her mommy to _____ _____ _____.
>>
>> What can this girl *do* so her mommy will buy her a box of cookies? [*Child answers.*]
>>
>> *Repeat child's response and say,* That's way number one.
>>
>> What's the idea of this game? [*Child answers.*] To think of lots of *different* ways.
>>
>> She could [*repeat number one*] or—she could _____?
>>
>> Let's ask *"or"?* Let's say that together, *"or"?*
>>
>> Can anybody think of way number two? *(If one child is playing, say,* "Can you think of way number two?"*)*
>>
>> Good, Sally [*shake hands*]—you gave way number two. Now we have [*repeat way number one and way number two, counting on fingers*]. She can [*repeat way number one*] or she can [*repeat way number two*].

All together, let's say, "What else?"

Can anybody think of way number three? What else could she *do?* What else could she *say?*

Keep going, always repeating all responses, always recognizing, and always asking, "What else?" If children begin to enumerate, classify it—that is, point out that hit, kick, bite are all hurting. *Then ask for a way that's different from* hurting.

If child suggests a trade, such as offering some cake, mother says:

How would that make her mother feel?

Do all people like cake?

No, all people do *not* like cake.

Maybe she would like cake.

How can we find out if she would like cake?

If the mother would *not* like cake, what else can the child do? *Continue same line of questioning.*

If the child suggests making her happy, without any specific ways as to how, ask, "How can the child make her mother happy?" and proceed with the same line of questioning.

At any point where the children run out of ideas, the mother can pick up any of the puppets provided and say (in the character voice of the puppet), "I wish I could think of an idea. Can you help me?" It has been found that a quiet or nonresponding child will often respond if he *is* the puppet character. The mother can let her child hold a puppet. With the child portraying the character of Terry, the mother follows with: "Terry, do you have an idea?" Often such a child will respond through the voice of the puppet, even though he does not yet respond as himself.

In the consequences section, composed of four contrived problem situations, the child first offers one solution to a problem. For example, a boy wants a girl to let him feed the animals. The child may suggest "He can push her out of the way." The mother then asks, "If the boy pushes the girl out of the way, what might happen next in the story?" Guiding questions such as, "What might the girl do?" or "What might the girl say?" or "How might the girl feel?" are asked, but the mother never suggests a consequence or in any way puts a value judgment on the child's solution. After the child offers all the possible consequences he can, the mother elicits another solution from the child and its possible consequences. This procedure is followed by the child deciding whether each solution offered is or is not a good one, based on the consequences he has given. Puppets can be utilized in the same manner as in the solutions section, either by letting the child *be* the puppet character or by the mother holding the puppet, saying "I wish I could think of something that might happen next; can you help me?"

For variety and interest, two stories are placed at this point in the script, each incorporating concepts learned thus far. Illustrated below is a further example of how puppets are used to represent real children when only one child is playing the game.

> [*To child.*] Whipple has your [*name toy*].
>
> Can you think of a way to get Whipple to give it back to you? Something you can do *or* say? *Let child answer.*
>
> Go ahead and try it. *Let child try it.*
>
> *Whipple:* [*Change voice*] No, I want it.
>
> Oh, that idea did not work. You'll have to think of something different. *Let child answer.*
>
> *Whipple answers:* Okay. You can have it.
>
> Very good, you thought of that all by yourself. *If the child suggests hitting or snatching, say:* Oh, how does that make Whipple feel? *Let child answer.* Can you think of an idea so Whipple will *not* feel sad (mad)? *Let child answer.*
>
> *Bring out Allie and Dilly. Put a piece of food, like a carrot, in Allie's mouth and have Dilly snatch it.*
>
> *Allie:* [*Change voice*] Dilly, why did you snatch that from me?
>
> *Dilly:* [*Change voice*] Because I wanted it.
>
> *Make Allie look sad.*
>
> How does Allie feel? *Let child answer.*
>
> What can Dilly do now so Allie will feel happy again? *Let child answer.*
>
> [*To Allie*] Allie, does that make you feel happy?

Allie: [*Change voice*] No, I'm still sad.

Oh, Allie is still sad. Can you think of a different idea? *Let child answer.*

[*To Allie*] Does that make you happy?

Allie: [*Change voice*] Yes, I like that idea.

Very good. You thought of that all by yourself.

Allie to Dilly: Dilly, will you let me draw with your crayon?

Dilly: No.

Allie to child: Can you help me? What can I do or say so Dilly will let me draw with his crayon? *Let child answer.*

Have Allie try each idea and have Dilly say yes or no.

At this point in the script an exercise is introduced to stimulate the mother to think more about alternative ways of dealing with real problem situations that her child may bring to or create for mother. She is encouraged to think about an actual problem she has had with her child recently—"Johnny keeps teasing his sister, hits her for no reason," for example. She is then asked to think about what she actually did or said, how the child reacted, what was said or done next—recreating as much as possible the actual conversation and actions that took place. The mother is then asked to think about whether she got all the facts from her child, how the child might have felt when the problem came up, how she found out (or could find out) how the child felt, and, finally, if there were any different ways she might have handled the same problem.

Solution-consequence pairing completes the part of the program that the mother teaches to her child. The child offers a solution to a problem, immediately followed by a potential consequence, then repeats the process with a new solution to the same problem. The goal is to associate the process of deciding upon a solution with the thought of a consequence. The mother then asks the child to tell whether he thinks each solution, paired with its consequence, is a good one or not a good one, and why.

The script ends with a final exercise for the mother to

think about. In suggesting the outline for mother-child dialogues, it incorporates each of the previous exercises. The details of any real dialogue naturally would depend on how the child responds to what the mother says. This exercise is presented in full because of its importance in the script.

FOR MOTHER
To Think About: VII
Encouraging Child to Solve Interpersonal Problems

Purpose: To think about how to encourage the child to think through and solve problems for himself based on the skills he has learned from the training program. At this point, both mother and child will be developing a problem-solving style of thinking and communication.

Type of Problem

Child engaged in interpersonal conflict.

Specific Problem

Child initiates hurting or grabbing behavior.

*Questions to Encourage
Problem-Solving Communication*

1. Why (did you hit him)?
2. (Hitting) is one thing you can do. How did that make (Judy) feel?
3. What happened when you (hit Peter)? What did Peter do or say?
4. Can you think of another way to *(repeat reasons child gave why he hit)* so that won't happen?
5. *(After child answers)* That's a different idea. What might happen if you try that?

Specific Problem

Child reciprocates hurting or grabbing behavior.

*Questions to Encourage
Problem-Solving Communication*

1. How did it make you feel when _____ (hit) you?
2. O.K., you felt (mad).
3. What happened when you (hit) him back?
4. (Hitting) is one thing you can do. Can you think of

something different to do that will make you feel happy?

5. *(After child answers)* That's a different idea. Is that a good idea? What might happen if you try that?

Type of Problem

Child pouts or cries.

Specific Problem

Child upset because he wants to fingerpaint right before dinner and mother does not want him to.

Child wants candy he sees in store and mother does not want him to have any.

Questions to Encourage
Problem-Solving Communication

1. I can't let you (fingerpaint now) because _____.
2. Do you know why I can't let you (fingerpaint) now?
3. What might happen if you (fingerpaint now)?
4. Can you think of something different to do now that will make you happy?

Type of Problem

Child in potentially dangerous situation or engaged in activity that could cause damage to property.

Specific Problems

Child is running inside.
Child is playing with water in the living room.
Child is climbing on furniture.
Child is painting on the wall.

Questions to Encourage
Problem-Solving Communication

1. Is that a good idea to (run inside)?
2. What might happen if you do that?
3. How will you feel if you (bump into something, dirty the furniture)?
4. Can you think of something different to do (in a different place) so that won't happen?

≋≋≋≋≋≋≋≋≋≋≋11≪≪≪≪≪≪≪≪≪≪≪

School Program
for Third- and
Fourth-Grade
Children

≋≋≋≋≋≋≋≋≋≋≋≋≋≋≋≪≪≪≪≪≪≪≪≪≪≪≪≪≪

This curriculum for third- and fourth-grade children in a public school setting was initially derived from the work of Larcen (see Larcen and others, 1974) and was later elaborated and tested further by McClure (1975). As with other ICPS programs, the purpose of the program is to enhance mediating thinking skills, thereby enhancing overt behavioral problem-solving behavior. The purposes of the program are: (1) to instill a problem-solving orientation, (2) to teach how to identify and define a problem, (3) to enhance capacity to generate alternative solutions and elaborate them, and (4) to sensitize to consequences.

Results of the Larcen study (see also Allen and others, 1976) indicate that the program does enhance capacity to think of alternative solutions and to elaborate on any one solution through means-ends thinking. Studies by these investigators also indicate that the actual tendency to conceptualize alternative solutions in a contrived but seemingly real situation may be enhanced in some children exposed to such a program. McClure elaborated upon the program, and compared effectiveness of the new program as a function of how it was administered: TV modeling tapes alone; TV modeling tapes plus small discussion groups; and TV modeling plus role playing. McClure discovered that, in general, small group discussion and/or role playing significantly enhances the effectiveness of training over mere TV video watching in developing alternative-thinking skills, that in general alternative-thinking ability is the best predictor of effectiveness of problem solving in a variety of settings, and that alternative thinking predicts sensitivity to a problem and persistence in dealing with it in a "real" situation. McClure found that the positive effects of Larcen's program on children did not persist four months after training had ended, suggesting that certain refinements as he has elaborated might make the difference and/or that more intense and extensive training may be required.

The program's teaching methods are based on the assumption that participation in learning is better than pure didactics. It emphasizes modeling effects, teacher reinforcement, brainstorming, and some role playing in the design of the learning settings. The point is made that the program is not a prescribed cookbook, but rather an approach accompanied by suggested techniques presented in a sequence. The findings of McClure suggest that different elements in the training program may have different effects, depending on one's interest.

The curriculum of the program has six parts. Within each part, a teacher may work with the entire class at once, work with small groups of four or five children, or assign a task to a small group to work by itself. The program, as reported in Allen and others, takes four and one-half months, the class meeting twice weekly for thirty minutes. In general, the more the approach requires small-group work, the more likely the teacher will need assistance in the classroom. The claim is made that small-group work is ideal for learning social problem solving, and the suggestion is made that parent volunteers may be one solution to the problem of classroom coverage.

Divergent Thinking Unit

The purpose of this unit is to give the group an opportunity to experience group problem solving and brainstorming, and to encourage the idea that problems are solvable. The problems dealt with in this unit are not interpersonal. The teacher might model brainstorming in front of the entire class, the problem being, for example, to think of all possible ways one might have gotten to school that day. The teacher gives extreme solutions, recording them all on the blackboard. The class is then broken into small groups, with the task of thinking up alternative uses for common objects. The teacher moves from one group to another during this process. Care is taken to avoid any judgments as to the quality of a solution, the focus being upon originality and quantity. Another format is to start with the entire group brainstorming about discarded home objects. These are listed on the blackboard. Small groups then brainstorm alternative uses, for about twenty minutes. The groups then come together, and prizes are given to the group that came up with the most ideas and the most original idea.

Problem Identification Unit

The purpose of this unit is to train in defining what the problem is and in identifying what the goals of the people involved may be. For example, in the large group, the teacher may select a typical problem and demonstrate in front of the group that the first thing in problem solving is to identify the problem and what the people involved want to achieve. Emphasis is placed on separating relevant from irrelevant aspects of the problem situation.

Small groups may be formed to practice this process, using unfinished problem stories or a pool of problems that the total class collected beforehand. The teacher elicts discussion with such probes as: "What is the problem as [*name of character*] sees it?" "What does he want to happen?" McClure has employed role-playing methods wherein the teacher presents the problem and the children explore different views through reenacting the scene many times. With role switching and subsequent discussion, the group explores the different ways different people see the problem and why it is important to define the problem specifically.

Alternative Solutions Unit

The purpose of this unit is to enhance capacity to generate alternative solutions to problems through the appreciation of divergent thinking and brainstorming methods. Working with the entire class, one technique uses a videotape wherein a child faces a problem and tries to generate alternative solutions. During pauses in the tape, the teacher asks the class for other options that the problem solver should consider.

In another exercise, small groups of children are given a list of unfinished problem stories or a list of problems previously generated by the group itself during the problem-identification exercises. The teacher prompts individual children with such questions as: "How can you . . . ?" "What else can you do?" "What other ways can you think of?" If the group begins to consider the consequences or implications of any solution, discussion is directed back to alternative solutions with a comment such as: "Since this solution causes a problem, what other solution can you think of that will not cause this problem?"

A variation of the above is when the teacher gives small groups of children problems—"How can a child get into a secret club?" or "What would you do if you borrowed a bike and you left it in the street and a car rode over it?"—and leaves them with the twenty-minute task of coming up with many solutions as well as original solutions. It is claimed that such a "set" motivates consideration of multiple alternatives, especially when prizes are offered.

McClure has designed an exercise for role playing alternative solutions. The group is given an unfinished problem story and asked to generate many alternative solutions. The teacher selects a negative or ineffective solution, the children enact it, and the teacher probes the group to consider whether the problem has been solved. Other solutions are then sought, and role playing continued.

Consideration of Consequences Unit

The purpose of this unit is to get the child to consider relevant outcomes before taking action and to think of obstacles that may arise and the consequences deriving from any given solution.

The techniques employed closely parallel those outlined above in the alternative-solution unit. For example, the class is shown a videotape dramatizing more than one child considering the possible consequences of solutions to problems. During a pause in the tape, the class is asked to expand further by coming up with other consequences they might see or obstacles that might arise in carrying out each solution portrayed on the videotape.

The teacher might work in small groups, using unfinished problem stories. The teacher discusses the importance of looking for consequences, emphasizing that there often is more than one possible consequence that follows any one problem solution. The group then goes through a list of possible solutions to a problem, seeking the solutions they judge would be most and least effective. The teacher then asks questions that will pinpoint the consequences that have led to these selections —"What will happen if . . . ?" "What will happen in the short run?" "In the long run?" and the like.

A variation of the above has the teacher give the group of children a problem and seven possible solutions. The group works alone listing possible consequences to each solution, discussing them, and selecting what they judge are the best and poorest. The group returns to the larger class and explains the choices.

McClure has developed a role-playing exercise wherein the teacher selects a solution to a problem which may be, in her judgment, a poor one. The group is directed to consider consequences. Children are selected to enact roles—if possible, roles their temperaments might not dispose them to actually play in real life. The session is concluded with discussion of the most effective solution enacted.

Elaboration of Solutions Unit

The purpose of this unit is to train children to consider the concrete steps (means) necessary in order to effectively carry out any one solution successfully. Training exercises follow the same teaching philosophy as previously described. A videotape may be shown of a child in the process of solving a problem like, for instance, obtaining parental permission to go camping. During pauses in the tape, the class is asked what steps the model might use to be most successful. The teacher reviews other possible solutions and their consequences.

When the teacher works in small groups, she emphasizes that a solution to a problem best works when one considers such details as when something is done or said, how others might react, and what interpersonal method may yield best results. Step-by-step elaborations are solicited from the group for a number of everyday interpersonal problems (for example, how to get a friend to do something he does not want to do), the teacher probing the group with such questions as: "What is the first thing to do?" The groups of children make lists of steps to use in carrying out each solution.

McClure's role-playing procedure has the children enact a solution after considering and discussing suggestions about how to carry it out. Inadequacies in the step-by-step plan are revealed, and the teacher may stop an enactment for discussion of what might be a problem in the plan and what specific steps might be taken to increase the likelihood of its being effective.

Integration of Problem-Solving Behaviors Unit

Employing videotape, small-group discussion, role playing, and teacher probing and guidance, the purpose of the final unit is to train children to integrate the previously trained parts of the problem-solving process. In each teaching format, a solution is sought, outcomes considered, and attention paid to maximizing success through attention to the step-by-step means comprising any solution plan. As in previous units, the problems selected are always true to life for children of this age, so that they can identify with the characters and find motivation for involvement.

Larcen did not find training to affect scores on his measure of adjustment, and McClure did not examine this issue. Training was shown to enhance internal locus of control and problem solving in a simulated social situation. Neither the Larcen or McClure studies related amount of change in cognitive problem-solving skill to amount of change in overt problem-solving behavior, although alternative thinking consistently emerged as a central capacity.

School Program for Fourth- and Fifth-Grade Children

A curriculum entitled *AWARE: A Curriculum for Social Development* has been designed by Elardo and Cooper (in press) to improve social competence and social development. Vehicles intended to accomplish this goal include: (1) the teaching of cognitive role-taking skills (including understanding the thoughts and feelings of other people) and (2) interpersonal cognitive problem-solving skills.

The problem-solving section is based on the research and, in part, on the general orientation of the nursery program of Shure and Spivack (see Shure, Spivack, and Gordon, 1972;

Spivack and Shure, 1974). Together with lessons in role-taking skills, the program was designed, adapted, and piloted for use by teachers of elementary-school-aged children (Elardo, 1974) and expanded in the form of a handbook for teachers (Elardo and Cooper, in press).

Evaluation has focused on the nine- and ten-year-olds (Elardo and Caldwell, in preparation *b*). While improvement in social role taking has been inconsistent, alternative-thinking skills have improved with use of the program. No test was made of the relationship between change in amount of alternative thinking and amount of behavioral improvement, but Elardo and Caldwell did find significant improvement in classroom adjustment as measured by the Devereux Elementary School Behavior Rating Scale (Spivack and Swift, 1967). Children initially most deviant in these behaviors improved the most. Trained children showed increased respect and concern for others, more ability to function without teacher guidance, a greater amount of attentiveness and less withdrawal, and more involvement and tendency to enter into classroom discussions. There was a tendency for trained children to decrease in amount of disruptive social behavior, and increase in positive behaviors with the teacher. Although comparisons were not made, the more consistent improvement in alternative thinking than in role-taking cognition suggests the behavioral improvement was more a function of the former than of the latter. The implications of these findings for alternative thinking as a mediator of adjustment are discussed in Chapter Three.

The program (Elardo and Cooper, in press) is divided into four sequenced units, with additional techniques for the teacher to use in discipline situations. Emphasis is placed on the incorporation of the program into the total school curriculum through enrichment activities in which learned skills can be exercised. Discussion and role-playing groups meet twice weekly for thirty to forty minutes, the total program being intended to become part of the school curriculum throughout the year.

Unit 1: Getting Acquainted

In the process of getting acquainted, the children suggest rules for the group discussions and reasons for these rules. Goals of the Aware group meetings are discussed with the children. On the second day, the children tell the group something about themselves, such as their hobby, what they did during the summer, what they like to do in their spare time. As a listening exercise, the children are encouraged to try to remember what each child said and, at the end of the session, to try to repeat what they heard about each child. These lessons are followed by an exercise wherein the children practice saying something positive about each other, an introduction to understanding the feelings of others.

Unit 2: Recognizing and Understanding Feelings

The purpose of the sixteen activities in this unit is to increase the children's awareness of their own feelings and those of others, by labeling and by talking about reasons people feel the way they do in a given situation. Emphasized throughout is the notion that causes for feelings differ. The first few lessons focus on vocabulary needed to recognize and understand feelings and are followed by guided group discussions. In one lesson, "Have you ever made someone feel?" the children discuss how their behavior affects the feelings of others. The children are asked questions, supplemented with photographs, designed to help them become aware that what they do affects how other people feel. Questions include, "Have you ever been able to make someone feel happy? What did you do?" Other emotions the children consider include surprise, disappointment, pride, fear, and loneliness. Questions about how the child can make another child experience these emotions are followed by focusing back on the child himself, as by asking, "How do you feel when you make someone else feel disappointed?"

Following the above, the children are guided to role-play

story sequences, taking into account how the different people might feel and the thoughts and feelings of all people involved. The goal of these lessons is to help children become better role-takers, one of the aims of project Aware. In the first role-playing lessons, the following story is told by the teacher:

> Jim screams at his friend, "Billy, you're always
> bugging me. Why do you always have to get in my way?
> I wish I would never see you again."

The sessions are divided into five steps: (1) discussing the situation; (2) rehearsing the situation; (3) explaining the participants' and audience's roles; (4) role playing, and (5) discussing the role playing.

Discussing the situation focuses upon such questions as: "How do you suppose Jim feels?" "How do you suppose Billy feels?" "What might happen next?" "If Billy becomes angry with Jim, what would he say?" (If necessary, a suggestion is given by the teacher, such as, "I don't want to play with you anyway.") "If Billy tries to understand Jim, what would he say?" (If necessary, a suggestion is given by the teacher, such as, "You're really angry. I guess I didn't know I got in your way. Sorry.")

In *rehearsing the situation*, a child pretends to be each character and shows the group how he would act in the situation (such as how Jim would talk to Billy, how Billy might react to Jim). The teacher then *explains* that two people are needed to role-play this situation, acting out several ways they could end the story.

In the fourth phase, that of *role playing*, children play the parts of the characters in the story, initially children who would likely be successful, to model for others.

Finally, the group *discusses the role playing*. The children are asked what they learned about each character, what way they thought was the best in solving the problem, and why. Beginning with the second story (focusing on feelings of pride and happiness), the children are encouraged to begin thinking about other things the role-players could say to each other in the situation.

After five such sessions and a total of seven story situations, the children discuss situations about feelings on days when things do not go well and how they can avoid the problem in the future. The children are given six possible situations such as, "Mary's team lost the game in P.E." Questions include, "How does Mary feel? Has this ever happened to you? Why? What could Mary do so this doesn't happen again?" Situations covering a wide range of feelings are included.

Unit 3: Understanding and Accepting Individual Differences

To help children understand their own uniqueness and to recognize and respect individual differences of others, twelve activities focus specifically on similarities and differences among people. In one game, each child writes down three good characteristics about himself or herself and, when the anonymous list is drawn from a box, the group guesses who wrote the characteristic being read. The idea here is for the group to learn something about each child and to understand that children can have different good characteristics. In another game, the focus switches to describing the strengths of *other* children in the group. Suggestions by the teacher are made, if necessary, with emphasis on how a person's strength can contribute to the group, such as, "If someone is kind and thoughtful this would help create harmony in the group."

Some games in this unit combine earlier games on people's feelings and individual differences. In one lesson, a story is read about how a child's difficulty with spelling creates conflict in the classroom. The child (Martin) is teased (by Howard) about his difficulty and ends up running out of the room. In the story, the teacher (Mrs. James) talks alone with the child and then to the class. In the context of individual differences among children, the group is asked the following questions.

What do you think Mrs. James said to the class? Why do you think Martin ran out of the room?

Why did Howard say something upsetting to Martin?

Why do you think Martin got so upset? What feelings do you suppose the class members have now?

How do you suppose Mrs. James feels? What should happen next? Why? How can the class work together to solve this problem?

Similar exercises are conducted for feelings of jealousy and differences in language ability and ability to express ideas. Except for the latter, each problem story is acted out by the children, if possible. Also included in the unit on individual differences are game activities focusing on people's preferences, physical differences, and attributes that a child values about himself, including awards received.

Unit 4: Developing Social Living Behaviors: Self-Reliance and Respect and Concern for Others

This unit, for which the first three units served as a foundation, has forty activities. The approach is similar to that employed in Unit 2, wherein the children (1) discuss the situation; (2) rehearse the situation; (3) are explained the participants' and audience's roles; and (4) role-play the situation. In addition to understanding feelings and individual differences, emphasis is placed on: (1) naming alternative solutions to problems; (2) naming consequences; and (3) stating causes for behavior.

In the first several lessons, interpersonal situations— typically, getting along with friends, two children in a fight, and what it means to be a friend—are taken through the above four steps and followed by a lesson on causality. Several example situations are presented, such as: "Let's look at 'Meddling Mary' (picture). Mary is always picking fights. Why is Mary always picking fights?" Among other examples are situations involving emotions of silliness, happiness, and jealousy.

After the words *alternative* and *consequences* are thoroughly explained, the group is introduced to problem solving with simple statements of a conflict situation, such as: "Lynn would like to use the jump rope that Andrea is using." First the children identify the problem, then name alternatives, and finally name a consequence for each alternative given.

The final problem-solving games include the complete cycle of discussing the problem through discussing the role playing.

One problem focuses on the difficult choices sometimes involved in making friends. In a story presented to the children, a child (Dick) is asked by the group leader (Phillip) to steal a magazine before he can become a member of the group. First the children identify Dick's problem and discuss how he feels, what he can do, and the possible consequences of what he does. Focus then turns to the other boys in the gang, what they want Dick to do and why. In the second phase, rehearsing the situation, the children choose one alternative given during the discussion and decide on what Dick would say and how he would feel if he used that idea. How the other boys in the gang would respond to Dick is then proposed by the children. In the third phase, that of explaining the participants' and audience's roles, the teacher tells the group that five people are needed to play the parts and the rest will listen and think about other ways to solve the problem. After the children role-play, the children are asked what they think about the alternative that Dick chose, the consequences that occurred, Dick's feelings, the feelings of the other boys, and why. The group role-plays the story a second time, in a different way.

Problems focus on interpersonal conflict between children and adults as well as between children and other children. Many are typical everyday situations that occur in the classroom or on the playground. Each problem is designed to help children recognize important facets involved in interpersonal relations—the reasons for feeling angry and how anger affects others, the value of thinking through a problem before getting angry, the importance of rules in playing games, how intentions must be considered in solving problems.

Interspersed in the final problem-solving section are activities designed to further help children analyze problem situations and to develop strategies for solving them. One such unit, "Solving Problems by Myself," encourages problem solving independent of adult supervision. Children offer as many solutions and consequences as they can to suggested situations, such as, "Your classmates tease you whenever you try to play kickball," "Your teacher leaves the room and someone begins pushing you," "You overhear someone calling your brother a name."

In another activity, "How Do Conflicts Begin and End?" the group is encouraged to observe and record conflicts that actually arise, possibly among younger children. Recorded are the number of children involved, the *cause* of the conflict (the first thing that was said or done), *alternatives* (ways used to resolve the conflict, if any), and *consequences* (how the conflict ended, feelings involved).

The program suggests that teachers use the training approach during the school day, including actual discipline situations that take place, such as fights (Elardo and Caldwell, in preparation *a*). In a manner similar to that developed by Shure and Spivack in their programs for younger children (described earlier in this chapter and in Spivack and Shure, 1974) teachers explore with the children their feelings, the feelings of others involved, alternatives for handling a problem, and the potential consequences.

Treatment Program
for Chronic
Psychiatric Patients

᚛᚛᚛᚛᚛᚛᚛᚛᚛᚛᚛᚛᚛᚛᚛᚛᚜᚜᚜᚜᚜᚜᚜᚜᚜᚜᚜᚜᚜᚜

Siegel and Spivack (1973) have developed a program entitled *Problem-Solving Therapy for Chronic Psychiatric Patients.* The initial success of the Shure and Spivack nursery-school program suggested that a variety of maladjusted groups of different ages might benefit from a structured, educational program designed to teach interpersonal cognitive problem-solving skills. Chronic psychiatric patients came to mind because of the general lack of therapeutic success reported with this group by other approaches. These are patients whose main characteristic (aside from their psychiatric symptomatology) is an obvious social incompetence that displays itself in many social situations. Such patients do not seem to know how to deal with other people in everyday situations. The hope was that a cognitive problem-solving program such as that to be described might teach them general cognitive strategies of use in coping more successfully with other people and dealing with problems that arise within the interpersonal matrix.

The program is designed for use by both professionals and paraprofessionals who work with chronic psychiatric patients. It can be employed either with individual patients or with small groups. It consists of a series of exercises that are gamelike in nature and simple enough for chronic patients to grasp their essentials. Patients find the exercises enjoyable and interesting. At every step there is an attempt to get the patients to relate their real-life problems and to use such problems as examples in which to apply the principles of the program. There are twelve exercises and each exercise takes from about twenty to forty-five minutes. Within exercises, more material can be added by the therapist to increase the depth of the learning experience. Similarly, exercises can be added to expand on each of the four stages.

The program has been employed on both an individual and group basis with about twenty chronic patients in extended aftercare programs following hospitalization. The majority had received a psychotic diagnosis. Regarding the efficacy of the program in changing problem-solving cognition, there is some evidence that patients exposed to the program change in the direction of being better able to think of alternate solutions to hypothetical real-life problems when compared with matched controls. Besides research evidence, there is anecdotal evidence that the program does have some therapeutic impact.

The training exercises that make up the program group themselves into four stages considered necessary for successful problem solving. These are:

(1) The ability to recognize problems
(2) The ability to define problems

    (3) The ability to think of alternative solutions to problems

    (4) The ability to deeide which of the alternative solutions is the best way to solve the problems.

During the initial meeting, when the program is used with individual patients, the therapist conducts a one-hour interview with the patient in which the purpose of the program is explained and the patient's real-life problems are explored.

It is explained to the patient that the program will be of benefit because it will help him deal more effectively with his real-life problems. (At the termination of the program, after the patient has been through the program stages, the therapist attempts to help the patient with these problems.) A brief typed description is given to the patient at the initial meeting. The patient is asked to read while the therapist reads aloud and then to memorize the four steps that make up successful problem solving. The description reads:

> The purpose of this program is to help people learn to solve problems that have caused them trouble. Many people do not know how to go about thinking of the ways to solve problems. There are a number of useful steps in the solving of problems. This program is intended to teach you these steps *and* to give you practice in mastering each of the steps.
> The steps are:
>
> 1. *Recognition of Problems*
> Problems are a part of *real life*. *Everybody* has them. Some people are just better at solving them than others. The *first step* in successful problem solving is to learn how to *recognize* problems. In this first step, you will be given a number of exercises to give you practice to be better at recognizing problems.
> 2. *Definition of Problems*
> After you learn how to better recognize problems, you will be given practice in how to *define* problems clearly by learning how to *find out* about problems and their solutions.

3. *Alternative Ways of Solving Problems*

The third and possibly most important step in problem solving is looking at *alternate ways* of solving
problems.

There may be more ways of solving a problem than
one. Some of the ways may be clearly better than
other ways. To learn this step you will practice
thinking about alternate ways to solve problems.

4. *Deciding Which Solution Is the Best Way To Solve the Problem*

The final step you learn is how to evaluate *different
solutions* to problems, and try to make a *decision*. In
this step you will get practice in looking at the pros
and cons of various solutions to problems, and trying to decide which one is best.

In group treatment the purpose of the program is similarly explained and the group's real-life problems are explored
with the goal of using the principles of the program to aid in
solution of the problems.

Description of the Program

Stage 1. Four exercises provide training in this initial
stage, "Recognition of Problems." The first exercise is intended
to give the patient an experience in paying attention to what he
sees, as a means of being better able to recognize problems when
they occur. The exercise involves the patient's being shown a
series of slides depicting a changing environment (an empty
conference room is first shown, then two women enter and
interact, and finally they exit, leaving the room empty again).
Following his viewing of the slides, the patient is asked questions about them (for example, "Which woman lit a ciga-
rette?"), which test his attention to the slides.

The second exercise is called "Memory for Faces" and is
an attempt to alert the patient to the importance of attentiveness to other people as a significant part of the ability to recognize problems. The patient is shown a slide of a group of peo-

ple. The next slide shows a new group of people with one familiar face from the earlier group. The patient's task is to recognize the familiar face—"Which of these people did you see in the last group?"

The third exercise is called "Magazine Faces." It involves pictures from magazines of people experiencing some emotion (happiness, depression, and so on) and the patient must describe the emotion. After doing this, the patient is asked to make up a story about why the people in the pictures are experiencing the emotion. The exercise is intended to highlight for the patient the importance of recognizing possible interpersonal problems concerning others' feelings.

The last exercise in Stage 1, "Finding Problems," involves showing the patient photographs of people in real-life problem situations. The patient's task is to look at the photographs and tell the therapist what the problem "is." Some problems are: a drunken husband, a fight at a party, and leaving a key in the door lock. The exercise is meant to give the patient some experience in the actual recognition of problems.

In the main, the exercises in Stage 1 are designed to establish a "set" to attend to and to find out about problems, employing simple situations that the patient can appreciate.

Stage 2.   The purpose of this stage is to train the ability to define problems through practice in seeking information about problems. Two exercises provide training in this stage. The first is called "Thirty Questions" and requires that the patient find out what the therapist is thinking about. For example, the therapist thinks of a problem such as "finding a job," or thinks of a common occupation, and the patient must find these out by asking the therapist questions. The task is intended to teach the patient the art of intelligent information gathering as one facet of the ability to define problems. The reasoning here is that the ability to define problems is dependent on being able to gather information about the problem in an organized and systematic fashion. The ostensible limit to the number of guesses is thirty questions, but the game continues until the patient guesses correctly. The therapist aids the patient by teaching him during the exercise to ask questions in a more organized, abstract manner. The therapist can respond to the questions only with yes or no. There are two problems, "finding a job" and "being late for appointments," and one occupation, "fireman." This exercise may be generally useful for patients with thought disturbance aside from its utility as a problem-solving exercise, because it forces the patient to be goal-directed and relevant in his thinking during the exercise. The exercise also draws the patient's attention to the function of language as communication, since it forces the patient to frame his questions to the therapist in an unambiguous and precise way; the questions must be phrased exactly, so that they can be answered by a yes or a no. Chronic psychotic patients are noted for the vagueness and ambiguity of their verbal communication.

Exercise 6 is called "Finding Out about People." This second exercise in Stage 2 is intended to teach the patient how to seek information about other people as part of the ability to define problems. It is explained to the patient that being a successful problem-solver involves the ability to be able to know what important people in one's life think and feel, since the thoughts and feelings of important others are frequently involved in the patient's interpersonal problems.

The patient listens to a series of three cassette tapes that contain little playlets illustrating various ways that people can find out what other people are thinking and feeling. The three ways of finding out about other people are: (1) asking direct questions about what they might be thinking and feeling, (2) indirectly bringing up the subject that you want information about, and (3) not taking the word of a third party about the person in whom you are interested but interacting with the person directly. For example, in a tape that exemplifies the first way of finding out what people might be thinking and feeling, two housewives are talking. One bemoans the fact that she and her husband cannot have children. The second wife suggests that adoption is also a way to have children. It develops that the first wife has thought about adoption but has never directly asked her husband how he feels about it. She is urged to ask him and does. She finds out that he is in favor of adopting a baby.

After the playlet, the therapist asks the patient how the child-less wife found out what she wanted to know from her husband. If the patient has difficulty in verbalizing the concept, the therapist aids him. After each of the other two playlets, the therapist attempts to ensure that the patient has grasped the principles. Following all three playlets, the therapist asks the patient three questions to determine whether or not the principles have been learned. These are:

(1) Is asking somebody what he thinks about something finding out about people directly or indirectly?
(2) How would you go about finding out something about somebody indirectly (that is, without coming right out and asking them)?
(3) A friend tells you that another person is not trust-worthy. How would you find out if this other person is untrustworthy without taking your friend's word?

Stage 3. Two exercises provide training for Stage 3, which is designed to train in the ability to think of alternative solutions for four interpersonal problems. Exercise 7 is called "Finding Alternatives." This task has the patient finding alternative solutions to four interpersonal problems. This exercise is meant to give the patient graphic practice in recognizing that there are different solutions to the same problem. The exercise requires that the patient look at a colored drawing of an interpersonal problem and then at a drawing that describes the person having resolved the problem. For example, the first problem is "loneliness." The problem picture that illustrates this has a young man sitting disconsolately in a chair thinking (in a comic-strip bubble above his head), "I'm lonely; I'd like to make some friends." The picture that illustrates the resolution of this problem depicts the same young man speaking on the phone, saying, "A party? Great! I'll come; . . . see you all later." After being shown these two drawings, the patient is shown eight separate drawings representing different means of solving the problem of loneliness. He is told that the drawings represent different ways of solving the problem and that his job is to name and pick out the different solutions and put the cards (within each solution) in logical order so as to solve the problem. Of the eight cards, two pictures show the young man meeting people at a church social club, three pictures show him interacting with coworkers, and three pictures show him interacting with his neighbors. The therapist guides the patient, if he has difficulty in picking out the separate solutions, and makes the point that there are different ways of solving problems or different paths to a common goal. This last point (different ways of solving problems) is made concretely by lining up the picture cards in the following fashion: problem, different sets of solutions, and, finally, resolution. The therapist points to the pictures while verbalizing that the different picture solutions will all get the lonely young man from the problem picture to the resolution picture. There are four problems: (1) loneliness, (2) finding a job, (3) making up after a marital quarrel, and (4) finding a girlfriend.

Exercise 8 is called "Creating Alternatives." This second exercise in Stage 3 has the patient generate his own solutions to given problems. The exercise is intended to give the patient practice in thinking of (rather than recognizing, as in Exercise 7) alternative solutions to problems. Stage 3 is viewed as quite important in the training of successful interpersonal problem solving. In this stage the patient is asked not only to recognize a number of alternate solutions to problems but to begin to generate, on his own, solutions to problems.

There are three problems: (1) getting along with your boss, (2) amusing yourself when alone, and (3) changing the annoying behavior of a friend. The patient is presented with the problems singly, provided with pencil and paper, and asked to write as many solutions as he can think of to each of the problems. The therapist encourages the patient to record as many possible solutions as he can think of and verbally reinforces whatever the patient produces. For example, for "amusing oneself when alone" one patient listed playing records, reading a book, listening to radio, and looking at TV.

Stage 4. Three exercises provide training for the final step, the ability to decide which alternative solution is the best way to solve a problem.

Exercise 9 is called "Impulsivity-Reflection Slides." The exercise is meant to dramatically demonstrate to the patient that the initial, frequently impulsively chosen solution to a problem is often not the best solution and that it is better to wait and reflect on other possible solutions before taking action. It involves the use of three sets of slides illustrating models coping with various problem situations, at first in an impulsive, ineffectual fashion and then coping with the same problem in a more reflective way. For example, in the first problem, a model is shown filling out an employment application impulsively, with the result that she puts her last name in the space on the form reserved for "first name," does not leave sufficient room in the address space to put in her city and state, and reverses two digits in her Social Security number. The result is a crossed-out, sloppy-looking application. Following this impulsive approach, the same model takes a fresh employment application, and reads the entire thing through slowly and carefully. She approaches each item on the form in a careful fashion; she looks up her Social Security number before she writes it, for example, and gets it down correctly. The result, in this reflective mode, is a neat, carefully filled-in form. In similar fashion, two other problems are depicted: getting change for a dollar (in the impulsive mode, the model doesn't count her change and claims that she has been shortchanged) and leaving one's handbag behind in a waiting room.

Before the slides are shown, the patient is oriented to the exercise by being told that doing the first thing that comes to mind to solve a problem may be the wrong thing to do since, if one waited, one might find a better solution to the problem. After the exercises the patient is asked a number of simple questions intended to determine how well he has learned the difference between an impulsive and a reflective solution. The questions are:

(1) Is taking an apartment that rents for $250.00 a month, when you earn only $2.00 an hour, an impulsive or a reflective solution to the problem of finding a place to live?

(2) Is making up a shopping list before you go to a supermarket reflective or impulsive?

(3) A company sends you a credit card. Is going out the same day and charging $300.00 worth of clothing on the card reflective or impulsive?

(4) Is having a set routine for doing housework that you follow every week reflective or impulsive?

Exercise 10 is called "Decision-Faces." It is intended to give the patient practice in generating solutions to problems and in considering the advantages and disadvantages of alternate solutions. This exercise is an important one, since it forces the patient not only to recognize different solutions to problems but also to enumerate the advantages and disadvantages of each solution. Then the patient makes a decision about which is the best solution to the problem, based on his consideration of the advantages and disadvantages. The exercise then provides the patient with an opportunity to actually make a decision after considering all possibilities.

The exercise involves three sets of slides of people caught in situations where they must make a decision between two choices. The three problems are: (1) whether or not to return a lost wallet to the owner, (2) whether to let somebody else use a pay phone first when their reason for using it seems important, and (3) whether or not to take your children to the zoo as promised or watch the Superbowl game with a friend also as promised. In the first set of slides, a man is depicted walking down the street. He discovers a wallet stuffed with money on the ground. He pockets the wallet and continues walking to a point where he encounters a second man who is searching the ground, obviously looking for something. The searcher confronts the finder and asks him if he has found a wallet. (The therapist explains the action even though the situation is apparent to patients without spoken dialogue.) The final slide shows a closeup of the finder's face after he has been asked if he found the wallet. He is obviously in a conflict situation and has two choices: to return the wallet or to lie to the seeker about finding it (and keep it). The patient is then asked what the finder's two choices are. After responding, the patient is then asked to list all of the advantages of his first named choice—for example, if he doesn't give the wallet back, he gets to keep all that money. He then is asked for disadvantages—for example, if he keeps the wallet he would feel bad. Similarly, the other choice has its advantages and disadvantages listed. After listing the advantages and disadvantages, the patient is then asked to think carefully about the two choices, their advantages and disadvantages, and to make a decision between choices as if he were the person in the slides who had to make the decision. The other two choice situations are presented in similar fashion.

Exercise 11 is called "Decision-Tapes." This exercise is essentially the same as Exercise 10, with the three choice situations on cassette tapes to give the patient further practice via an audio rather than a visual modality. The three choices are: (1) whether to go to a movie with your best friend or go to a party, (2) whether to take an immediately available $2.00-an-hour job or wait for a $4.00-an-hour job that may or may not materialize, and (3) whether to marry an older person now or wait to marry a younger one.

Exercise 12 is called "Plays." This final exercise is intended to give the patient practice in all four stages of problem solving. This exercise is also on cassette tapes. Six problem situations are presented in dramatic form as little playlets. These are: (1) a lonely bored wife whose husband works nights, (2) a dispute between roommates, (3) loneliness, (4) speech anxiety, (5) an unfair, demanding husband, and (6) a snoring husband. The patient is told at the beginning of the exercise that he is going to listen to a series of skits on tape about people in various problem situations. His job is to listen to the skits closely and tell the therapist what the problem is, how the people involved might be feeling, and the different ways that the problem might be solved with the advantages and disadvantages of each solution; finally, he is to decide on the best possible solution. For example, Skit 4, "Speech Anxiety," consists of the following dialogue:

> Narrator: In this skit Bob has just met his friend Herb.
> Bob: Hi, Herb. How ya doin'?
> Herb: Okay. How are you? How's college?
> Bob: (Worriedly) Okay I guess. Well, maybe not okay.

Herb: What's the matter?
Bob: (With feeling) Aw, I have to give a short talk
          in my speech class, and I'm scared to death.
          Talking in front of groups of people really
          makes me terrified.

Patients identify the problem here readily, a frequent
solution in this instance being, "Memorize the speech so that
he knows it very well." During the process of identifying the
problem, generating alternate solutions, and deciding which is
the best solution, the therapist positively reinforces the
patient's efforts and keeps encouraging the patient to continue
with the problem solution process if he seems resistant.
Regarding the final decision process, it is stressed to the patient
that if what seems to be the best solution is tried and does not
work, then the next best solution can be tried, and so on down
the line. This final exercise builds on all the previous 11 exercises since it involves all the skills they teach.

At the completion of the program, the therapist refers to
the list of personal problems that the patient raised in the initial interview. He encourages the patient to bring his newly
acquired problem-solving skills to bear upon his own
problems.

For example, finding a job was a problem listed by one
patient. During the postprogram discussion between the therapist and the patient, the patient was able to list a number of possible solutions to this problem. He included newspaper ads,
talking to friends about possible jobs, and the state employment office. The interplay between therapist and patient in
the postprogram session went generally in the following
fashion: After the problem was mentioned by the therapist, the
patient was asked how many solutions he could think of to
solve the problem. Every solution was positively reinforced by
the therapist, even though in his judgment some solutions were
obviously going to be ineffective in solving the problem. The
therapist's comment following a poor solution was, "Okay,
good, you've thought of another solution. We'll see how good
or bad it is when we look at the advantages and disadvantages."

During the generating of alternative solutions, the therapist constantly encouraged the patient to think of more solutions— "That's good. Can you think of anything else?"

The therapist may also suggest solutions to the patient when the patient has obviously stopped trying to generate new solutions. When the therapist decides that there are no more possible solutions to the problem, he asks the patient to consider the advantages and disadvantages of each of the possible solutions. For example, one patient gave "going to bars" as a solution to the problem of meeting women.

Therapist: Any good points about that solution?

Patient: I may meet some person I like.

Therapist: Sure. That's what you're in there for—you could meet somebody. Okay, any bad points about that solution compared to the others?

Patient: I always have a fear of meeting people off-hand, you know? Because sometimes they may be setting up just to rob me.

Therapist: Okay, so there's kind of a danger about going to a bar. You never know what you're going to run into—what kind of people. The girl might be setting you up for a guy to rob you. Any other bad points about the bar to meet girls?

Patient: No. I can't think of any offhand.

Therapist: Well, you might get drunk. Compared to the other two solutions [buying new clothes and having a popular female relative introduce him to her friends] this one might get you into a fight. That happens in bars too. So the bar could be very unpleasant. Okay. So you've got three solutions to this problem of meeting girls and you kind of looked at the good points and the bad points just the way I taught you in the program. Can you make a decision? Which solution do you think you would try first?

Patient: Meeting girls by having my sister introduce me. Meeting girls she knows.

Therapist: Okay, that certainly sounds like a good first solution. Good. Do you get the idea? Just like we did in the program, I'd like you to think about solutions in this way. Think of all the possible solutions and then look at the good points and the bad points. Then after you've kind of thought it over, then try to make a decision as to which solution is the best—it's got more in it for you: the advantages are bigger, the good points are bigger and the bad points are smaller.

It is stressed to the patient that if his first solution doesn't work, he can always try the second solution.

The program has been employed mostly with individuals but has been tried with a small group of chronic patients in a partial-hospitalization setting. This was an ongoing therapy group and not an experimental one. During the course of the twelve exercises which, for various reasons, were strung out over several months, new members came into the group and others departed. It was impossible to orient new members to everything that had gone on before they arrived, but there was a brief orientation to the four stages of successful problem solving.

During the actual exercises, every attempt was made to involve even the most withdrawn patients by such remarks as, "Sue, you haven't said anything so far about the advantages of going to the party rather than going to the movies. What do you think?" In the actual exercises, the group achieved a richness of problem solution greater than was achieved by most of the individual patients because the more verbal and active members seemed to try to outdo each other in responding. At every session, every attempt was made to hear an actual problem of one of the patients, and the group attempted to help the patient with the problem. The therapist guided the group in the successive stages of problem solving. In effect this meant that, during the early sessions dealing with the first two stages, the therapist had to jump ahead conceptually and make sure the group was also knowledgeable about later stages of problem solving. This did not seem to noticeably confuse the patients.

Experience with the program has suggested that patients who will not benefit from the program fall into the following classes:

(1) *Patients who are acutely disturbed:* This is the case because extreme anxiety is generally found in such patients, and the patient is so concerned with his anxiety that he cannot concentrate on the program.

(2) *Brain-damaged patients:* The program does have a certain complexity and brain-damaged patients seem to become confused by this. They persist on earlier exercises when the later exercises are being taught.

(3) *Mentally retarded patients:* The program is generally too complex for such patients.

The therapist, in carrying out the program with both individuals and groups, should be directive, emotive, enthusiastic, and optimistic. Chronic patients are generally so apathetic that they have to be constantly motivated and inspired in the belief that they can make constructive changes in their lives through the program.

Group Therapy
Program for
Young Adults
and Adults

Platt, Spivack, and Swift (1974) originally designed, and Platt and Spivack (1976) further developed, a highly structured program for adolescents and adults entitled *Interpersonal Problem-Solving Group Therapy*. This therapy program is based on three separate areas of knowledge. The first and primary one is the research by Platt, Spivack, and their associates, which has identified specific areas of problem solving in which psychiatric patients and other maladjusted groups are deficient and which thus should be the focus of any attempt at effecting adjustment through the modification of problem-solving thinking.

A second body of research provided specific tasks and techniques that were adapted for use in this program. For instance, Spohn and Wolk (1963) successfully used a discussion task to improve social participation in schizophrenics, and this task has been incorporated in Unit 5 of the program. Likewise Sarason and Ganzer (1969) have reported the successful use of a modeling and discussion technique in the treatment of institutionalized delinquents, and this general technique has been used throughout the nineteen units. Similar use has been made of Meichenbaum and Cameron's (1973) technique of training patients to talk to themselves, and McFall's (McFall and Marston, 1970; McFall and Lillesand, 1971) behavioral rehearsal technique. A modification of Kagan's (1965) Matching Familiar Figures Task has also been adapted as a training task, as has a modification of Draughton's (1973) technique of duplicating facial expressions (Unit 5) and Morton's (1955) use of the TAT as a training technique (Unit 5).

The third body of knowledge, again in the area of techniques on which the program has drawn, consists of the training exercises developed by Siegel and Spivack (1973) specifically for the training of interpersonal problem-solving skills in chronic schizophrenic patients. These include the exercises that deal with finding new facts, making decisions, and presenting one's point of view.

The program originally took the form of a detailed script intended for use by the group leader. The script included suggested instructions to the group, including the dialogues to be used, as well as instructional guidelines for the group leader in dealing with problem situations. Also included were basic materials for group exercises on specific problem-solving skills. A parallel workbook (Platt and Spivack, 1976) was subsequently developed for use by the group members themselves. This workbook includes most of the exercises and illustrations that are to be found in the leader's script, as well as additional exercises developed after the original group leader's manual was prepared, omitting only the detailed instructions for the group leader.

A set of procedural guidelines for users of the program is also available. These guidelines evolved out of experience in using the program with various types of maladjusted groups, including acute and chronic psychiatric patients and incarcerated youthful heroin offenders. Formal evaluation of this program is currently in progress.

Intagliata (1976) has already evaluated a 10-session adaptation of this program as part of a treatment program for male alcoholics. The results of his evaluation indicate that the treatment group showed significantly more improvement from pre- to post-testing in the number of relevant and effective means generated on the MEPS procedure than did the controls. In a structured discharge readiness interview administered shortly before leaving the hospital, treatment subjects also told of significantly more specific plans, anticipated more obstacles, reported having considered a greater number of alternative strategies for dealing with anticipated problems, and said that they had already taken more steps to formulate and activate plans than had controls. Furthermore, a preliminary follow-up of treatment subjects showed that 14 of the 22 subjects contacted one month after the completion of the program had made use, in a variety of specific problem situations that they encountered, of the problem-solving principles they had been taught.

Structure of the Program

The program consists of nineteen units roughly divided into two major groupings. The first half of the nineteen-unit program comprises a sequenced series of lessons to train skills deemed necessary to enable an individual to implement the specific problem-solving skills focused on in the second half of the program. The decision to include these specific prerequisite skills (such as the ability to differentiate fact from opinion) was based on experience in piloting problem-solving programs with a number of patient and offender groups. Experience indicates that the units dealing with prerequisite skills are most useful for groups that are significantly deficient in problem-solving skills. Where the social competence of the group is more optimal, certain of the early units may be omitted without seriously affecting the program. For instance, when using the program with a group of relatively competent outpatients who have a high level of educational attainment, the use of the earlier units may be inappropriate. On the other hand, these same units may be particularly valuable when the group is composed of patients with serious impairment, a low level of social skills and educational attainment, or history of failure at even relatively uncomplicated interpersonal situations. A general overriding consideration should be the recognition that the program was designed to be flexible. Where the use of a particular unit seems to the therapist to be unrealistic or inappropriate for a particular group, it should be deleted.

The early units should also be seen as a useful introduction to the notion of problem solving as an important element in interpersonal relationships. They also establish a didactic or teaching/learning set, and aid in establishing rapport between the leader(s) and the group members.

The time period required for implementation of the program is somewhat flexible. Therefore, while the original conception was that at least a single weekly session should be devoted to each of the units, with more than one session for a group that started with a particularly low level of social skills, it is recognized that in many clinical situations a nineteen-week period of time for the program may be unrealistic because of instability of group membership. Again, where units must be omitted because of time constraints, it is suggested that it be the earlier ones, dealing with prerequisite skills, that are omitted.

Certain general themes are emphasized throughout the program. These ideas include: (1) that problems are solvable; (2) that the focus of the program is on problems of an interpersonal nature; (3) that interpersonal problems are a common part of everyday life for everybody; (4) that the group members should see the group as a place to bring immediate problems with which they are now faced and which they are attempting to solve; and (5) that the proper temporal focus of the group is the present and the future, not the past. This last point deserves further elaboration. The group leader clearly states that the group is different in its time orientation from others in which the patients may have been involved. In interpersonal problem-solving therapy, the appropriate focus is on how to solve the problems with which one is now faced and *not* upon events that have already occurred, such as those that led to the development of one's "problem."

In carrying out the program, major emphasis is placed on encouraging the group members themselves to *generate* as many of the elements of the problem-solving process as possible. Also, where possible, the focus of the group is on actual, current problems rather than on hypothetical ones. The only exceptions to this rule might be during the first session, when the group leader wishes to initiate group discussion about a problem in order to illustrate some aspects of the problem-solving process or, later in the program, when he knows there is a problem in the group or a common problem among members that has not been spontaneously brought forth for discussion. For instance, the group members may be having common difficulties in coping with a fellow patient or even a staff member over a particular issue, and the group leader may wish to discuss ways of solving this kind of problem by applying the principles covered up to that point by the program without referring directly to the actual situation.

Finally, group members are encouraged to bring their *current* problems to the group for assistance in solving them. To facilitate this, the last part of each group session is specifically designated as a time during which the group members may (and should) do this.

The Program

Unit 1. "Get Set To Be a Problem-Solver in Your Own Life." Unit 1 attempts to establish a noncritical and productive group atmosphere in which problems can be recognized and

discussed. To do this the leader makes the following statement
to the group:

> Problems are recognizable. There are skills you
> can learn . . . skills to help you feel better and happier . . .
> skills to solve your problems. To solve your problems
> and be happier you have to *want* to try. . . . In this group
> we will listen to problems and try to think of ways to
> solve them. Everyone in the group will have to help try-
> ing to solve his own problems and will have chances to
> try to help others. In other words, this is a place where
> we will listen to one another. We will NOT be talking
> about why a problem can not be solved or how hard it is
> to solve a problem which keeps one from being happy.
> Anybody can tell you why you can't solve your prob-
> lems. We all know people who say *you can't do it,* and
> put you down. Maybe even you have said, *I can't do it,*
> and put yourself down. In everything that happens we
> will look for our part in it.

The first task is designed to help the group define problems by learning how to recognize them. The first step in this
process focuses on the subjective feelings associated with having problems. To do this the group leader asks each member of
the group to suggest a way in which he or she is able to tell
when he or she has a problem. Questions useful in priming the
group might be, "Do you feel differently when you have a problem?" or "Do you ever notice that people act differently when
they have a problem?" or "What kinds of things do people do
when they have problems?" The aim of using these questions
is to generate discussion of how to identify cues involved in
problem recognition. As a concluding statement, the leader
would review what had been said by the group members by
saying:

> Yes, you have a problem when you feel unhappy,
> you feel that something is wrong, or you notice that
> somebody acts a certain way toward you, like they don't

listen to you. Other ways in which we know where we
have a problem are. . . .

As part of the real-life problem discussion period concluding the session, the group members are asked to generate a
list of common problems people have, with the focus on those
of an interpersonal nature. In doing this, the leader continually
focuses attention on the interpersonal aspects of problems,
encourages group members to contribute their ideas to the discussion, and maintains a nonjudgmental attitude toward the
suggestions made by the group.

A final part of the first meeting is devoted to providing a
problem for the group to work on before the next meeting. One
form this assignment takes is to suggest a problem to the group
for which they must "write down all the ideas you can think of
as to how to solve this problem."

Unit 2. "Learn the Facts: I." The second unit attempts
to delineate the essential differences between facts and opinions
in human interactions as an important element in problem
solving. The group members are told:

It is necessary to learn the difference between
what we actually see and what we assume about what
we see if we are to solve our problems successfully. In
order to be able to separate facts from opinions we
watch and we listen carefully to really find out what is
happening.

The first task, employing TAT cards, requires the group
to decide what constitutes fact or opinion in a description of
each pictured scene. The aim here is to highlight the distinction between reality and fantasy, imagination, or opinion by
establishing that facts in interpersonal situations are facts
because we actually see them (that is, we can answer yes to the
question, "Do you actually *see* it?"). *Opinion,* on the other
hand, is presented as reflecting what we feel, imagine, or believe
about a situation while not actually seeing it. We infer it, however, from what we actually *do* see.

A second task stresses the importance of being observant by requiring the group to listen to a skit and then answer certain "factual" questions about what they've seen. The group leader then introduces a discussion of "How might we find out if our *opinion* is also a fact?" This is intended to elicit statements such as, "You could ask him how he felt," "You could look for yourself to see if it were really that way," and so forth.

Unit 3. "Learn the Facts: II." This unit deals with the importance of being observant in discovering facts about the environment. The necessity to pay attention to details is introduced in the first task. TAT cards are flashed at the group, which is then required to describe as much of the scene as they can remember. The second task focuses on the kinds of cues that could be used in remembering faces. Throughout the session, the following principle is referred to by the group leader: "It is important to distinguish fact from feeling or opinion, as we learned last time. But it is also very important to look for all the facts and details in a problem situation. Pay attention. Look carefully."

Unit 4. "Learn the Facts: III." This unit focuses on ways of obtaining more information about interpersonal situations than that which is available through observation. As the group members are told: "Stop! Look! And *ask!* To get information you need you have to ask questions. You can't depend *only* on what you see. Sometimes you don't see everything present in a situation because all the facts you need to solve the problem are not readily available. In these cases you have to reach out and obtain more information by asking someone who has it. Today we will learn how to get more information from other people."

For the first task, a tape is presented that illustrates the principle of asking direct questions. A second tape, of fragmented sentences, requires the group to ask questions designed to obtain the missing information. The essential characteristics of good questions are discussed in light of efficiently obtaining information. These tasks were adopted from the program developed by Siegel and Spivack (1973; see also Chapter Thirteen of this book).

For one home study task, each group member obtains another group member's telephone number and address. He must contact this individual to practice asking questions to obtain more information. The focus is to be on finding out about a problem the other person was having that week, which includes using the training elements learned up to this point, and generating with the person alternative ways of solving his problem.

Unit 5. "The Facts As Others See Them." The tasks in this unit were designed to illustrate the fact that people often have different points of view and that understanding this is important to solving problems. The first task is simply to list favorite foods and TV programs to show that within the group not everyone shares the same likes and dislikes. The principle is reinforced in the second task of interpreting a TAT card scene, in which individual differences in interpretations are pointed out—for instance, the fact that one group member sees a figure as a "father" and another as just "an older man," while this figure may be seen as "upset" by one individual or as "not being in any particular mood" by another group member. Such conflicting interpretations serve as good points of departure for the group leader, who should suggest that because of our unique perceptions of things, people, moods, and so forth, we may each be prepared to respond differently to the same stimuli. Thus, the "facts" may be different to each of us, and furthermore, even when we do tend to agree on them, we may still wish to take different courses of action as a result. The session ends with the leader asking the group how they may apply the lessons learned in the session to their own lives. He may ask, for instance, if we should expect others to agree entirely with us when we form an opinion about what the facts are or, more importantly, about whether or not we should undertake a particular course of action.

Unit 6. "Recognizing Feelings: I." Unit 6 deals with recognizing how other people feel as an important guide in solving problems. As the leader indicates: "Being able to recognize the way other people feel about things or letting them know how you feel is very important to your being a good problem-solver. Why should this be so? Because it will help you to decide what you should do or should not do. Suppose that someone you are with is doing something you don't like. How could you let him know you didn't like it? You might ask him to stop doing it. But sometimes you're embarrassed or feel it's impolite and so you don't say anything. Now how else can you let the person know you want him to stop?" The group leader then guides the group to generate more subtle ways of informing someone of your displeasure, such as by acting uncomfortable (fidgeting, frowning, and so on) or changing the subject. The first task encourages the group to distinguish between verbal and nonverbal methods of communicating. The second provides group members with practice in nonverbal communication in structured situations, with the group evaluating methods of individual effectiveness.

The real-life problem discussion period involves the group members in presenting situations from their own lives where being able to recognize the way someone else is feeling could be important. Group members are guided to discuss how ideas learned in this unit could be applied to these situations. In this regard, the group leader might say, "Now that we have discussed how to tell someone something without actually doing so directly, can you think of any recent instances where someone was trying to give you a message without telling you directly?" or "Have you used any of these cues we have discussed to give a message to anyone else recently?"

Unit 7. "Communicating Feelings: II." Unit 7 concentrates on recognizing and generating facial expressions as an important mode of communication. The first two tasks require the group to identify feelings from facial expressions in photographs and to imitate these expressions. To facilitate learning of these facial expressions, the group members practice in pairs before the group, with the group providing feedback to the actors. Each group member is also provided with a small mirror so that he or she can obtain feedback at any time. This mirror is also used outside the group. The group members are told, "Take out the mirror and look at your expression when you are feeling a strong emotion. Also, practice trying to let someone know by your facial expression alone how you feel about something. Do this in front of a mirror at first, and maybe later on, after you're good at it, try to have other people guess what you're feeling. Do this all without using any words at all. Do it just for ten minutes each day. The feelings you should try communicating are [happiness, sadness, and so on]." In the third task the group members role-play situations in which one member must communicate his response to a request solely through facial expressions. For instance, each group member is told to respond, by means of facial expression, to such requests as, "How would you like to go to Joe's party?" or "Can you loan me five dollars?" The group then decides if the answer is unambiguous, and is asked to demonstrate other ways of communicating the reply by facial expression.

Unit 8. "Tricks of the Problem-Solving Trade: I." This unit concentrates on specific methods that may be used to aid one's memory. In the tasks, the group members describe various techniques they have used to remember specific conversations while a list is made of all their suggestions and then discussed. The group members draw on this list in obtaining information over the telephone, regarding such things as train schedules, show times, and so forth.

Unit 9. "Tricks of the Problem-Solving Trade: II." Building upon material presented in Units 5 and 6, Unit 9 attempts to train memory for faces as well as continuing to indirectly train attentiveness to facial expression. Photographs of faces are shown to the group members, and they are then required to pick these faces out of a larger group of pictures. In doing so, attention is drawn by the leader to the facial expressions shown by the models, and the group is asked to infer the mood of the model. An additional purpose of this unit is to begin to introduce self-directed language as a mediating mechanism in problem solving. Another exercise often used requires group members to pick a familiar face out of a crowd of people in a photograph. Attention to detail is stressed as a necessary part of a self-directed verbal statement. For instance, when a face is identified, the leader may ask the group member: "Joe, how did you know it was B?" The leader tries to shape the group member's response until an indication that some self-directed verbal statement is used is obtained. When it is obtained, or it becomes obvious that the group member cannot provide it, the leader goes on to another group member, repeating the process until the entire group is covered.

The leader then shares with the group a "trick" he uses to remember faces himself. He carefully goes over the picture, talking (as if to himself) about specific details of the face (hair color, facial shape, and so on). He tries to point out unusual characteristics, sometimes suggesting, "He looks like _____." The leader uses the same picture as previously, then has the group members repeat the process together. Then he says, "Okay. Now let's go on to the next picture, using the system we just learned."

Unit 10. "Don't Leap to Conclusions." Unit 10 introduces the concept of taking time to think before coming to a decision as necessary in reaching the right decision. This is illustrated in the first exercise, in which the group, using a procedure similar to Kagan's Matching Familiar Figures Task, must correctly match a figure with an identical one from a group of very similar figures. The similarity of the figures requires careful attention to detail. As the group performs, discussion focuses on the advantages of "thinking before acting." The use of self-directed statements is emphasized here as a guide in making the correct choice. This is evident in the following statement by the group leader:

> Now, before we look at the next figure, let me show you a trick I use to help me pick the right one. Watch how I do it. [*Leader looks at task and says out loud.*] Now, what is it that I have to do? I have to find the one picture which is just like the one on the other page. Is it the first one? Are the ears the same? Let me look back at the other page. Yes, they are. What about the hair? Yes, it's the same as in the other picture. What about the mouth—is it the same? No, it's not. In the other picture the mouth is open, here it is closed. So it's not this first picture. Okay, now I'll look at the second picture, but I have to take my time and not hurry. First,

the ears. Yes, they're the same. Now the hair. Yes, it's
the same. Now the mouth. Yes, it's the same; . . . okay,
this one is exactly the same as the picture on the other
page. Finished. I did it. Now, I want you all to look at
your books and follow along with me while I do the task
again. Now, you do the task, talking out loud as you do
it. Now do it again, whispering to yourself this time.
Now do it without talking out loud. Good, now let's try
another one. This time by yourselves, talking out loud
while you do it. Now, do it once, but don't talk out loud
this time. Just talk to yourself silently.

The real-life problem discussion and home study assignment attempt to introduce the notions of taking time to make a
decision and also the usefulness of self-directed statements in
such situations in the daily life of the group member. In the
real-life problem discussion, the group leader emphasizes the
former point by introducing the following discussion after the
matching tasks have been completed.

Now, see how much better you are at picking the
right thing when you take your time. Has anyone ever
been in a situation where they did the wrong thing or
came to the wrong conclusion, because they did it too
fast? Make believe you had to do it over again. How
would you approach the situation now? What would
you say to yourself while you were doing it?

The leader concludes the group session by giving the following assignment to the group:

Practice talking to yourself during the week
while you are trying to apply problem solving to your
own life. If you feel bad about something, say to yourself, "Why do I feel this way? Is it because of _____, or
is it because of _____?" and so on until you find out
what it is. Before you decide how to deal with your
problem, say to yourself, "I'm going to take my time
solving this problem and not rush into it."

Unit 11. "Tricks of the Problem-Solving Trade: III." Unit 11 further emphasizes the principle of thinking out loud as one of the ways to clearly define and think through a problem. Several stories are presented as exercises in which the group must state the problem facing the protagonist. Defining the problem is shown to be the first step in arriving at a solution. Use is made again in this unit of cartoons presenting problem situations in which Sam and Fred, two characters who were introduced earlier, are faced with problems that they must solve:

> Here are some other problem situations Sam is in. Help him state what the problem is. Your second task is to think of ways for Sam to solve his problem. Say them out loud and then write down all the ideas you can think of to solve the problem.

One problem situation in which Sam is depicted is that of being stopped by a traffic policeman. Sam is saying to himself, "I'm sure I wasn't speeding, but how do I convince him [the policeman]?"

Use is also made of situations from the means-ends procedure, such as, "Sam had just moved in that day and didn't know anyone. He wanted to have friends in the neighborhood. What can he do to make friends?"

The group leader guides the group to statements of the problem, such as, "Sam is lonely" or "Sam has no one to call upon for help if he should need it." After the possible problems are exhausted, the group turns to generating as many solutions as possible for this problem.

Unit 12. "Generating Alternatives." This unit focuses specifically on generating alternative solutions to interpersonal problem situations. The leader points out:

> We are more likely to be successful at solving our problems if we can think of and talk about a lot of ways of handling our problems. That way if one way does not work, we can try another way.

The group then discusses the possible *additional* ways of solving the problems they were given as homework in the preceding unit. The emphasis here is exclusively on the *generation* of alternatives rather than on an evaluation of their appropriateness. A series of problems with which Sam has been confronted are presented.

> A problem Sam has at times, even when he knows the problem, is how to tell someone he does not want to do something. Sometimes, for instance, the boss tells Sam to do something that he really does not want to do or that he thinks he should not do. When this happens, how can Sam tell the boss that he does not want to do it? Below are several other situations Sam sometimes finds himself in. Help him get out of them by giving him things to say or to do. Remember that the more ways of solving these problems that Sam has available, the more likely it is that he will be successful in doing so.

Unit 13. "Consequences." Building upon Unit 12, this unit orients the group toward evaluating alternative courses of action. The first task involves careful consideration of possible consequences of each alternative suggested in the preceding unit discussion.

> Last time, we tried to think of all the things Sam could do or say when he had certain problems with other people. Let's go over them now and see if we thought of *all* of the possible things that Sam could have done.
> Now, which of these do you think he should have done? What could have happened if he had chosen _____? What else could have happened? What might have happened if he had decided to do _____? Which do you think was the best thing to do? Why? That's right, because it resulted in his getting what he wanted, namely, _____. So maybe we not only have to think of a number of things to do in a problem situation, that is, of solving the problem, but also of what might happen

if we try each of these ways. Now, let's try another of the problems from last time.

The second exercise presents a series of sets of illustrations depicting people caught in situations where they have to make a choice between two alternatives. The exercise is intended to give the group members practice in considering the advantages and disadvantages of alternative solutions to problems, as an aid in teaching them to be better decision-makers. The group practices considering the advantages and the disadvantages of the two choices in accordance with the following principle:

> Every time we think of something we could do to solve a problem, we have to think about what might happen if we do that particular thing. If we think about this *before* we actually do anything it helps us to see what is really the best thing to do.

After the presentation of each problem situation, the leader asks the group for the possible choices in the situations, and all the possible advantages and disadvantages of each. Each group member is then asked for the choice he or she would make in that situation and for the reasoning behind that choice.

Unit 14. "Practicing What You Have Learned." Three central concepts have been introduced in the immediately preceding units: Defining the problem, thinking of alternatives, and considering consequences. Unit 14 serves as a review of these problem-solving principles and introduces the idea of defining a goal: "What do you want; what are you after with this person?"

As part of the review process, the self-interrogation/direction sequence to follow in a problem situation is presented for discussion by the group members:

(1) Why do I feel this way?
(2) I'm going to take my time solving this problem and not rush into it.
(3) What can I do to solve this problem and make myself feel good? What else, what else?

(4) What will happen if I do the first thing I thought of?
     What else?
(5) What will happen if I do the second thing I thought
     of? What else?
(6) What is the thing to do that will lead to what I want
     to happen?
(7) Okay, now, that's what I'll do!

Individual group member's problems often serve as focal
points for discussion at this time.

Unit 15. "The Facts as Others See Them." Unit 15
deals with the ability to see a situation from another person's
viewpoint. As the group leader says,

> We now know that, once we have sensed that a
> problem exists, we need a plan or an approach to solv-
> ing that problem. But interpersonal problem situations
> are complicated. One reason they are complicated is
> because different people see the problem differently.
> Seeing the situation from the viewpoints or perspec-
> tives of others helps us plan. That is, knowing how
> someone else feels about a particular plan of action
> helps us to anticipate any obstacle that this other person
> may put in our way. When we anticipate these obsta-
> cles, we are better able to think of which means will be
> best in overcoming them."

As an illustrative exercise the group members write several stories based on TAT cards. The differences in point of
view evidenced in these stories are used for a discussion by the
group at the next session. Between the two sessions, the group
leader identifies pairs of differing stories and, dividing the
group into pairs, has the writer of each discuss with his or her
partner why he thought what he did about the characters' motivations and so on. The purpose of this exercise is to have the
group members develop a greater appreciation of another person's viewpoint about a particular situation. The second exercise involves a careful analysis of a taped argument between
husband and wife regarding their respective viewpoints.

Unit 16. "Communicating with Others: I." This unit attempts to deal with the problems associated with presenting one's own viewpoint. This unit, as well as Unit 17, is placed at this point in the program because of the observation that many patients in pilot runs of the program had difficulty keeping to the point of a discussion and not digressing. If this problem has not arisen in the course of the program, the leader may omit these two units and proceed to Unit 18.

A skit is enacted by the group following the script presented in the workbook. This skit serves as a focal point in a discussion regarding the most effective way to present a point of view and to deal with the feelings associated with changing one's mind.

Unit 17. "Communicating with Others: II." The importance of keeping to the point is emphasized in Unit 17. The exercises involve acting out skits, following a script provided by the leader, illustrating the problem of digression. The discussion centers on specific methods of keeping a conversation focused on the problem at hand, such as by learning not to be distracted or by telling someone that a specific question is not relevant to the immediate discussion.

Unit 18. "Final Steps Toward Effective Problem Solving." Unit 18 attempts to consolidate the principles of problem solving into a series of logical consecutive steps. The principle here is stated in the following way:

> In solving our problems, not only must we not rush into trying to solve them, but we must carefully think of the step-by-step things that we have to do. For instance, Fred may say, "I know I have a problem with my girlfriend, but I've got it solved because I am going to try to change." Is this enough to solve the problem? It's an important first step, but Fred would probably try and think of the specific steps that he would have to take to solve the problem and that's what we are going to learn to do in this unit.

To emphasize the importance of thinking in terms of specific and detailed steps, the group is asked to relate exactly what they will do upon leaving for the evening. The second task requires them to detail a series of step-by-step actions to be taken in solving three problems of their old friend Sam. After listing all the possible courses of action that Sam might take in a particular situation and the pros and cons of each one, one is decided upon and the necessary steps to implement it are listed. A typical story might involve Sam being at a party where he doesn't know anyone and wanting to make friends with someone.

Unit 19. "Putting Your Problem-Solving Skills into Practice." The final structured unit deals with organizing all of the principles of problem solving and applying them to various problem situations. In the first task, the group is provided with a problem situation in the form of a story and several skits. In the second, the group uses each stage of problem solving in reaching the goal stated for a story situation and three skits. In the third task, the group is on its own in bringing to bear what they have learned for solving given interpersonal problems. From this point on, the group becomes involved in ongoing real-life problems of its individual members.

Group Therapy
Program for
Hospitalized
Psychiatric Patients

Coche and Flick (1975a) have developed a short-term, intensive small-group training procedure for use with psychiatric adults entering inpatient care for no more than two or three weeks. There is no reason to believe the same approach would not be useful in a variety of inpatient or residential settings, although data are available only from work in a private psychiatric hospital (Coche and Flick, 1975b; Coche, 1976). In the earlier study the program was found to significantly enhance means-ends thinking over a two-week period, to reduce the tendency to think in terms of irrelevant means, and to increase the ratio of relevant to irrelevant means generated by these psychotic patients. Trained patients left the hospital sooner than control patients, although this may have been due to the special attention they received. The second study suggested that ICPS training decreased depressive affect, enhanced self-esteem and introspectiveness, and increased the sense of mastery and positive social competence.

The program is designed to work with patient groups varying in size from four to ten, although evidence suggests that groups of four to six may get more out of it than larger groups. The groups meet each day, or almost each day, so that as many sessions as possible are held during the time available. The leader's role is that of participant-observer. He initially sets the tone and defines the objectives of the group, he keeps discussion on the track by reminding the group whenever necessary of the goal to present and solve problems, and he guides group members through the training process.

The first session begins with the leader stating that the purpose of the group is to help people gain more experience in problem solving and that members will therefore be encouraged to bring up everyday problems for discussion and the group will then try to come up with as many possible solutions as can be found. The leader emphasizes that all solutions are welcome and that only when no one can think of any new solutions will the usefulness of solutions be discussed. He also explains that he will keep a log of all the problems and solutions and will read from the log when this is needed to refresh people's memories. Use of a blackboard during training was found to be disruptive and uncomfortable to leader and patients alike.

Step 1: Bringing up a Problem

The group experience begins with a request by the leader for some member to present a problem, either personal or practical. It has been found that the first few sessions are usually concerned with general problems involving situations on the ward with aides, nurses, or doctors, and other aspects of hospital life (for example, taking medication). Over time, as group members become more relaxed, they present more personal or emotional problems to the group for consideration. If one person starts out with a highly personal problem, the group may move at that level, or it may become uneasy. In the latter case, group members shy away from personal issues for a while.

The group leader does not ask a particular group member for a problem or a solution, although other group members at times exert some group pressure to encourage a silent comember to present a problem.

On the rare occasion when group members are unable to bring up any problems, the group leader has a prepared set of hypothetical problems, one of which he can present to the group. These problems are similar in structure to those used in the Means-Ends Problem Solving (MEPS) technique (Platt and Spivack, 1975a), but of different content. Despite the availability of such hypothetical problems, the members are encouraged to think of problems themselves.

Step 2: Clarifying the Problem

Patients often do not pose a problem in a clear, concise manner, and this leads to confusion among the other members. In this case, the group leader encourages the patient to restate the problem, or he seeks clarification by asking the patient specific questions. The group leader assumes responsibility for clearing up any remaining confusion by restating the problem to the group. As solutions are being presented, the leader may restate the problem in order to maintain clarity in the discussion and increase chances that solutions do not stray from the problem at hand. By bringing the patients back to the present problem, the leader helps the group to avoid presenting solutions that are not relevant to the specific problem to be worked on.

Step 3: Presenting Solutions

Coche and Flick report that the reduced capacity of the mentally ill patient to effectively solve interpersonal problems is often reflected in a tendency to respond to problems with a habitual solution employed repeatedly without much regard to applicability and without the realization that alternatives exist. Therefore, after a problem has been presented and clarified, the leader asks for possible solutions from the group. As solutions are verbalized, a log is kept by the leader recording all problems and solutions presented during each hourly session. The log serves as a reference to remind the group of solutions already suggested, aiding the members in further exploration of other possible alternate solutions. The log also serves as a reinforcer, in that having the solution written down underscores its official acceptance.

During this brainstorming phase of the problem-solving training, frequent social reinforcement is given to encourage the process of presenting as many solutions as possible to each problem brought up in the group. The leader is not concerned with the content of the solutions offered. No value judgments or criticisms are made as to the appropriateness of the solutions offered. An alternative suggested is rewarded by "thanks" and a smile and by entering it into the group log.

The group continues to provide alternate solutions until it is apparent that the members have exhausted their resources for that particular problem. This determination is usually made by the leader, although with experience the group naturally moves on to the next step.

Step 4: Discussion of Feasibility

The final step in the training process is the discussion of the feasibility of each solution, to determine what appears to be the most appropriate solution for the particular problem. The leader begins this phase by rereading the problem and the alternate solutions presented from the log. At this point, reinforcement by the leader takes the form of a comment about the variety or quantity of alternatives given, perhaps accompanied by a restatement of the group's goal to handle problems in this manner. The leader then asks the group, again not specifying any particular group member, for opinions as to what appears to be the most feasible or "likely to succeed" solution. The point is made that a solution may be appropriate for one person but be less so, or even inappropriate, for another. This distinction encourages patients to consider the wisdom of different solutions and helps to allay fears of group rejection when considering why one solution may be "best." Again the leader refrains from giving his option, functioning mainly as a catalyst in group discussion.

Step 5: Role Playing

Coche and Flick are in the process of incorporating role playing into the group design to further promote the transfer of problem solving into real-life situations. One or more patients may assume a role within the problem situation and enact some of the solutions presented. Coche and Flick feel that role playing promotes active participation and would encourage members to discuss the feasibility of solutions in preparation for role-playing enactment. The group should feel a sense of participation and satisfaction when they actively see the effects their solutions have on others. The use of role playing provides the patients with the experience of seeing their ideas put into immediate use, which, in turn, should reinforce in the group the tendency to supply each problem with a large number of solutions.

Coche and Flick have described one instance of their procedure in action. The problem was presented by a middle-aged patient who was unhappy about her medication. She described some of the effects it had on her and expressed extreme dislike at being "forced" to take her pills. The leader asked the patient to pose the problem to the group for their suggestions and further encouraged her to clarify the problem so as to help the group focus attention on the next step, that of generating alternative possible solutions. The problem, after clarification, was stated as: "What can you do when your medication is bothering you and you dislike taking it?" The leader then asked the group to think of solutions, and several were verbalized:

(1) Refuse to take your medication.

(2) Talk to your doctor about how you feel.
(3) Have patience and realize there is a trial period to get used to drugs.
(4) Pray to God that the nurse may forget to give it to you.
(5) Ask the doctor if there is another drug you can take that may have fewer side effects.

When the group felt it had exhausted its supply of solutions, a discussion ensued concerning the feasibility or practicality of each solution. The group suggested it might be best to combine two solutions. They judged that talking to one's doctor about one's feelings and fears, as well as asking for a different medication, would be the most appropriate solution. Several patients volunteered to enact the problem and suggested solution. The patient who posed the problem participated, assuming the role of herself during the particular problem situation.

As noted earlier, such a structured yet flexible group discussion process would appear to have broad potential applicability. The nature of interpersonal problems dealt with would always reflect the composition of the group and its specific situation, thus making discussion relevant to their real lives. After the group enumerates possible solutions and there is discussion of the feasibility of each, the leader can review the process for the person who initiated the problem and ask: "What looks good to you? What do you think would work best for you?" A group member may also be encouraged to try out a solution he judges to be best and asked at a subsequent session how well his solution worked for him.

⤳⤳⤳⤳⤳⤳⤳⤳⤳⤳16⤳⤳⤳⤳⤳⤳⤳⤳⤳⤳

Related Programs

⤳⤳⤳⤳⤳⤳⤳⤳⤳⤳⤳⤳⤳⤳⤳⤳⤳⤳⤳⤳⤳⤳⤳

Certain training and therapeutic programs, or parts of broader programs in the area of interpersonal problem solving that have also been described in the literature, are similar to ICPS programs in overall purpose or use of specific techniques. However, they do not focus specifically on the training of interpersonal cognitive problem-solving skills as means of effecting behavioral adjustment. Since they do emphasize interpersonal problem solving and involve thinking skills said to define the problem-solving process, they are summarized briefly for the reader's interest. In each instance a brief background comment will be made, the program or approach described, and comparison made with interpersonal cognitive problem-solving programs developed to date.

Understanding Our Feelings (LaRue and LaRue, 1969)

This program consists of a number of problem situations presented in picture and story form, serving as a point of departure for role playing in which children have an opportunity "to analyze a social dilemma, explore their feelings about it, and then consider many different solutions to the problem and the consequences of those solutions." The stimuli leading to role playing are categorized into general themes dealing with adult-child relationships, learning, work and responsibility, friendship, aloneness, and discord. The program is intended for use with latency-period children in group situations. Its emphasis is on role playing as a natural play situation wherein children learn about their affective lives as well as how to deal with problems that will be confronted in life. The suggestion is made that the materials may be used as part of a social science program or of a language arts program, in light of its emphasis on self-expression and discussion.

The role-playing process is described as a five-step process. Having selected the right time, place, and atmosphere for the role playing, the "problem" picture (or story) is presented. In Step I the children are asked: "What is happening in this picture?"; "How do you think they feel?"; "What will happen next?" The children are encouraged to give as many answers to each question as possible, the teacher functioning only as discussion leader (never offering a suggestion, opinion, or correction). Once a problem has been identified, players for Step II are selected (or volunteer), sometimes including the teacher. The "stage" is set, the teacher instructing that the audience must show sympathetic attention. Throughout the enactment (Step III), the teacher helps when necessary to keep the enactment going, although with experience the group manages well without the teacher assuming such a role.

When the enactment ends, Step IV takes place: discussion and evaluation. The teacher poses three questions: "What will be the consequences? (How will each person feel now?)"; "What can you tell us about a similar experience?"; "Is there any other way this situation could be resolved?" Responses to the first question tap how each child felt (as an actor) or thinks actors felt about the problem solution and why. The question about "similar experiences" is intended to assist children in thinking about solutions to similar problems. The third question is intended to lead children to speculate on other possible solutions or explore further steps in the solution that was enacted.

The final step requires a reenactment, following the same process. At completion, however, discussion may also focus on comparing the solutions and consequences of the two enactments, with the possibility of noting other possibilities. Further enactments become possible, although it is suggested that no more than one problem situation be presented during any one role-playing session.

In many respects, this program purports to train processes that make up ICPS ability: problem identity, generating ideas about solutions and consequences, and means-ends thinking. While consideration of consequences is limited to consideration of how people feel after enactment, the format would likely allow of broader discussion of what might happen next. As with ICPS training programs, the adult is not to pass judgment on solutions offered (that is, there are no rights and wrongs). In the absence of data, it is an open question whether the use of role playing as presented in this program actually produces enhanced ICPS skills. Its intent is obviously to affect each child's problem-solving ability, even though LaRue and LaRue feel the need to assert that the program "is not intended to be used for personal or group therapy."

The program manual does not specify any limits or requirements on the program as these might relate to age or intellectual or emotional issues, nor does it suggest any prerequisite skills for ensuring a child's benefit. The claim is made that children can benefit without actively role playing or even participating in discussion.

Words and Action (Shaftel and Shaftel, 1967)

This program is quite similar in both conception and procedures to the program of LaRue and LaRue just described. It employs role playing as the major vehicle of intervention, with the claim that role playing helps children gain perspective, learn how to deal with interpersonal situations, and acquire ability to analyze problems and practice solutions. As with LaRue and LaRue, no evaluative data are offered or referred to with respect to their specific program. The stimuli employed as points of departure for discussion and role playing are twenty pictorial representations of problem situations between young children of school age and between children and adults. The program is offered for teachers of children in early school years, especially children from disadvantaged homes wherein there may have been deficient learning in verbalizing feelings and discussing problems that arise between people. Role playing is seen as a stimulator of talk and self-expression rather than as a vehicle to learn ways of thinking, but the choice of pictures depicting interpersonal situations and the methods of procedure limit the discussion to interpersonal problems.

The program offers instructions to the teacher on how to proceed, including example dialogues and hints about how to handle special situations, and specific things to say and do as the teacher leads the group through the required procedure. After an initial warm-up period with a picture, the group is asked, "What is happening in this picture?" Responses are elicited and encouraged, and some children may be asked to show, in pantomime if necessary, what is happening. The teacher may participate at this point as a model. The question, "What do you think will happen now?" is then posed as a means of generating thought as to the solution to the problem. Teacher questions must be carefully used to assist in this process, since the purpose is to zero in on a solution (for example, "What can the boy do now?"; "What would you do?"). Role playing proceeds from this point, with the understanding that the ease of entering into it and the level to be attained depend greatly upon the age of the child and the experience of the group.

Following enactment, the teacher directs discussion to how the characters in the enactment felt or might have felt and how pleased everyone was with the way the enactment ended. This is followed by, "Is there something else the[se] child[ren] might do?" The intent here is to elicit other possible resolutions to the problem situation, using subtle suggestions and cues as needed. New alternatives are enacted and discussed, at this point including discussion of effectiveness of the solutions enacted, relative to consequences. The main thrust of consequences discussions is apparently upon the effects of solutions on how people feel and the reality of the solution.

This program is quite similar to ICPS programs in its focus upon getting children to generate problem-solving thinking in a nonjudgmental atmosphere. With the exception that Shaftel and Shaftel recommend that the teacher avoid discussions of solution options that might upset the group, the focus is on getting children to verbalize through teacher-guided discussions.

While the creators of the program designed the program to teach children how to solve problems, they do not specify prerequisite skills or what goes into the problem-solving process itself. As noted earlier, they appear to be more interested in the program as a vehicle to encourage verbalization and thinking in general than in its potential to teach specific problem-solving cognitive skills. Mention is made of the fact that children of different ages will differ in their ability to discuss and role-play, and that the teacher must adjust himself and the program to these constraints.

SeeLab (Howe and Achterman, 1975)

The SeeLab program presents an overall training package that is much broader in its goals than the training of problem-solving methods. It attempts to teach an appreciation of a variety of human-behavior dynamics and ways people should relate to each other in general, as well as to train children in educational environments specifically. Program elements deal with a variety of issues related to interpersonal relationships, with a heavy focus on how people should communicate with each other to maximize understanding and good feeling and minimize conflict and bad feeling. A very significant element is what is termed reflective listening, which consists of nonjudgmental reactions to others in a problem situation in conjunction with sensitive reflection of feelings aimed at helping the other person clarify his situation.

Of relevance here is a subsection of the training program that describes methods of dialoguing with others in conflict situations, employing first reflective listening and/or specific methods of sending clear messages and then encouragement to generate solutions to the problem situation. Sample dialogues are provided for situations in which the adult is confronted with a resistant child, a person has to respond to another person who is having a conflict with a third party, a person feels he must confront someone about a problem they are having, and a person (for example, a teacher) must intervene in the conflict between two others because he is accountable for them (for example, students). In all instances, the point is made that the person must, in a nonjudgmental manner, reflect back the feelings he perceives as present in the other person(s), so as to help identify the problem or dilemma, and then invite the alternative solutions that the other person judges to be appropriate. If one is a sensitive listener and sender of information and an accurate reflector of the other person's actual feelings, the point is made that guiding toward consideration of optional solutions will work. Suggested technique does not include any discussion of potential consequences, although such consideration may be implicit in the invitation to consider "appropriate" solutions.

Methods are also suggested in the handling of problems that confront a group of people, including adult-child, child-child, and adult-adult groupings. Success in the process is said to occur because adults or others in power stop admonishing, commanding, and controlling, all contributions are accepted, cooperation replaces power relationships, and everyone's contribution is received and respected. Again, the facilitator in the group must practice reflective listening, and help everyone "own" his or her feelings and express them. Steps in the group process include acknowledgment of concern about the issue, inviting discussion, the facilitator's reflecting feelings and thoughts of participants as they emerge, the invitation that the group suggest solutions, the facilitator's accepting these without evaluation, the listing of all solutions offered, the elimination of any solution requiring illegal or other acts that the facilitator may feel would be too uncomfortable for him to carry out, the suggestion that group members now decide for themselves what solution they wish to employ, and establishing a time in the future to meet and assess how well solutions are working. A dialogue between a teacher and the class is provided in the manual as an example of this process.

While no data on program effectiveness are offered, the problem-solving segments of the SeeLab program are similar to ICPS programs in encouraging generation of ideas about the nature and possible cause of a problem (through reflective listening) and in requesting enumeration of possible solutions. Suggested methods do not deal with the issue of consequences in any consistent way. SeeLab encourages the person to evaluate what he does in terms of what happens as a result of his action but not the pros and cons of what he might do before he takes action. The program places some limit on acceptable alternative solutions insofar as the use of force or social power is concerned. This is probably in part due to the broader mission of the program to deal with human values and overall self-enhancement. Thus, while ICPS programs focus upon the cognitive operations at work in problem solving, the SeeLab program focuses relatively more on acceptance and articulating of feelings and the facilitator's role as a reflective listener.

Decision-Making Skills for Children
(Branca, D'Augelli, and Evans, 1975)

This program for fourth to sixth graders is in its developmental phase and is an attempt to adapt a newer, more general guidance approach to the field of primary prevention in drug abuse. The work is predicated on the recognition that informa-

tion giving alone is not effective as a general guidance strategy
or in drug education specifically.

From the literature on decision making, the authors
define eight components of the decision-making process, under
the assumption that the process is a sequential and logical pro-
gression of thought. They also assume, drawing upon Piaget,
that the required abstract ability to successfully carry out the
decision-making process does not emerge in children younger
than ten years of age. Thus, the program is designed for use
with ten- to twelve-year-olds. The eight components in decision making, converted to training goals, are to:

(1) Define the problem or dilemma.
(2) Identify all the relevant alternative courses of action.
(3) Identify all probable consequences or outcomes of
    each alternative.
(4) Identify the risks involved in pursuing each
    alternative.
(5) Identify and rank all salient personal values.
(6) Select the alternative characterized by consequences
    of greatest satisfaction of personal values and least
    risk.
(7) Take the chosen course of action.
(8) Review the selection.

In designing the program, the idea has been to attend to
and teach the *process* of decision making and not "right" or
"wrong" decisions and outcomes. The philosophy of training
is to involve children in guided decisions and role playing
around lifelike dilemmas. The program consists of six forty-
minute sessions. The first five are instructional and the sixth is
used for review. Each of the first five sessions has two segments.
The first segment consists of introducing a "problem family"
saga that moves from session to session, wherein a different
family member confronts a dilemma on each occasion. During
the second segment, other characters are presented who must
face and decide on action in new situations. Throughout all
sessions, the vocabulary of decision making is informally

emphasized, including the concepts of choice, risk, value, decision, alternative, and consequence.

Considering the "problem family" segment first, during the first session the entire class is encouraged to discuss and define the characteristics of the members of a hypothetical family group. In subsequent sessions, as the family saga emerges, different family members face decisions about school work, leisure activity, personal development, family responsibility, or a moral question. The group leader guides the class through the steps involved in the decision-making process, and then the class decides on a final best decision and its possible consequences. In the following session, a new dilemma is presented, often deriving from the decision of the previous session. The group leader points up consequences and asks the class to review its last decision.

In the second segment of each session, the new characters introduced differ in their values from the family members. The aim of this contrast is to highlight the fact that the decision-making process remains the same even though the content of a decision may vary as a function of one's values. Activity during this segment involves small-group discussions, followed by role playing of the decision-making process and a final review of the process and its consequences. During the final, sixth session, the group leader reviews the steps in the decision-making process and the decision-making vocabulary involved.

One study has been reported on the effects of the program upon fourth- through sixth-grade elementary school children (Evans, D'Augelli, and Branca, 1975; Branca, D'Augelli, and Evans, 1975). Strong evidence is presented indicating that the program significantly enhances the vocabulary of decision making and influences thinking into consequences of one's acts. Only weak support was noted relative to program effects on decision-making orientation, the generation of alternative solutions, and elimination of nonalternative and nonconsequential thinking. No effect was noted on self-concept, or on a role-repertoire test. The authors noted the likelihood of stronger effects in the fifth and sixth grades than fourth grade, and conclude that more work is needed to tighten up and improve program effectiveness. No measure of effects on overt behavioral adjustment was attempted.

While still in its early developmental stages, the present program bears some striking similarities to ICPS programs. It places emphasis on the processes of thought rather than its content, and on teaching the language of thought as important tools in the thought processes to be affected. The group leader or teacher is seen as a guide but not didactic instructor, and the recipients are drawn into active discussion and involvement during the program. The program differs from ICPS programs in that it has a broader focus than interpersonal relationships and starts out with the goal of influencing a very complex set of cognitive processes that may or may not be equally relevant to decision making or problem solving. Nevertheless, it is very much in the current stream of work that focuses on the education of thought processes felt to underlie the solving of real-life problems.

The Family Contract Game
(Blechman, 1974; Blechman and Olson, 1975)

This board game is a training procedure the purpose of which is to guide family members through steps in solving concrete interpersonal problems between individual family members. The underlying assumption of the training procedure is that family conflict is a social and not psychological issue, involving struggles over values, status, power, and scarce resources, wherein the goal is not only to achieve individual goals but also to neutralize, hurt, or negate the other person. Conflicts may not be approached with an idea of solution, there is as a consequence little opportunity for shared rewarding interpersonal experience, and finally family members withdraw from one another. The assumption of the training program is that this process may be reversed if the family setting can be brought under the "stimulus control" of the game, which is structured to teach family members to be more efficient in solving their problems, and to obtain rewards for the effort.

If this happens, it is hoped that the family will be motivated to exercise this method on an ongoing basis, begin to evaluate each other more positively, and do more things together.

Following the analysis of Aldous (1971), it is posed that there are five logical steps in efficient problem solving: (1) identification and definition of the problem, (2) collection of information relevant to the problem, (3) innovation of active alternatives, (4) choice of course of action, and (5) evaluation of the consequences of action. Communication in the game is aimed at avoiding the interruptions, unresponsiveness, tendencies toward excuse making and denial of responsibility, and the criticisms and complaints that usually characterize interactions of families in conflict. The game setting attempts to alter the social environment by providing rules of procedure and therapist support and guidance so that discussion focuses on a problem in operational terms, attempts to identify a solution, and suggests concrete rewards each family member can apply as a result of the problem-solving behavior of another. If agreement is reached about how to solve a specific problem, a written contract is completed and the results of the plan recorded during the subsequent week.

Some families are said to be able to use the Family Contract Game by relying solely on the written instructions, while others need supervision during initial weeks. Details of how the game is played have been described by Blechman (1974). Family members play together. Essentially, family members record on cards in very specific terms what someone else does that creates a problem (for example, "Mother, you interrupt when I talk on the phone") and write their names on the back. Each member also makes his own reward cards, again in specific language (for example, more time watching television). All members displeased about something throw dice to begin. The winner (DP) puts his problem card on top of the family stack of problem cards, and invites the family member or members (OP) who he thinks can help solve the problem to play with him.

As the dyad or group play the game, the process moves

them to see the specific problem, who is involved, what DP sees OP doing to solve the problem (for example, "Mother, please hand me a note when I'm on the telephone"), and what rewards OP might supply DP for this new behavior out of the "reward" deck of cards. The negotiation that occurs as players move around the board must consider whether the new behavior will really please DP, is possible for OP to carry out, will lead to reward, and ends up in a contract that includes who will record daily the new behaviors as they emerge. Contracts are honored for one week, discussed again, and perhaps renegotiated. The game may supply a list of typical family problems as an aid to family thinking and includes "fun" bonus and risk cards to enrich the game quality. The emphasis throughout is to specify in concrete behavioral terms the behavior that displeases, the behavior to replace it that will please the other person, and the specific reward to follow. The contract that specifies these is signed.

Since the Family Contract Game conceives of family problems wholly as social in nature, no reference is made to the problem-solving capacities or skills of individual members in either carrying out this process or in relation to change as a function of the program. Since the game may take as little as fifteen minutes to play each week and the family engages in it largely or totally in the absence of a therapist, any success may be viewed as an actual experience and thus serve as motivation for continuation. While it is noted that the therapist's role may vary as a function of the need of a family for direction and guidance in playing the game, the issue of family willingness to engage in talk about interpersonal problems is not dealt with. The creators of the program see the game's advantages for clinical and primary prevention work with families that have a short attention span, a concrete approach to life, tend to be secretive, and have meager social skills. One small study of effectiveness (see Blechman and Olson, 1975) included four single-parent family pairs (parent-child pairs). The results suggested some positive effects of training on parental ratings of child problems, and that game procedures alter problem-solving interactions during training.

Thresholds (Burglass and Duffy, 1974)

This program is designed to serve clients in the correctional system, the purpose being to foster the processes that underlie independent decision making. The program is offered as a philosophical system established on theological premises, based upon the principles of self-determination and community responsibility and the ethics of autonomy and individual commitment. The creators of the program emphasize the individual's right to make and live out his own decisions, and they see the purpose of the program as furthering the thought processes that enable this to happen.

> We are concerned with the thougnt processes, the cognitive mechanisms, that individuals use to conduct their lives. Our efforts are directed toward helping individuals discover, develop, and preserve their personal autonomy by freeing themselves from construction of narrow thinking, habitual patterns of thought, and unwarranted assumptions and unreasonable expectations. We do this directly by helping the individual analyze his own thought processes and by teaching the process of decision-making [ch. 3, p. 2].

A manual and client workbook are available as guides. These describe the philosophic underpinnings of the program, definition of concepts, and the structure of the course. The program is delivered in seventeen one-to-one sessions and three group sessions. The first three individual sessions are introductory, aimed at establishing rapport, informing the client about the program, obtaining information about him, and eliciting his intent to participate. In the subsequent fourteen sessions, each of the seven steps in decision making is presented one at a time, in order, in didactic form. This is followed by a dialogue on each step during the subsequent session, which employs the workbook. The seven steps, and a brief outline of what goes into the training of each, are presented below.

Definition of the situation.   Every decision is said to be made in a situational context, and the first step in the program is that of learning that there are external as well as internal circumstances in one's life, some that occur or exist in the past, present, or future, that may or may not limit the decision-maker. The point is also made that some situations are a consequence of a previous decision the client made, some are a reaction to some other situation, while others are only assumptions on his part or a product of chance. During the dialogue session, the client lists a series of situations in response to a hypothetical person in a story and then lists and analyzes some in his own life. The goal of the program is to have situations derive from decisions and chance, but not reaction and assumption.

Expanding possibilities. The focus is to teach the importance of an open mind, ready to consider all possibilities for decision. Brainstorming is the method used, pointing out that insufficient information, premature rejection of an idea, and unwarranted assumptions can get in the way. The workbook requires the client to define situations and list possibilities for discussion.

Evaluating possibilities. The purpose of this step is to teach the client to think about each possibility in terms of its desirability, likelihood of succeeding, and risks involved. The idea is conveyed that there are desirable and undesirable outcomes, that both are important to consider, and that in any one decision these may have to be balanced and weighed. The workbook provides examples and requires the client to record his own.

Decisional criteria. In this step the client is taught four rationales or criteria for decision making. One tells the client to choose a possibility that minimizes chances of negative outcome for himself (that is, minimal risk or "play it safe"). Another asks for the possibility that might yield maximal return, forgetting risk. A third emphasizes a decision of which the outcome has the least negative and the most positive consequences on the client as well as others involved in the situation, and the fourth calls for a decision made "on principle," ignoring its effects on self and others. In the workbook, the client attempts to learn these by using them to categorize decisions he and others have made or might make.

Decision. In this step the focus is placed upon the making of a decision. The point is made that the process of deciding is crucial, that it should be self-conscious and thus willful, and that it signifies future action. A good decision is said to be defined by the process gone through and not its outcome. In the workbook, the client goes through prior decision-making steps for a hypothetical person and then himself, ending up by recording a decision on which he would act. The program attempts to convey that not to decide is also a decision, that action alone makes the future, that one must dare to decide, and that one is acceptable regardless of the outcome.

Acting on a decision. The purpose of this step is to highlight the need to create detailed strategies and tactics in carrying out a decision toward a goal, defining the means whereby the client can monitor his own progress. This process involves a time-line, and the program recommends daily lists that the client can check himself. (The process defines a means-ends way of thinking in its emphasis on strategies and tactics in carrying out a decision toward a goal.) An attempt is made to make the distinction between goals and tactics, and to emphasize that the client controls his plan and not vice versa. Throughout the workbook, the client draws up strategies and tactics to achieve goals and is asked to put them in temporal order and create means of self-monitoring.

Ratification. The final step has as its goal clarifying the idea that, having made a decision, it is necessary to reaffirm it and stick to it. The point is conveyed that this can be done by the client's creating a symbol and/or ritual as a reminder to follow through. Examples are provided, suggesting that through conscious participation in some ritual (thing done or said), "one consents to the action and ratifies the decision, and thus preserves what might otherwise be lost: intentionality."

The manual recommends that visual displays be used each individual session and that the orientation should be one of drawing out the client. The teacher must do his own homework and design sessions to be tailor-made for the client, considering his sophistication and personal situation. The three group sessions employ art and films as a focus for structured questions by the teacher aimed at: (1) emphasizing that one's decisions in life give meaning, (2) pointing out that one is always free to make decisions no matter how limited the situation seems to be, and (3) demonstrating how strategies and tactics are employed and can be put together in a plan.

Since the *Thresholds* program focuses on decision making, its cognitive focus is broader than that demanded of interpersonal problem solving. In fact, the program does not focus directly upon interpersonal issues, except as consequences come up for discussion when dealing with decisional criteria (Step 4). It has been outlined, here, however, because of its expressed concern with teaching cognitive processes, including generation of alternative possibilities, consequences, and means-ends strategies and tactics. To date no data have been collected evaluating the impact of the program upon the cognitive processes or behavioral adjustment of those who have experienced the program. Qualitative appraisal raises questions as to whether many of the philosophical and ethical concepts that underlie the exercises in the workbook could be appreciated by those with modest educational background, despite attempts that might be made by a teacher to translate them into more understandable terms. Question might also be raised regarding the required reading level of the workbook. It would also seem that teachers would have to be trained quite carefully in the approach, since some of the materials must be created out of what the client produces and the concepts underlying each step are left to the teacher to translate into terms that fit the client.

Problem-Solving Training Procedure
(Goldfried and Goldfried, 1975)

This procedure derives from the behavior therapy field, specifically its advances in theory and technique beyond the use of methods arising solely from principles of classical and instrumental conditioning. It recognizes that any therapeutic intervention, if it is to be effective in dealing with the complex issues of human adjustment, must attend to cognitive and other mediational processes. In this case, Goldfried and Goldfried propose procedures and techniques to help people "figure things out" so that they can better cope with the world around them.

> The general goal in problem-solving training is not to provide individuals with specific solutions to specific problematic situations, but rather to provide a general coping strategy, so that they may be in a better position to deal more effectively with a wide variety of situational problems [p. 104].

According to Goldfried and Goldfried, the problem-solving process follows five steps: (1) general orientation, (2) problem definition and formulation, (3) generation of alternatives, (4) decision making, and (5) verification. General orientation involves a general attitude that includes a recognition that problem situations are a normal part of life, an assumption that one can cope with such situations, a sensitivity to the existence of a problem, and a readiness to think before doing anything. Problem definition and formulation means defining the problem situation in detailed and concrete terms. Generation of alternatives involves the stating of a quantity of possible solutions, holding in check any preconceived judgments of agreeability or effectiveness. Decision making is the process of selecting among possible solutions the one that is best, considering the circumstances and/or personal issues involved and the personal issues to be resolved. Verification requires that the problem-solver act upon his decision and verify whether the consequences were as expected and his problem satisfactorily resolved.

People are said to differ in the stage in which they typically have difficulty and thus require training, and training is therefore to be focused where the client is weakest. Training is viewed as a procedure wherein modeling after the therapist, practice, automatization, and reinforcement for successful solutions come into play.

During initial phases of training, the therapist may

model the problem-solving procedures, speaking out his
thoughts as he carries out the process with the client watching,
the client slowly becoming more active in the process. The initial focus of the training is in establishing a problem-solving
"set." The therapist explains that problems are natural and
must be recognized when they arise but that one should not act
impulsively. Emotion may serve as a signal that a problem
exists and that the client should then seek to find the exact
events that may have triggered things off. The client may be
asked to identify common problem situations that have
occurred in his life and even to keep a record of occasions that
set off the emotions signaling a problem.

The next step is to work with the client in spelling out all
the details of his problem situation, both external (interpersonal) and internal (the client's own thoughts and feelings,
conflicts, and mixed feelings). The purpose is to identify the
"real" problem or question. Often this means identifying what
exactly the client wants. In some cases, the authors state, this
may be enough, while in other cases it is necessary to move on
to the next stage.

In the third stage, the concretely defined problem having
been stated, the client is instructed to think of as many possible
solutions as he can, without prejudging their likelihood of success, personal consequences, or the details that would be necessary if actually carried out as a solution plan. The therapist
may actually suggest added possibilities.

In the fourth stage the client is guided to evaluate each
general solution strategy in terms of its personal, social, and
short- and long-term consequences, making estimates as to
how good he feels about each and its likelihood of success. Having decided on one solution (or perhaps more than one in combination), the client is then guided by the therapist to elaborate
on the details of the solution(s). These specific tactics may cover
in detail what the client might say or do, exactly when, how
others might react, and so forth.

In the final stage the client must carry out the chosen
course of action, attending to how well it achieves what was
desired. The therapist encourages action and helps the client

verify whether or not it has worked. If results are not satisfactory, the problem-solving procedure is resumed and another solution is sought.

While D'Zurilla and Goldfried (1971) have reviewed research to justify the notion of specific problem-solving stages, no evidence has yet appeared as to the efficacy of the specific therapeutic approach outlined above. The research reviewed in the 1971 article covers mostly studies of impersonal problem solving or studies that suggest but by no means prove the significance of such stages. It is not clear at times whether the therapeutic approach suggested is offered as a training program in itself to teach the cognitive elements of problem solving or as a way of going about doing therapy. Certainly these are not incompatible issues, and one might wish to assume that whatever approach a therapist takes with a client in helping him solve problems will be taken over by the client himself as his way of doing things. In any case, Goldfried and Goldfried offer their individual approach as a set of therapeutic guidelines rather than a cookbook.

Goldfried and Goldfried view their procedure as only one method among many that may be necessary within a total therapeutic program. Thus, if a client decides upon a course of action but cannot act on it because of excessive anxiety, the therapist might then choose specific procedures to decrease the anxiety. The implication is that the stages of problem solving as defined described an "ideal," normal, "healthy" process of mind, and that points within this process wherein a person cannot function define areas in which a client needs therapeutic help.

The guidelines offered by Goldfried and Goldfried very closely approximate some elements of programs directly emerging from ICPS research. The emphasis is on training a way of thinking rather than what to think. Specifically, they emphasize the importance of the generation of possible solutions and possible consequences. Their focus upon spelling out the specific things a client must do in carrying out a particular solution closely approaches the ICPS focus on learning means-ends cognition. The overall approach is educational in the sense that cognitive changes are presumed to play a significant role in changing overt behavior.

Problem Solving in Brief Psychotherapy
(McGuire and Sifneos, 1970)

McGuire and Sifneos describe an approach they have used in brief psychotherapy, the goal of which is to teach patients how to resolve conflicts by viewing what happens to them in the language of a problem-solving model. They note that many patients exhibit a deficit in learning with regard to solving internal conflicts, suggesting that the handicap may be more cognitive than emotional, and reflect an inability of the patient with a problem to look at himself and what he does in a way that is useful in initiating change. Having been taught a useful way during the therapeutic process, the client can apply it in new situations. They report on fifteen cases treated using two forms of their approach and explain why the approach presented below is preferable.

The therapist using this approach attempts to conceptualize what the patient says in terms of an ends-means-conditions-response paradigm. Most conflicts discussed in therapy are said to be capable of conceptualization within this framework, although the patient initially may be aware only of one or two elements. Ordering of elements of the conflict in terms of these four elements enables the patient to grasp more of what is going on. In the process the patient may learn that he has certain wishes or motives (that is, ends), which may or may not be in conflict or unrealistic. He may learn he has personal or physical capacity (that is, means) to achieve these ends and about how realistic they are. Beyond these, there are circumstances (that is, conditions) which may or may not facilitate or obstruct utilization of means. Finally, there are the patient's responses to fulfillment or nonfulfillment of his ends, which often trouble or baffle him. For example, a patient may seek competitive success (end), work hard to do this (means), and do this in a setting wherein such striving is accepted if not encouraged (conditions). His response to success, however, may be guilty feelings and withdrawal because of unrecognized associated hostile or sadistic ends.

In employing their approach, McGuire and Sifneos place special emphasis on the order in which problem elements are approached in the therapy and therefore learned by the patient. They term this the "natural sequence." They claim that of the two groups they studied, the group that learned quicker, and exhibited better therapeutic results, first recognized the nature of their own responses, then recognized the limiting conditions, and finally identified the means and ends. Patients in treatment worked backwards, and therapeutic results indicated the therapist should move in this direction in his work. An example might help. A young woman had a history of being frightened in close relationships with men. In other areas of her life she did quite well.

> Therapy began with the patient describing in detail the many occurrences which frightened her (responses and conditions). It was clear to the therapist that the patient feared that men would take advantage of her, that her only response was to react to this fear, and that her conflict centered around her desire for intimacy coupled with fear of such intimacy. The therapist avoided making any comments about the conflict early in treatment. Rather, through a series of clarifications, she gradually became aware of the repetitive nature of her fright. Next she began to sense the conditions, mainly that she often found herself in the presence of men who were known for their interest in sexual activity. From there she began to work back to the means with which she dealt with men (mainly seduction and rejection) and eventually to her ends, which were both to be close to and to dominate men.
>
> At this point therapy had continued for eight weeks (one session per week). The conflict had been reformulated in terms of the model, the patient understood it, and for weeks nine and ten she proceeded to identify a variety of additional hostile acts which she had carried out toward men, how such acts were inevitable if she perceived men as close to her, and how

her past responses to intimacy were obviously unsuccessful.

McGuire and Sifneos note that when the therapist attempts to structure the therapy in the "logical" order of ends-means-conditions-response, there results a highly intellectual investigation into causes, plans for behavior change, and attempts at change that fail. They claim that failure results from attempts to eliminate personal conflicts through new forms of behavior without sufficient prior appreciation of the effects and consequences of the conflict. They add that too-hasty exploration into ends (wishes, motives) may lead to premature conceptualizing of the problem, that the patient usually recognizes his responses more easily and quickly, and that it makes sense to pursue a conflict in a manner that seems most natural for the patient. Further, patients trained in the logical order tended to explain their distress in terms of the model, rather than use it as a process of investigation, and were less able to apply it to novel situations.

McGuire and Sifneos suggest their technique as only one approach within a broader spectrum of therapeutic concepts and tools. They state that while the approach may not be applicable to all patients, the model helps order the therapist's thinking while working with patients and helps pinpoint where, in a complex set of events, a deficit of thought exists. Thus, distress may follow from misunderstood wishes or ends in one patient but, in another, from a lack of appreciation of the realism or effectiveness of means or from a lack of awareness of the circumstances in which the patient is functioning.

The Art of Problem Solving (Carkhuff, 1973)

This booklet is offered as a guide in helping others to develop problem-solving skills. It is intended for use by those in the role of helping others, whether as parent, teacher, counsellor, or administrator. It is not oriented to mental health but purportedly may be of use to anyone who works with others because he is interested in enhancing the other person's personal effectiveness.

Essentially, the program is a didactic presentation of elements said to compose a rational problem-solving methodology. It is meant for "responsible people" willing to "take responsibility for the hard work needed to resolve problems in their lives." The goal in applying the method is to help a person with a problem (the "helpee") gain knowledge of the problem-solving process through interaction with the helper, the latter working with the helpee in going through and learning the process. No evidence is offered as to the effectiveness of the method.

Carkhuff presents in his booklet the steps the helper should use, exemplifying through a case that runs throughout. Initial stages involve the helper in guiding the helpee to explore and understand his problem. Much of the work during these stages involves the helper in reflecting helpee feelings, this aimed at uncovering the precise nature of the problem(s) and what the helpee values in his life that has become involved in the problem. Next, the helper works with the helpee to break down and define the problem and put it in concrete and even measurable terms. Out of what may be a complex problem, one aspect is chosen that can be seen clearly and very likely solved. This is converted to goals to be achieved and even subgoals. The next stage involves developing courses of action that are workable or likely to achieve the goal, aside from any consideration of negative side effects. The helper engages in this process with the helpee, the potential courses of action being written down so that they can be looked at.

The next stage is aimed at developing what is called a value hierarchy, which is in essence a ranked listing of the things in life that the helpee values which are touched by or involved in his problem (for example, people, ideas, things, activities). Many of these are supposedly revealed to the helper during initial stages of exploring the problem. Through questioning, numerical weights are assigned these values to describe their relative importance to the helpee. At this point each potential course of action is evaluated on the basis of the degree to which it helps the helpee realize his values. A chart is prepared whereon are recorded the numerical values of each course of action for each value and the numerical values for each course of action are summed. In this fashion, courses of action may be compared relative to helping the helpee achieve his or her valued life goals in the problem situation. The final stages include helper-helpee discussion aimed at the design of a step-by-step procedure to successfully carry out the course of action selected, including the building in of self-reinforcements and deprivations for the helpee to experience at appropriate points as substeps are achieved or not achieved.

While it is not clear from the material presented in *The Art of Problem Solving,* it would seem that carrying out the process as described essentially consists of sensitive counselling, didactics, the modeling of certain problem-solving thinking skills, and a touch of behavior therapy. Little is said about the requirements needed to be an effective helper, although it is clear that certain therapeutic skills would be needed before the program could be used effectively. The program itself shares with ICPS programs a focus on generating alternative courses of action and the defining of step-by-step means in planning action, although the helper apparently is more active in completing this process than is typical of ICPS procedures.

One unique element in this program is the suggested technique of graphing the lattice of alternative courses of action against the helpee's problem-solving values and assigning numerical values to each coordinate, so that a total numerical value emerges for each potential course of action. This method is consistent with the emphasis placed throughout on defining and concretizing the problem-solving process.

Major Elements
of Interpersonal
Problem-Solving
Programs

XXXXXXXXXXXXXXXXXXXXXXXXXX

Evaluation of programs to date consistently indicates effectiveness in enhancing ICPS skills and improving behavioral adjustment. It is still too early in the development and evaluation of such programs, however, to pinpoint specifically the necessary and sufficient properties of a successful training program. Nevertheless, programs that have been used and shown to enhance ICPS skills have certain qualities in common that warrant mention. Effective programs create and employ ways to stimulate thought and discussion in and around interpersonal problem situations with which participants can identify. The ways to stimulate may vary, including videotapes, cassette audio tapes, puppets, pictures, and story roots, the choice depending on the age, diagnosis, and interest level of the recipient as well as ingenuity of the program designer and the setting in which the program is being used. These initiating stimuli are crucial because their function is to engage recipients in an active process of thinking that is relevant to the solving of real-life interpersonal problems. It appears necessary to have active participation (as opposed to passive listening) or at least provide actively involved models for those who may be slow to become actively involved. A key feature of this participation is having the recipient generate thought, rather than choose from the offerings of others or merely follow the thoughts offered by the teacher, parent, or therapist.

Most programs that have emerged specifically out of ICPS research have also been highly structured and sequenced. While allowing of some flexibility, the implication is that learning ICPS skills requires structured guidance on the part of the person administering the program, repeated exercises in the use of the thinking skills by the recipient, and a presentation of clearly defined goals to the recipient. The sequencing of program elements also suggests that certain things should be learned before others (for example, generating problem solutions comes before thoughts about consequences). However, sequencing has also derived from another property of programs: the assumption it is necessary to cover certain prerequisite skills before teaching ICPS skills. These prerequisites may include the language of problem solving, an orientation to problem-solve, or certain social skills (for example, social cues —that different people may think and feel differently; how one knows there is a problem).

Despite these similarities, much remains to be discovered about programing style, aside from the obvious issue of which ICPS skills are to be the end-point goal. It is necessary to determine which prerequisite skills are in fact necessary to program before moving into the training of ICPS skills. Presumably, this becomes a serious issue the younger the child receiving training or the more disturbed the patient. Experience suggests it is best not to overestimate the cognitive and/or linguistic capacity of special groups. One can program prerequisites, or one can bypass or move quickly through them if particular recipients are not stimulated or otherwise indicate that they do not require this prerequisite training.

While some programs employ role playing as well as group discussion, there is no evidence that role playing significantly enhances learning beyond what is acquired from participation in active discussion in which ideas are generated. Stone and others (1975) have demonstrated that nine- to ten-year-old children, given a chance to practice in small groups certain elements of problem solving after watching a videotaped model, show enhancement in these elements. Only further studies, such as one completed by McClure (1975), comparing techniques (for example, group discussion, modeling, role playing) will shed light on this issue. It is likely that role playing has suggested itself as a method to some programers because implicit in it is a training in ability to take or appreciate different roles. If role taking is specially designed and used this way, it is likely that programs for adolescents and adults would profit from use of this technique. Evidence reported in Chapter Five suggests that perspective taking may play a more significant role in interpersonal problem solving in these age groups than in young children.

Most of the programs developed are composed of numerous elements organized into a sequenced complex of learning experiences. While such a quality may be necessary for effectiveness, this quality raises the question of what element or elements are doing what job and how important one element is versus another in enhancing ICPS thought and behavioral adjustment. Research in program development must in the future examine and manipulate elements so that programs can be refined and streamlined without loss of effectiveness. It would also be of interest to examine if there are qualities or any background experiences required of those administering such programs. One advantage of most ICPS programs is that learning to use them does not require prior professional training as a therapist or teacher. This fact has very practical financial implications for program managers. Further, experience indicates that once a teacher, mental health worker, or parent learns the program, he or she can successfully train peers to use the program with others. In this fashion, once a single person in a clinic or school, for example, is trained, it is possible to build a cadre of staff and a group of ICPS programs relevant to the recipients being trained. All programs to date have used professional, paraprofessional, or other adults, and an interesting question is whether in some instances older children exposed to the program can train younger children or even children their own age with only guiding supervision from an adult. A study by Wilcox (1972), employing a program similar in some respects to typical ICPS programs, suggested that a trained eleven-year-old may be as effective an agent as a teacher in working with small groups of children his own age in group discussion around problem situations.

Little is known about how well and in what ways the training of ICPS skills or a general problem-solving approach may become part of a more general therapeutic effort that involves other techniques. Experience suggests that the manner in which this is done may differ, depending upon one's broader treatment approach and theory. A behavioristic orientation (for example, Goldfried and Goldfried, 1975) may suggest a logical sequencing of discussion with the patient, with the therapist leading the way, starting with orientation toward and defining of the problem and ending with a choice of what to do. Problems encountered in the process along the way (for example, anxiety) are dealt with through the use of special therapeutic techniques (for example, desensitization), so that the end point is reached. A more traditional psychodynamic orientation (for example, McGuire and Sifneos, 1970) may suggest a different sequence, starting perhaps with what the patient has been doing and feeling in problem situations, only slowly working backwards to discover the details of the stimuli that elicit his trouble and what appear to be his motives (and conflicts in motives) and goals. Both approaches attempt to orient the patient to a problem-solving approach, both may focus on the task of defining goals, articulating options and consequences, and appreciating the fact that certain goals or potential solutions have become associated with negative or inhibiting emotions.

Continued effort should go into evaluating the effectiveness of ICPS programs. Some program developers or suggesters of therapeutic methods assume that a program must be worthwhile because what they intend to use as a teaching technique seems reasonable or has been found to work in other contexts, or that what is being taught is so worthwhile that any program to teach it is acceptable without examination. In some instances, evaluation of social cognitive programs has only included cognitive change, not measuring change in social behavior or adjustment. In other cases, behavioral changes have been studied but no relation to cognitive change has been examined. In these instances, the mediational element of ICPS skills is left unexplored.

A fruitful approach to evaluating ICPS programs is suggested in the work of Shure and Spivack (1973; 1975a, b). ICPS skills were measured before and after training, as was overt behavioral adjustment. Changes in both cognition and social adjustment were examined as a function of training, as well as the relationship between amount of change in cognition and likelihood or amount of change in social adjustment. The fact that trained youngsters who improved most in certain ICPS skills as a function of training also improved most at the overt behavioral level provided strong evidence that it was change in ICPS skills that mediated improved social adjustment, and not an extraneous selective feature of the work with the trained (but not control) group that brought about improved overt behavior (see also Spivack and Shure, 1974). This design also provides other safety features. A complex ICPS training program may not do equally well in training all ICPS skills it intends to train. The fact that a particular program does not alter social adjustment may not be evidence that the thinking skills are irrelevant but that the program does not affect the most important ICPS skills, or enough of them. If the program improves social adjustment and some cognitive skills, and amount of social adjustment relates to change in these cognitive skills, the latter become highlighted as significant mediators. The program may not need to incorporate training in other cognitive skills. Thus the measurement of both cognitive and behavioral change, and the relating of the two, makes it possible to carry out the kind of program refinement suggested earlier as needed.

It has been noted that typical ICPS programs provide relatively structured learning experiences aimed at enhancing specific thinking skills. In a few instances (Shure and Spivack, 1975e; Spivack and Shure, 1974) it has been suggested that there may be ways of talking or dialoguing with a person in a real problem situation that will promote his problem-solving ability (see also Howe and Achterman, 1975). Spivack and Shure suggest that the style and techniques of the formal training programs may be incorporated into conversations that spontaneously arise during the day with children. In such instances the most important principles are to guide the child to "think things through, make his own decisions, and carry out his own ideas." They provide typical dialogues that occur between adult and child in problem situations, such as when the child hurts another child, grabs something, cries about something, or has failed in something with another child, pinpointing how adult response and guiding questions may encourage and lead a child to generate problem-solving thought. Research reported in Chapter Six has demonstrated specific ways in which dialoguing methods differ between mothers of high and low ICPS children. Howe and Achterman suggest steps that an adult may follow in helping children resolve conflicts arising between them, one significant element being the invitation (after certain feelings have been explored and clarified) to consider appropriate alternative solutions. The advantage to such techniques is that they afford potential learning experiences continuously in actual situations, reinforcing whatever is learned in formal training. At this point it is not known how well exclusive focus on such informal methods of intervention dialoguing might work to enhance ICPS skills without prior or concurrent formal training to teach ICPS skills and certain prerequisite skills. Study of such a possibility would seem well worthwhile. Experience with very young children suggests that prior formal training helps substantially in successful informal dialoguing. Experience also has indicated that, despite protestations to the contrary, it is the rare adult who employs these methods when dealing with children (or adults) in real problem situations. We are all much more prone than we realize to react judgmentally to others in a problem situation by telling the other person what we think is the problem or the "right" solution, to presume we know what the other person is thinking or feeling, and to focus on achieving in that particular situation a solution that suits us. We are less prone than we realize to draw out or extract from the child (or other adult) his view of a problem situation, his reactions to and feelings about it, or what he views as possible solutions and their consequences and effects. Especially with children, adults reacting in problem situations are usually determined to have matters end up the way they judge best for the child, rather than view the goal of interaction as being the encouragement of problem-solving thinking on the part of the child, irrespective of the final solution that emerges.

References

ALDOUS, J. "A Framework for the Analysis of Family Problem Solving." In J. Aldous, T. Condon, R. Hill, M. Straus, and I. Tallman (Eds.), *Family Problem Solving*. Hinsdale, Illinois: Dryden Press, 1971.

ALLEN, G., CHINSKY, J., LARCEN, S., LOCHMAN, J., AND SELINGER, H. *Community Psychology and the Schools: A Behaviorally Oriented Multilevel Preventive Approach*. Hillsdale, New Jersey: Earlbaum, 1976.

ANDERSON, S., AND MESSICK, S. "Social Competency in Young

Children." *Developmental Psychology*, 1974, *10*, 282–293.

BEARISON, D. J., AND CASSEL, T. Z. "Cognitive Decentralization and Social Codes: Communicative Effectiveness in Young Children from Differing Family Contexts." *Developmental Psychology*, 1975, *11*, 29–36.

BEE, H. L. "Socializing for Problem Solving." In J. Aldous, T. Condon, R. Hill, M. Straus, and I. Tallman (Eds.), *Family Problem Solving*. Hinsdale, Illinois: Dryden Press, 1971.

BLECHMAN, E. A. "The Family Contract Game." *The Family Coordinator*, 1974, *23*, 269–281.

BLECHMAN, E. A., AND OLSON, D. H. L. "The Family Contract Game: Description and Effectiveness." In D. H. Olson (Ed.), *Treating Relationships*. Lake Mills, Iowa: Graphic Publishing, 1975.

BLOOM, B. *Stability and Change in Human Characteristics*. New York: Wiley, 1964.

BRANCA, M. C., D'AUGELLI, J. F., AND EVANS, K. L. "Development of a Decision-Making Skills Education Program: Study I." Unpublished manuscript. University Park: Pennsylvania State University, College of Education, Department of Counsellor Education, 1975.

BURGLASS, M. E., AND DUFFY, M. G. *Thresholds: Teachers Manual*. Cambridge: Correctional Solutions Foundation, Inc., 1974.

BUSSE, T. V. "Childrearing Antecedents of Flexible Thinking." Thesis. Chicago: University of Chicago, Department of Education, 1967.

CAMP, B. N., AND BASH, M. A. "Think Aloud Program Group Manual." Unpublished manuscript. Boulder: University of Colorado Medical Center, 1975.

CARKHUFF, R. R. *The Art of Problem Solving*. Amherst, Massachusetts: Human Resource Development Press, 1973.

CERESNIE, S. "Communication and Cooperation in Dyads of Children of Varying Levels of Egocentrism." Unpublished master's thesis. Detroit: Wayne State University, 1974.

CHANDLER, M. J. "Egocentrism and Antisocial Behavior: The Assessment and Training of Social Perspective-Taking Skills." *Developmental Psychology,* 1973, *9,* 326–332.

CHANDLER, M. J., GREENSPAN, S., AND BARENBOIM, C. "The Assessment and Training of Role-Taking and Referential Communication Skills in Institutionalized Emotionally Disturbed Children." *Developmental Psychology,* 1974, *10,* 546–553.

CHILMAN, C. S. *Growing Up Poor.* Publication 13. Washington, D.C.: Welfare Administration, 1966.

CLINE, V. "Ability to Judge Personality Assessed with a Stress Interview and Sound-Film Technique." *Journal of Abnormal and Social Psychology,* 1955, *50,* 183–187.

COCHE, E. "Therapeutic Benefits of a Problem-Solving Training Program for Hospitalized Psychiatric Patients." Paper presented at Society for Psychotherapy Research, San Diego, California, 1976.

COCHE, E., AND FLICK, A. "Problem-Solving Training Groups for Psychiatric Patients: A Manual." Unpublished manuscript. Friends Hospital, Philadelphia, Pennsylvania, 1975*a.*

COCHE, E., AND FLICK, A. "Problem-Solving Training Groups for Hospitalized Psychiatric Patients." *Journal of Psychology,* 1975*b, 91,* 19–29.

DAVIS, G. "Current Status of Research and Theory in Human Problem Solving." *Psychological Bulletin,* 1966, *66,* 36–54.

DEUTSCH, F. "Observational and Sociometric Measures of Peer Popularity and Their Relationship to Egocentric Communication in Female Pre-Schoolers." *Developmental Psychology,* in press.

DRAUGHTON, M. "Duplication of Facial Expressions: Conditions Affecting Task and Possible Clinical Usefulness." *Journal of Personality,* 1973, *41,* 140–150.

DUDEK, S. Z., LESTER, E. P., GOLDBERG, J. S., AND DYER, G. B. "Relationship of Piaget Measures to Standard Intelligence and Motor Scales." *Perceptual and Motor Skills,* 1969, *28,* 351–362.

DUNCAN, C. P. "Recent Research on Human Problem-Solving." *Psychological Bulletin,* 1959, *56,* 397–429.

DYMOND, R. "Personality and Empathy." *Journal of Consulting Psychology,* 1950, *14,* 343–350.

D'ZURILLA, T. J., AND GOLDFRIED, M. R. "Problem-Solving and Behavior Modification." *Journal of Abnormal Psychology,* 1971, *78,* 107–126.

ELARDO, P. T. "Project AWARE: A School Program to Facilitate the Social Development of Children." Paper presented at the 4th Annual H. Blumberg Symposium, Chapel Hill, North Carolina, 1974.

ELARDO, P. T., AND CALDWELL, B. M. "An Examination of the Relationship Between Role-Taking and Social Competence." Paper presented at Southeastern Conference on Human Development, Nashville, 1976.

ELARDO, P. T., AND CALDWELL, B. M. "Project AWARE: A School Program to Facilitate the Social Development of Kindergarten-Elementary Children." In preparation *a.*

ELARDO, P. T., AND CALDWELL, B. M. "The Effects of an Experimental Social Development Program on Children in the Middle Childhood Period." In preparation *b.*

ELARDO, P. T., AND COOPER, M. *Project AWARE: A Handbook for Teachers.* Reading, Massachusetts: Addison-Wesley, in press.

EPSTEIN, A. S., AND RADIN, N. "Motivational Components Related to Father Behavior and Cognitive Functioning in Pre-Schoolers." *Child Development,* 1975, *46,* 831–839.

EVANS, K. L., D'AUGELLI, J. F., AND BRANCA, M. C. "Development of a Primary Prevention Program: Decision-Making Skills Training for Children." Paper presented at Annual Meeting of the Eastern Psychological Association, New York, 1975.

FEFFER, M. H., AND GOUREVITCH, V. "Cognitive Aspects of Role-Taking in Children." *Journal of Personality,* 1960, *28,* 383–396.

FEFFER, M. H., AND JAHELKA, M. "Implications of the Decentering Concept for the Structuring of Projective Content."

Journal of Consulting and Clinical Psychology, 1968, *32,* 434–441.

FEFFER, M. H., AND SUCHOTLIFF, L. "Decentering Implications of Social Interactions." *Journal of Personality and Social Psychology,* 1966, *4,* 415–422.

FESHBACH, N. D. "Empathy: An Interpersonal Process." Paper presented at the American Psychological Association, Montreal, 1973.

FESHBACH, N. D., AND FESHBACH, S. "The Relationship Between Empathy and Aggression in Two Age Groups." *Developmental Psychology,* 1969, *1,* 102–107.

FINLEY, G. E., FRENCH, D., AND COWAN, P. "Egocentrism and Popularity." Presented at the XIV Inter-American Congress of Psychology, Sao Paulo, Brazil, 1973.

FRIEDMAN, A. A., BOSZORMENYI-NAGY, I., JUNGREIS, J. E., LINCOLN, G., MITCHELL, H. E., SONNE, J. C., SPECK, R. V., AND SPIVACK, G. *Psychotherapy for the Whole Family.* New York: Springer, 1965.

GARDINER, R. W., HOLZMAN, P. L., KLEIN, G. S., LINTON, H. B., AND SPENCE, D. P. "Cognitive Control: A Study of Individual Consistencies in Cognitive Behavior." *Psychological Issues,* 1959, *1,* Monograph No. 4.

GELATT, H. B., NARENHORST, B., AND CAREY, R. *Deciding: A Leader's Guide.* New York: College Entrance Examination Board, 1972.

GIEBINK, J. W., STOVER, D. S., AND FAHL, M. A. "Teaching Adaptive Responses to Frustration to Emotionally Disturbed Boys." *Journal of Consulting and Clinical Psychology,* 1968, *32,* 366–368.

GOLDBERG, S., AND LEWIS, M. "Play Behavior in the Year-Old Infant: Early Sex Differences." *Child Development,* 1969, *40,* 21–32.

GOLDFRIED, M. R., AND GOLDFRIED, A. P. "Cognitive Change Methods." In F. H. Kaufer and A. P. Goldstein (Eds.), *Helping People Change.* New York: Pergamon Press, 1975.

GRAY, S., AND MILLER, J. D. "Early Experience in Relation to

Cognitive Development." *Review of Educational Research,* 1967, *37,* 475–493.

GUILFORD, J. P. *The Nature of Human Intelligence.* New York: McGraw-Hill, 1967.

HAERTZEN, C. T., AND HILL, H. E. "Effects of Morphine and Pentobarbital on Differential MMPI Profiles." *Journal of Clinical Psychology,* 1959, *15,* 434–437.

HERTZIG, M. E., BIRCH, H. G., THOMAS, A., AND MENDEZ, D. A. "Class and Ethnic Differences in the Responsiveness of Preschool Children to Cognitive Demands." *Monographs of the Society for Research in Child Development,* 1968, *33,* 1.

HESS, R. D., AND SHIPMAN, V. C. "Early Experience and the Socialization of Cognitive Modes in Children." *Child Development,* 1965, *36,* 869–886.

HESS, R. D., SHIPMAN, V. C., BROPHY, J. E., AND BEAR, R. M. *The Cognitive Environments of Urban Preschool Children.* Chicago: University of Chicago, Graduate School of Education, 1968.

HOEPFNER, R., AND O'SULLIVAN, M. "Social Intelligence and IQ." *Educational and Psychological Measurement,* 1968, *28,* 339–344.

HOLZWORTH, W. A. *Effects of Selective Reinforcement Therapy in a Miniature Situation in Nursery School Children.* Unpublished thesis. University of Illinois, Urbana, 1964.

HOOVER, C. F. "The Embroiled Family: A Blueprint for Schizophrenia." *Family Process,* 1965, *4,* 291–310.

HOWE, W., AND ACHTERMAN, E. *SeeLab.* Santa Clara, California: See Inc., 1975.

IANNOTTI, R. J. "The Effect of Role-taking Experiences on Role-Taking, Altruism, Empathy, and Aggression." Paper presented at the Society for Research in Child Development, Denver, 1975.

INTAGLIATA, J. "Increasing the Interpersonal Problem-Solving Effectiveness of an Alcoholic Population." Unpublished doctoral dissertation. State University of New York at Buffalo, 1976.

JAHODA, M. "The Meaning of Psychological Health." *Social Casework*, 1953, *34*, 349–354.

JAHODA, M. *Current Concepts of Positive Mental Health*. New York: Basic Books, 1958.

JENNINGS, K. D. "People Versus Object Orientation, Social Behavior, and Intellectual Abilities in Preschool Children." *Developmental Psychology*, 1975, *11*, 511–519.

KAGAN, J. "Reflection-Impulsivity and Reading Ability in Primary Grade Children." *Child Development*, 1965, *36*, 609–628.

KAMEYA, L. I. "The Effect of Empathy Level and Role-Taking Training upon Prosocial Behavior." Paper presented at the Society for Research in Child Development, Denver, 1975.

KERR, B. (Illust.) Good Manners Posters. Set 1, Primary Grades. Wilkinsburg, Pa.: Hayes, 1957.

KURDEK, L. A., AND RODGON, M. M. "Perceptual, Cognitive, and Affective Perspective Taking in Kindergarten Through Sixth Grade Children." *Developmental Psychology*, 1975, *11*, 643–650.

LARCEN, S. W., CHINSKY, J. M., ALLEN, G., LOCHMAN, J., AND SELINGER, H. V. "Training Children in Social Problem Solving Strategies." Paper presented at Midwestern Psychological Association, Chicago, 1974.

LARCEN, S. W., SPIVACK, G., AND SHURE, M. "Problem-solving Thinking and Adjustment Among Dependent-Neglected Pre-Adolescents." Paper presented at Eastern Psychological Association, Boston, 1972.

LA RUE, W., AND LA RUE, S. *Understanding Our Feelings*. San Francisco: Century Communications, 1969.

LEVINE, M., AND SPIVACK, G. *The Rorschach Index of Repressive Style*. Springfield, Illinois: Thomas, 1964.

MC CLURE, L. F. "Social Problem-solving Training and Assessment: An Experimental Intervention in an Elementary School Setting." Unpublished dissertation. University of Connecticut, Storrs, 1975.

MC FALL, R. M., AND LILLESAND, D. B. "Behavioral Rehearsal with Modeling and Coaching in Assertion Training."

Journal of Abnormal Psychology, 1971, *77*, 313–323.

MC FALL, R. M., AND MARSTON, A. R. "An Experimental Investigation of Behavior Rehearsal in Assertive Training." *Journal of Abnormal Psychology*, 1970, *76*, 295–303.

MC GUIRE, M. T., AND SIFNEOS, P. E. "Problem-solving in Psychotherapy." *Psychiatric Quarterly*, 1970, *44*, 667–673.

MAHONEY, M. J. *Cognitive and Behavior Modification.* Cambridge, Massachusetts: Ballinger, 1974.

MARGOLIN, E. *Sociocultural Elements in Early Childhood Education.* New York: Macmillan, 1974.

MARGOLIN, G., AND PATTERSON, G. R. "Differential Consequences Provided by Mothers and Fathers for Their Sons and Daughters." *Developmental Psychology*, 1975, *11*, 537–538.

MEICHENBAUM, D., AND CAMERON, R. "Training Schizophrenics To Talk to Themselves: A Means of Developing Attentional Controls." *Behavior Therapy*, 1973, *4*, 515–534.

MEICHENBAUM, D., AND GOODMAN, J. "Training Impulsive Children To Talk to Themselves." *Journal of Abnormal Psychology*, 1971, *77*, 115–126.

MILGRAM, N. A. "Cognitive and Emphatic Factors in Role-Taking by Schizophrenic and Brain Damaged Patients." *Journal of Abnormal and Social Psychology*, 1960, *60*, 219–224.

MINUCHIN, S., CHAMBERLAIN, P., AND GRAMBARD, P. "A Project to Teach Learning Skills to Disturbed, Delinquent Children." *American Journal of Orthopsychiatry*, 1967, *37*, 558–567.

MISHLER, E. G., AND WAXLER, N. E. *Interaction in Families: An Experimental Study of Family Processes and Schizophrenia.* New York: Wiley, 1968.

MORTON, R. B. "An Experiment in Brief Psychotherapy." *Psychological Monographs*, 1955, *69* (Whole No. 386).

MUUSS, R. E. "Mental Health Implications of a Preventive Psychiatry Program in the Light of Research Findings." *Marriage and Family Living*, 1960a, *22*, 150–156.

MUUSS, R. E. "The Relationship Between 'Causal' Orientation, Anxiety, and Insecurity in Elementary School Children." *Journal of Educational Psychology*, 1960*b*, *51*, 122–129.

OJEMANN, R. H. *Manual for Elementary Problem Series III.* Iowa City: Iowa Child Welfare Station, University of Iowa, 1962.

OJEMANN, R. H. "Incorporating Psychological Concepts in the School Curriculum." *Journal of School Psychology*, 1967, *5*, 195–204.

OJEMANN, R. H., LEVITT, E. L., LYLE, W. H., AND WHITESIDE, M. F. "The Effects of 'Causal' Teacher Training Program and Certain Curricular Changes on Grade School Children." *Journal of Experimental Education*, 1955, *24*, 95–114.

O'SULLIVAN, M., AND GUILFORD, J. P. *Six Factor Tests of Social Intelligence: A Manual of Instructions and Interpretations.* Beverly Hills, California: Sheridan Psychological Services, 1966.

PLATT, J. J., SCURA, W. C., AND HANNON, J. R. "Problem-Solving Thinking of Youthful Incarcerated Heroin Addicts." *Journal of Community Psychology*, 1973, *1*, 278–281.

PLATT, J. J., AND SIEGEL, J. M. "MMPI Characteristics of Good and Poor Social Problem-Solvers Among Psychiatric Patients." *Journal of Psychology*, in press.

PLATT, J. J., SIEGEL, J. M., AND SPIVACK, G. "Do Psychiatric Patients and Normals See the Same Solutions as Effective in Solving Interpersonal Problems?" *Journal of Consulting and Clinical Psychology*, 1975, *43*, 279.

PLATT, J. J., AND SPIVACK, G. "Real-Life Problem-Solving Thinking in Neuropsychiatric Patients and Controls." Paper presented at the Meeting of the Eastern Psychological Association, Atlantic City, New Jersey, 1970.

PLATT, J. J., AND SPIVACK, G. "Problem-Solving Thinking of Psychiatric Patients." *Journal of Consulting and Clinical Psychology*, 1972*a*, *39*, 148–151.

PLATT, J. J., AND SPIVACK, G. "Social Competence and Effective Problem-Solving Thinking in Psychiatric Patients." *Journal of Clinical Psychology*, 1972*b*, *28*, 3–5.

PLATT, J. J., AND SPIVACK, G. "Studies in Problem-Solving Thinking of Psychiatric Patients: Patient-Control Differences and Factorial Structure of Problem-Solving Thinking." Paper presented at American Psychological Association, Montreal, 1973. In *Proceedings, 81st Annual Convention of the American Psychological Association*, 1973, *8*, 461–462.

PLATT, J. J., AND SPIVACK, G. "Means of Solving Real-Life Problems: I. Psychiatric Patients Versus Controls, and Cross-Cultural Comparisons of Normal Females." *Journal of Community Psychology*, 1974, *2*, 45–48.

PLATT, J. J., AND SPIVACK, G. *Manual for the Means-Ends-Problem-Solving Procedure*. Philadelphia: Department of Mental Health Sciences, Hahnemann Community Mental Health/Mental Retardation Center, 1975*a*.

PLATT, J. J., AND SPIVACK, G. "Unidimensionality of the Means-Ends Problem-Solving (MEPS) Procedure." *Journal of Clinical Psychology*, 1975*b*, *31*, 15–16.

PLATT, J. J., AND SPIVACK, G. *Workbook for Training in Inter-Personal Problem Solving Thinking*. Philadelphia: Department of Mental Health Sciences, Hahnemann Community Mental Health/Mental Retardation Center, 1976.

PLATT, J. J., SPIVACK, G., ALTMAN, N., ALTMAN, D., AND PEIZER, S. B. "Adolescent Problem-Solving Thinking." *Journal of Consulting and Clinical Psychology*, 1974, *42*, 787–793.

PLATT, J. J., SPIVACK, G., AND SWIFT, M. S. *Problem-Solving Therapy with Maladjusted Groups* (Research and Evaluation Report No. 28). Philadelphia: Department of Mental Health Sciences, Hahnemann Medical College and Hospital, 1974.

RAPAPORT, D. *Organization and Pathology of Thought*. New York: Columbia University Press, 1951.

RARDIN, D. R., AND MOAN, C. E. "Peer Interaction and Cognitive Development." *Child Development*, 1971, *42*, 1685–1699.

REISS, D. "Individual Thinking and Family Interaction, II. A Study of Pattern Recognition and Hypothesis Testing in Families of Normals, Those with Character Disorders, and Schizophrenics." *Journal of Psychiatric Research*, 1967, *5*, 193–211.

REISS, D. "Individual Thinking and Family Interaction, III. An Experimental Study of Categorization Performance in Families of Normals, Those with Character Disorders, and Schizophrenics." *Journal of Nervous and Mental Diseases,* 1968, *146,* 384–403.

REISS, D. "Individual Thinking and Family Interaction, IV. A Study of Information Exchange in Families of Normals, Those with Character Disorders, and Schizophrenics." *Journal of Nervous and Mental Diseases,* 1969, *149,* 473–490.

REISS, D. "Varieties of Consensual Experience, I. A Theory Relating Family Interaction to Individual Thinking." *Family Process,* 1971, *10,* 1–28.

ROTHENBERG, B. "Children's Social Sensitivity and the Relationship to Interpersonal Competence, Intrapersonal Comfort, and Intellectual Level." *Developmental Psychology,* 1970, *2,* 335–350.

RUBIN, K. H. "Egocentrism in Childhood: A Unitary Construct?" *Child Development,* 1973, *44,* 102–110.

RUBIN, K. H., AND SCHNIEDER, F. W. "The Relationship Between Moral Judgement, Egocentrism, and Altruistic Behavior." *Child Development,* 1973, *44,* 661–665.

SARASON, I. G., AND GANZER, V. J. "Social Influence Techniques in Clinical and Community Psychology." In C. D. Spielberger (Ed.), *Current Topics in Clinical and Community Psychology,* Vol. 1. New York: Academic Press, 1969.

SCHNALL, M., AND FEFFER, M. *Role-Taking Task Scoring Criteria.* Unpublished manuscript. Yeshiva University, New York, 1970.

SCOTT, R. D., AND ASKWORTH, P. L. " 'Closure' at the First Schizophrenic Breakdown: A Family Study." *British Journal of Medical Psychology,* 1967, *40,* 109–145.

SHAFTEL, F., AND SHAFTEL, G. *Words and Action.* New York: Holt, Rinehart and Winston, 1967.

SHANLEY, L. A., WALKER, R. E., AND FOLEY, J. M. "Social Intelligence: A Concept in Search of Data." *Psychological Reports,* 1971, *29,* 1123–1132.

SHANTZ, C. U. "The Development of Social Cognition." In E. M.

Hetherington (Ed.), *Review of Child Development Research*, Vol. 5. Chicago: University of Chicago Press, 1975.

SHURE, M. B., NEWMAN, S., AND SILVER, S. "Problem-Solving Thinking Among Adjusted, Impulsive and Inhibited Head Start Children." Paper presented at Eastern Psychological Association, Washington, D.C., 1973.

SHURE, M. B., AND SPIVACK, G. "Cognitive Problem-Solving Skills, Adjustment and Social Class." Research and Evaluation Report #26. Philadelphia: Department of Mental Health Sciences, Hahnemann Community Mental Health/Mental Retardation Center, 1970*a*.

SHURE, M. B., AND SPIVACK, G. "Problem-Solving Capacity, Social Class and Adjustment Among Nursery School Children." Paper presented at Eastern Psychological Association, Atlantic City, New Jersey, 1970*b*.

SHURE, M. B., AND SPIVACK, G. "Means-Ends Thinking, Adjustment and Social Class Among Elementary School-Aged Children." *Journal of Consulting and Clinical Psychology*, 1972, *38*, 348–353.

SHURE, M. B., AND SPIVACK, G. "A Preventive Mental Health Program for Four-Year-Old Head Start Children." Paper presented at the Society for Research in Child Development, Philadelphia, 1973.

SHURE, M. B., AND SPIVACK, G. *A Mental Health Program for Kindergarten Children: Training Script.* Philadelphia: Department of Mental Health Sciences, Hahnemann Community Mental Health/Mental Retardation Center, 1974*a*.

SHURE, M. B., AND SPIVACK, G. *Preschool Interpersonal Problem-Solving (PIPS) Test: Manual.* Philadelphia: Department of Mental Health Sciences, Hahnemann Community Mental Health/Mental Retardation Center, 1974*b*.

SHURE, M. B., AND SPIVACK, G. *A Mental Health Program for Preschool and Kindergarten Children,* and *A Mental Health Program for Mothers of Young Children: An Interpersonal Problem-Solving Approach Toward Social Adjustment.* A Comprehensive Report of Research and

Training. No. MH-20372. Washington, D.C.: National Institute of Mental Health, 1975a. (Available from the authors.)

SHURE, M. B., AND SPIVACK, G. *A Mental Health Program for Preschool (and Kindergarten) Children* and *A Mental Health Program for Mothers of Young Children*. Final Summary Report MH-20372. Washington, D.C.: National Institute of Mental Health, 1975b.

SHURE, M. B., AND SPIVACK, G. "Interpersonal Cognitive Problem-solving Intervention: The Second (Kindergarten) Year." Paper presented at the American Psychological Association, Chicago, 1975c.

SHURE, M. B., AND SPIVACK, G. *Problem-Solving Techniques in Childrearing: Training Script for Parents of Young Children*. Philadelphia: Department of Mental Health Sciences, Hahnemann Community Mental Health/ Mental Retardation Center, 1975d.

SHURE, M. B., AND SPIVACK, G. "Training Mothers to Help Their Children Solve Real-Life Problems." Paper presented at the Society for Research in Child Development, Denver, 1975e.

SHURE, M. B., SPIVACK, G., AND GORDON, R. "Problem-Solving Thinking: A Preventive Mental Health Program for Preschool Children." *Reading World*, 1972, *11*, 259–273.

SHURE, M. B., SPIVACK, G., AND JAEGER, M. A. "Problem-Solving Thinking and Adjustment among Disadvantaged Preschool Children." *Child Development*, 1971, *42*, 1791–1803.

SHURE, M. B., SPIVACK, G., AND POWELL, L. "A Problem-Solving Intervention Program for Disadvantaged Preschool Children." Paper presented at Eastern Psychological Association, Boston, 1972.

SIEGEL, J. M., PLATT, J. J., AND PEIZER, S. B. "Emotional and Social Real-Life Problem-Solving Thinking in Adolescent and Adult Psychiatric Patients." *Journal of Clinical Psychology*, 1976, *32*, 230–232.

SIEGEL, J. M., PLATT, J. J., AND SPIVACK, G. "Means of Solving Real-Life Problems: II: Do Professionals and Laymen

See the Same Solutions as Effective in Solving Problems?" *Journal of Community Psychology*, 1974, *2*, 49–50.

SIEGEL, J. M., AND SPIVACK, G. "Problem-Solving Therapy: A New Program for Chronic Schizophrenic Patients." Research and Evaluation Report No. 23. Hahnemann Medical College and Hospital, Philadelphia, 1973.

SIMON, H. A., AND NEWELL, A. "Human Problem-Solving: The State of the Theory in 1970." *American Psychologist*, 1971, *26*, 145–159.

SPIVACK, G., AND LEVINE, M. "Self-Regulation in Acting-Out and Normal Adolescents." Report M-4531, National Institute of Health, Washington, D.C., 1963.

SPIVACK, G., AND SHURE, M. B. *Social Adjustment of Young Children: A Cognitive Approach to Solving Real-Life Problems.* San Francisco: Jossey-Bass, 1974.

SPIVACK, G., AND SHURE, M. B. "Maternal Childrearing and the Interpersonal Cognitive Problem-Solving Ability of Four-Year-Olds." Paper presented at the Society for Research in Child Development, Denver, 1975.

SPIVACK, G., AND SPOTTS, J. "Childhood Symptomatology: Further Data Defining the Meaning of the Devereux Child Behavior (DCB) Rating Scale Factors." Devon, Pa.: Devereux Foundation, 1966*a*.

SPIVACK, G., AND SPOTTS, J. *Devereux Child Behavior Rating Scale Manual.* Devon, Pa.: Devereux Foundation, 1966*b*.

SPIVACK, G., AND SWIFT, M. "The Devereux Elementary School Behavior Rating Scale: A Study of the Nature and Organization of Achievement Related Disturbed Classroom Behavior." *Journal of Special Education*, 1966, *1*, 71–90.

SPIVACK, G., AND SWIFT, M. *Devereux Elementary School Behavior Rating Scale.* Devon, Pa.: Devereux Foundation, 1967.

SPOHN, H. E., AND WOLK, W. "Effect of Group Problem-Solving Experience upon Social Withdrawal in Chronic Schizophrenics." *Journal of Abnormal and Social Psychology*, 1963, *66*, 187–190.

STONE, G. L., HINDS, W. C., AND SCHMIDT, G. W. "Teaching Mental

Health Behaviors to Elementary School Children." *Professional Psychology*, 1975, *6*, 34–40.

STRAUSS, M. A. "Communication, Creativity, and Problem-Solving Ability of Middle and Working-Class Families in Three Societies." *American Journal of Sociology*, 1968, *73*, 417–430.

SUCHOTLIFF, L. "Relation of Formal Thought Disorder to the Communication Deficit of Schizophrenics." *Journal of Abnormal Psychology,* 1970, *76*, 250–257.

THORNDIKE, R. L. "Intelligence and Its Uses." *Harper's Magazine*, 1920, *140*, 227–235.

TURNER, R. H. *Family Interaction*. New York: Wiley, 1970.

TURNURE, C. "Cognitive Development and Role-Taking Ability in Boys and Girls from 7 to 12." *Developmental Psychology*, 1975, *11*, 202–209.

WEINSTEIN, E. A. "The Development of Interpersonal Competence." In D. A. Goslin (Ed.), *Handbook of Socialization Theory and Research*. Chicago: McNally, 1969.

WEINSTOCK, A. R. "Family Background and Defense Mechanisms." *Journal of Personality and Social Psychology*, 1967*a*, *5*, 67–75.

WEINSTOCK, A. R. "Longitudinal Study of Social Class and Defense Preferences." *Journal of Consulting Psychology*, 1967*b*, *31*, 539–541.

WILCOX, M. A. "Comparison of Elementary School Children's Interaction in Teacher-led and Student-led Small Groups." Doctoral dissertation. Stanford University, 1972. Reprinted in part by Stanford Research Institute, Menlo Park, California, 1972.

WITKIN, H. A., DYK, R. B., FATHERSON, H. F., GOODENOUGH, D. R., AND KARP, S. A. *Psychological Differentiation*. New York: Wiley, 1962.

WITTICK, J. "The Generality of Prediction of Self Reports." *Journal of Community Psychology*, 1955, *19*, 445–448.

ZIGLER, E., AND PHILLIPS, L. "Social Competence and the Process-Reactive Distinction in Psychopathology." *Journal of Abnormal and Social Psychology*, 1962, *65*, 215–222.

Index

Aberrant behavior: inability to generate alternatives as key indicator of, 51; preschool, defined, 22; preschool, predictable on basis of ICPS scores. *See also* Behavioral adjustment

ACHTERMAN, E., 271-273, 296

"Acting out," in preschoolers, 23

Adolescence, adjustment relative to ICPS skills in, 82-101; delinquency, and family problem solving in, 127, 128; ICPS training programs in, 242-260

Affect, unpleasant, and means-ends thinking, 106

Aggression: conceptualized vs. acted out, 160; as consequence of frustration, 19; as force, 25-26; in means-ends stories of disturbed vs. normal children, 69-70

ALDOUS, J., 125, 154, 155, 277

ALLEN, G., 61-63, 71, 213

Alternative consequences, 32; and mothers, 140; and preschoolers, 166

Alternative-solution thinking: in adolescence, 83, 91-92, 99; in adults, 116, 122-123; and behavioral adjustment, 21-22, 24, 29-31, 43, 58-59, 62-64, 122-123, 160, 166; dominance of, in middle childhood, 166, 215; in group therapy, 253; in interpersonal problems, preschool, 224-226; and IQ, preschool, 27-29; and language ability, 26; and means-ends, middle childhood, 77; in middle childhood generally, 58-59, 62-64, 77, 166; in mothers, 139; in preschool children, 18-31; not reflected in willingness to talk, 28-29. *See*

also Mothers; Tests; Training

Anxiety, 75, 106

Art of Problem Solving (program), 288-290

ASKWORTH, P., 128

Authoritarian personality, 153

Authority-type problem: for fifth graders, 58; for preschoolers, 20-21

Autonomy: and causal thinking, 43-44; and consequential thinking, 37; not an interpersonal attribute, 28

AWARE: A Curriculum for Social Development (program), 219

Awareness of interpersonal problems, 19. *See also* Emotional awareness; Sensitivity to interpersonal problems

BASH, M., 190

BEARISON, D., 133, 134

BEE, H., 130

Behavioral adjustment: in adults, 122-123; and alternative thinking, 21-24, 43, 122-123, 160, 166; categories of, 24, 141; and causal thinking, 42, 76-77; and consequential thinking, 33-35; and interpersonal sensitivity, 43. *See also* Impulsivity; Inhibition; Tests; Training

BIRCH, H., 126

Blame, assignment of, 13-14

BLECHMAN, E., 276-282

BLOOM, B., 131

Board games, as training tools, 276-278

Brain-damaged patients, 16

BRANCA, M., 273-276

BURGLASS, M., 279-282

313